THE PRE-TRIBULATION RAPTURE

Allen Beechick

This book was written for personal reading pleasure and study, but it is easily adapted for classes or discussion groups. A guide is available for the leader's use.

ACCENT BOOKS
Denver, Colorado

236.4
Bee

ACCENT BOOKS

A division of Accent Publications, Inc.
12100 W. Sixth Avenue
P.O. Box 15337
Denver, Colorado 80215

Copyright © 1981 Accent Publications, Inc.
Printed in the United States of America

All rights reserved. No portion of this book may be reproduced in any form without the written permission of the publishers, with the exception of brief excerpts in magazine reviews.

Library of Congress Catalog Card Number 79-53291

ISBN 0-89636-040-7

1980 First Printing
1981 Second Printing

CONTENTS

1. **How It All Began** — 5
   ". . . Seal not the sayings of the prophecy of this book: for the time is at hand" (Revelation 22:10).

2. **Will Believers Know the Day?** — 7
   ". . . a thousand two hundred and threescore days" (Revelation 12:6).
   ". . . ye know neither the day nor the hour wherein the Son of man cometh" (Matthew 25:13).

3. **Who Will Populate the Millennium?** — 39
   "And they shall not escape" (1 Thessalonians 5:3).

4. **When Is the Wedding?** — 58
   "Return from the wedding" (Luke 12:36).

5. **First Thessalonians: Salvation** — 81
   "Therefore . . . watch" (1 Thessalonians 5:6).

6. **Second Thessalonians: Glory** — 120
   "Therefore, brethren, stand fast, and hold the traditions which ye have been taught" (2 Thessalonians 2:15).

7. **Revelation** — 161
   "And they had on their heads crowns of gold" (Revelation 4:4).

8. **Which Comes First?** — 190
   "Gather ye together first the tares" (Matthew 13:30).

9. **Luke Seventeen** — 204
   "The one shall be taken, and the other shall be left" (Luke 17:34).

10.	**The Winepress**	214

"And the angel thrust in his sickle into the earth, and gathered the vine of the earth, and cast it into the great winepress of the wrath of God. And the winepress was trodden without the city, and blood came out of the winepress, even unto the horse bridles, by the space of a thousand and six hundred furlongs [200 miles]" (Revelation 14:19-20).

11.	**The Olivet Solution**	231

"So shall also the coming of the Son of man be" (Matthew 24:37).

12.	**Now What?**	269

"All the law is fulfilled in one word . . ." (Galatians 5:14).

Appendix I 277
Outlines of First and Second Thessalonians

Appendix II 287
Points to Remember When Studying the Bible

"... Seal not the sayings of the prophecy of this book: for the time is at hand" (Revelation 22:10).

1
How It All Began

I never thought I would get wrapped up in it so soon. I had always heard about the controversy between "pre-tribulationists" and "post-tribulationists." I had learned that the difference between the two was only seven years. But what a seven years! The "tribulation" it is called, because this seven years unleashes that terrible time we read about in Revelation, the last book of the Bible. So great are the calamities as God bombards this planet with one global catastrophe after another to try to shake men to their senses, to give them one last chance to believe and be saved, that only one-half of the earth's population will survive.

I had learned that post-tribulationists believe that Christ will not return until *after* the tribulation; that is why we call them *post*-tribulationists. In other words, if I am part of the final generation, then I can expect to live on earth and endure the tribulation before I meet Christ. On the other hand, I learned that pre-tribulationists believe that Christ will come for all Christians, those who trust solely in the shed blood of Christ to save them from their sins, and He will evacuate them from the earth and take them to heaven *before* the tribulation. That is

THE PRE-TRIBULATION RAPTURE

why we call them *pre*-tribulationists. For short we will call the two groups pre-tribs and post-tribs.

In the back of my mind I figured that someday I would look into the controversy and examine the Bible for myself so that I could decide which side was right. I wasn't satisfied to believe something just because my pastors and teachers said it was so. I wanted to make sure that I had solid Biblical reasons for what I believed. So this was a project that I had in mind for the far-off future. But I never expected to tackle it so soon.

It all began when my brother walked into the house one day and surprised me with this statement: "I've read this post-trib book by Gundry[1] and it makes a lot of sense to me. I believe post-tribulationism is correct. I think we will go through the tribulation."

This surprised me, as I said, but it did not make me antagonistic. I asked him, "What are some of the strong points you learned from this book?" As he presented some of the points I interjected with statements like, "Wow! That's very interesting. That's a good point. Oh, I never thought of that before."

So I could delay it no longer. I had to make a study for myself from the Bible. I came to the study casting aside all preconceived notions as much as is humanly possible. I determined to let the Bible speak for itself.

I was in for another surprise. The more that I studied and prayed and meditated, the more the pieces began to fall into place. God's Word was not an obscure maze of unfathomable riddles. I discovered a beauty and a harmony that gets me so excited I want to shout.

Psalm 138:2 is true after all: ". . . Thou hast magnified thy word above all thy name." I stand simply amazed before the Word of God.

---

1. Robert H. Gundry, *The Church and the Tribulation* (Grand Rapids, MI: Zondervan Publishing House, 1973).

". . . a thousand two hundred and threescore days" (Revelation 12:6).

". . . ye know neither the day nor the hour wherein the Son of man cometh" (Matthew 25:13).

2
Will Believers Know the Day?

Have you ever put a puzzle together and almost finished it, but found some pieces were missing? Do you remember how you felt about that gaping hole right in the middle of your beautiful picture? If you could only find those missing pieces (maybe they're still in the box or under the table, or worse yet, mixed in with another puzzle), then you would have a complete picture at last.

I would like to give you a missing piece. Not a piece to your table puzzle, of course, but this chapter will give you a missing piece in the pre-post controversy.

You see, in the back of my brain there has always been one little question that has bothered me. Ever since that first day when my brother walked into the living room and shared his post-trib arguments and I asked him this question, I have never yet found a satisfactory answer from any post-trib. As long as this question remains unanswered, it leaves a gaping hole right in the middle of the picture.

My question is this: Can believers living during the tribulation know the day Christ will return? Think about it. If the tribulation is seven years long, and if Christ will return at the end of the tribulation, then what prevents believers from knowing when Christ will return?

Some readers will have a ready answer for me. They will respond immediately, "Watch therefore, for ye know neither the day nor the hour wherein the Son of man cometh" (Matthew 25:13). If the day and hour cannot be known, doesn't that contradict any idea that believers during the tribulation can know the day? Well, maybe and maybe not. Let us examine all the evidence first before we jump to any conclusions.

Would it surprise you if I told you that other Scriptures indicate that tribulation saints *can* know the day? Where are these missing pieces to the puzzle? How do they fit into the picture? Let's find out.

MISSING PIECES IN THE PUZZLE

I peek under the table and the first piece I spot is Daniel 9:27:

> And he shall confirm the covenant [or more correctly, "a" covenant] with many for one week: and *in the midst of the week* he shall cause the sacrifice and the oblation to cease, and for the overspreading of abominations he shall make it desolate, even until the consummation, and that determined shall be poured upon the desolate. (Italics are added in Scripture verses throughout this work to emphasize points.)

"In the Midst of the Week." Some terms in this verse need defining. "Week" is agreed by many Bible scholars to mean "week of years" rather than a week of days. How do they know this? The Hebrew word translated "week" simply means "seven." It could refer to seven days, seven years, or seven anything. The word is simply "seven." Now Genesis 29:27 is a case where the word obviously refers to seven years, because Jacob served one "week" or seven years for Rachel. Likewise, in Daniel 9:27 the meaning "seven years" best fits the context. I won't go into all the reasons for that here since other writers have already done that. Many post-tribs agree that this means seven years; so I think we can go on to define our next term.

Will Believers Know the Day?

"*Abomination of Desolation.*" What is this? Jesus describes it more fully: "When ye therefore shall see the abomination of desolation, spoken of by Daniel the prophet, stand in the holy place, (whoso readeth, let him understand:)" (Matthew 24:15). Paul gives even a fuller account of this event: "Let no man deceive you by any means: for that day shall not come, except there come a falling away first, and that man of sin be revealed, the son of perdition; who opposeth and exalteth himself above all that is called God, or that is worshipped; so that he as God sitteth in the temple of God, showing himself that he is God" (2 Thessalonians 2:3-4).

According to these passages the abomination of desolation involves a desecration of the temple by the man of sin. At the time of this writing the Jews have no temple, but they will build one again someday in Jerusalem. Into this temple will strut the man of sin, acting as if he owned the place, and he will try to usurp God's position by broadcasting to the world that he is God. This abomination climaxes all abominations.

Perhaps the abomination of desolation also includes an image set up in the temple, because Daniel says it is "set up" and Jesus says it is "standing" in the holy place. Certainly that would be an abomination almost as great as the man of sin entering the temple in person.

We don't need to know every little thing that is going to happen at the abomination of desolation. All we need to know is what the Bible tells us. At least we know this. We know that it is a prominent and pivotal incident. The minute it occurs any believer can spot it for what it is.

"*In the Midst of the Week.*" Now that we have defined these terms, let us reread Daniel 9:27:

> And he shall confirm the covenant with many for one week: and *in the midst of the week* he shall cause the sacrifice and the oblation to cease, and for the overspreading of abominations he shall make it desolate, even until the consummation, and that determined shall be poured upon the desolate.

I want you to notice one thing. The abomination of desola-

THE PRE-TRIBULATION RAPTURE

tion splits the seven years in half. In other words, it occurs at the three-and-one-half-year point, three and one-half years before Christ returns to earth.

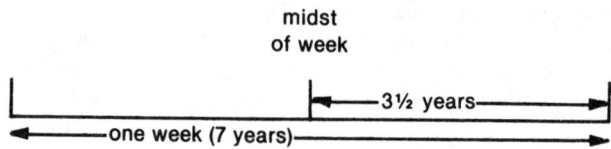

Think about it now. Doesn't this tell us the time? If your lover went overseas and was scheduled to return in three and one-half years, wouldn't you have the date circled in red on your calendar? Likewise, if I were on earth during the tribulation, and if I spotted the abomination of desolation, I would immediately count three and one-half years and I would know the time of Christ's return. Simple isn't it? What is there to prevent me from doing that?

"Forty-two Months." Well, three and one-half years is only approximate, you say. That still doesn't give away the exact day.

Is it only approximate? Or did God really mean three and one-half years *exactly?*

Before we shove everything back under the table again, I think I see another missing piece peeking out at me. Ah, look at this one. Revelation 13:5 says:

> And there was given unto him a mouth speaking great things and blasphemies; and power was given unto him to continue *forty and two months.*

Forty-two months! How long is that? Exactly three and one-half years.

Will Believers Know the Day?

"Twelve Hundred Sixty Days." Oh, but forty-two months still doesn't tell us much, you say. Some months have thirty days, some thirty-one, one has twenty-eight; so that still doesn't reveal the exact day.

Don't give up yet. Look! I spy another missing piece. Revelation 12:6 says:

> And the woman fled into the wilderness, where she hath a place prepared of God, that they should feed her there *a thousand two hundred and threescore days.*

"A Thousand Two Hundred and Threescore Days." Oh, the beauty and harmony of God's Word! How long is 1260 days? Precisely 42 months or 3½ years. The Biblical month, therefore, is thirty days long. (See also Genesis 7:11 and 8:3-4 where 150 days are five months.)

When God said three and one-half years, He meant it after all, right down to the very day.

SUCH HARMONY!

Isn't it beautiful how the Word of God harmonizes? God expresses the same period of time in three different ways: 3½ years, 42 months, and 1260 days.

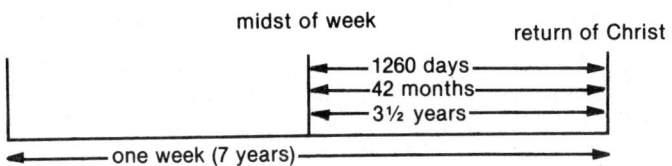

If He repeats the same thing over and over again He must be trying to make it clear enough to erase all doubt. It must be that He wants us to know precisely how long this period of time is.

THE PRE-TRIBULATION RAPTURE

But maybe I'm assuming too much. Maybe all these verses do not refer to the same time period. Maybe I'm pretending harmony when there really isn't.

Let's check it out.

The Last Three and One-half Years. When we check out these time periods, we will discover that they *all* refer to the *last three and one-half years before* Christ returns. Going back to our first verse, Daniel 9:27, remember that seven years are sliced in half, giving us three and one-half years for the last half of the tribulation. To make this doubly clear, let us reinforce this with another verse from Daniel. Daniel 12:7 says:

> And I heard the man clothed in linen, which was upon the waters of the river, when he held up his right hand and his left hand unto heaven, and sware by him that liveth for ever that it shall be for *a time, times, and an half;* and when he shall have accomplished to scatter the power of the holy people, all these things shall be finished.

What is "a time, times, and an half"? We can dream up all kinds of interpretations for this, but the Bible itself gives the correct interpretation. This mysterious phrase comes to light in Revelation 12:6 and 14:

> And the woman fled into the wilderness, where she hath a place prepared of God, that they should feed her there *a thousand two hundred and threescore days.*

> And to the woman were given two wings of a great eagle, that she might fly into the wilderness into her place, where she is nourished for *a time, and times, and half a time,* from the face of the serpent.

From these verses we see that "a time, times, and an half" equals 1260 days. "Time" means one year, "times" means two years, and "an half a time" means one-half year. So "a time, times, and an half" is just another way of saying three and one-half years. (Daniel puts the time obscurely, but Revelation clears it up for us. Why? Daniel was temporarily sealed, Daniel 12:4, but Revelation is unsealed, Revelation 22:10.)

Will Believers Know the Day?

Now to the main point. This three and one-half years, according to Daniel 12:6, is "unto the end." This reinforces our conviction that this is *the last three and one-half years of the tribulation.*

The Last Forty-two Months. We previously mentioned the man of sin who will desecrate the temple with the abomination of desolation. This evil character is called by several other names in Scripture. He is called the "beast" in Revelation 13 and "antichrist" in 1 John 4:3.

It doesn't matter to me what your favorite terminology happens to be for this man, but let me ask you one question. When will he be destroyed? When? I know that some people try to say that antichrist has already lived in past history, but my Bible clearly states that he will be destroyed *at the coming of Christ.* (Revelation 19:11-21; 2 Thessalonians 2:8).

May we use some simple logic? If the beast has power for forty-two months, and if the beast is destroyed at Christ's coming, then the forty-two-month period has to be *the last forty-two months before Christ's return.* (Revelation 13 mentions two beasts, but both share the identical forty-two-month duration. Both beasts may be alluded to in 2 Thessalonians 2:3-4 and 8-10.)

The Last Twelve Hundred Sixty Days. Why is the woman nourished for only 1260 days? Why not longer? Maybe God will nourish her for only 1260 days and then allow her to go hungry after that. No, I don't think so. I believe Christ returns at the end of the 1260th day, and that explains why protection is no longer needed. So this is the *last 1260 days* before Christ returns.

WHEN DOES THE COUNTDOWN BEGIN?

So far we have seen that the 3½ years, the 42 months, and the 1260 days all refer to the same period of time, that last period immediately before Christ returns to earth. With this information believers during the tribulation can calculate the exact day of Christ's return.

But wait a minute. How will these tribulation saints know when to start counting? How will they recognize Day One of the 1260 days?

Very simple. The *abomination of desolation.*

The Three-and-One-Half-Year Countdown. Let's reread Daniel 9:27:

> And he shall confirm the covenant with many *for one week:* and *in the midst of the week* he shall cause the sacrifice and the oblation to cease, and for the overspreading of abominations he shall make it desolate, even until the consummation, and that determined shall be poured upon the desolate.

You see, it is the abomination of desolation in the midst of the week that begins the three-and-one-half-year countdown.

"The Forty-two-Month Countdown. Does the abomination of desolation also begin the forty-two-month countdown? No one verse gives the answer for this, but two passages combined provide more insight. First let us read Revelation 13:5-7:

> And there was given unto him a mouth speaking great things and blasphemies; and power was given unto him to continue forty and two months. And he opened his mouth in blasphemy against God, to blaspheme his name, and his tabernacle, and them that dwell in heaven. And it was given unto him to make war with the saints, and to overcome them: and power was given unto him over all kindreds, and tongues, and nations.

This passage does not pinpoint the beginning of the forty-two-month countdown. It does tell us something else, though. It spells out the powers that God will allow the beast to have. Two of these powers especially I want you notice. First, he is given power to speak great things against God. We'll call this "mouth power." Second, he is given power to war against the saints. We'll call this "persecution power."

If you're thinking ahead about his mouth power and

Will Believers Know the Day?

persecution power, then you know already what I'm getting at. If you don't know what I'm getting at, then 2 Thessalonians 2:3-4 should give it away:

> Let no man deceive you by any means: for that day shall not come, except there come a falling away first, and that man of sin be revealed, the son of perdition; who opposeth and exalteth himself above all that is called God, or that is worshipped; so that he as God sitteth in the temple of God, showing himself that he is God.

When does the beast's mouth power begin? This passage connects it with the *abomination of desolation.* What we couldn't find in one passage alone, we discovered by comparing two passages. Revelation 13:5 gives the timespan and 2 Thessalonians 2:3-4 gives the beginning point.

Let us examine 2 Thessalonians 2 more carefully to see if the context supports our interpretation. Paul's whole purpose is to prove to the Thessalonians that the day of the Lord is *not* at hand yet, and to prove his point he appeals to one observable sign. Imagine a stairway with only two steps. These two steps represent Paul's steps of logic in this passage. On step number one is the question, "How can we tell when the day of the Lord is at hand?" The answer, "We know the day of the Lord is at hand when the man of sin is revealed."

That's fine, but how do we know when the man of sin is revealed? If Paul were standing in front of me, I would say to him, "Paul, it still seems nebulous. How in the world can anyone tell when the man of sin is revealed? Some think he has already been revealed in past history. Others think he might now be on the scene. Still others insist that his revelation is yet future. It looks like a lot of guesswork to me. That is why I'm glad you did not stop at step number one. I'm glad you gave step number two."

On step number two is the next question, "How can we tell when the man of sin is revealed?" The answer, "We know he is revealed when he sits in the temple boasting to be God." In other words, this momentous event is a signpost. Thank you,

THE PRE-TRIBULATION RAPTURE

Paul. Without this signpost we would have no way of recognizing if the man of sin were revealed or not, and we would never know when to say, "The day of the Lord is at hand."

PAUL'S LOGIC IN SECOND THESSALONIANS 2

Step Two
Answer: We recognize the man of sin when he sits in the temple boasting to be God.
Question: How can we tell when the man of sin is revealed?

Step One
Answer: We know the day of the Lord is at hand when the man of sin is revealed.
Question: How can we tell when the day of the Lord is at hand?

Paul is saying, "You have a signpost. You all can easily identify it. It is obvious that this momentous event has not yet occurred, and so we know that the man of sin has not yet been revealed, and therefore, it is premature to say, "The day of the Lord is at hand."

Even today some people try to say that the tribulation is past, and so the day of the Lord could come at any moment. I think 2 Thessalonians 2 was made to order for this view.

After going through all the logic in this passage, I want you to notice one thing. Notice that the abomination of desolation, that momentous event when the man of sin sits in the temple claiming to be God, marks the grand entrance of the man of sin onto the scene. How else can we know him? This is how he reveals himself. For the first time he unmasks, and he is revealed for what he is. Perhaps he has been a prominent political figure for some time, but never before has he spoken such blasphemies against God as he does at the abomination of

Will Believers Know the Day?

desolation. God allows him this "mouth power" for only forty-two months, and the *abomination of desolation is our signpost at the beginning of this forty-two-month countdown.*

The Twelve-Hundred-Sixty-Day Countdown. It fascinates me to watch Scripture harmonize. For quite awhile, even after being convinced that tribulation believers can know the day of Christ's return, I had not discovered this next pair of verses that I want to show you. But they were there all the time. Now they are the clearest and most convincing evidence, at least to me, that tribulation saints can calculate the exact day.

Recall from Revelation 13:5-7 two powers given to the beast. One was "mouth power" which we just finished talking about. Now let's talk about the other, "persecution power." This next pair of passages deals with his persecution power and its forty-two-month duration.

So far we have seen that it is the abomination of desolation which begins the three and one-half years, and it is the abomination which begins the forty-two months. But what about the twelve hundred sixty days? Does the abomination begin that too?

Revelation 12:6 does not reveal the occasion of fleeing for safety for the twelve hundred sixty days. But if you are thinking ahead, you know already what I'm getting at. If not, Matthew 24:15-16 will give it away.

> When ye therefore shall see the abomination of desolation spoken of by Daniel the prophet, stand in the holy place, (whoso readeth, let him understand:) then let them which be in Judaea flee into the mountains.

Amazing, isn't it? Jesus pinpoints the moment of fleeing for safety, namely, the abomination of desolation.

Revelation 12 and Matthew 24 make a great team. Matthew 24 *names* the event ("abomination of desolation") while Revelation 12 *dates* the event (1260 days).

Yes, if I were going through the tribulation and spotted the abomination, you can be sure I would calculate the twelve hun-

THE PRE-TRIBULATION RAPTURE

dred sixty days very carefully on my calendar or on the wall of my cave.

Let's summarize our findings with a diagram. You don't have to be a great theologian to figure this out. Or even a great mathematician. All you have to do is read the Scriptures and accept them for what they say. No fancy interpretation is needed. It's so simple.

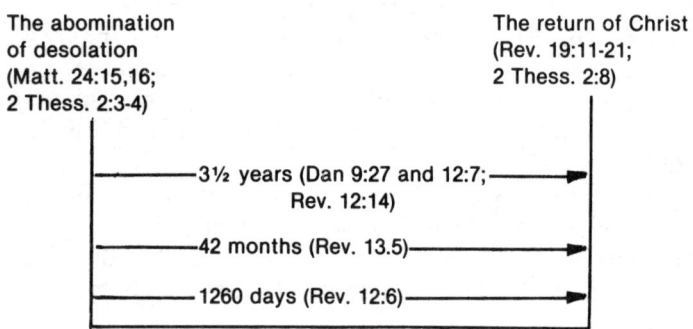

If any area seems hazy or doubtful, why not just look up the passages in the above diagram and read them slowly. See if anything but the abomination of desolation begins this period. See if anything but the return of Christ ends this period. And see if God didn't express the identical period of time in three different ways in order to remove all doubt as to how long this period of time is.

HOW DO THE PIECES FIT?

The missing pieces we found under the table fit together very nicely, didn't they? The Scriptures harmonized beautifully. But how do the missing pieces fit into the larger puzzle? How am I going to use this to prove the timing of the rapture?

It took us a long time to get here. But we have finally arrived at the big point of this chapter. On the one hand we have all these passages which reveal the exact day. On the other hand, we have passages like, "Watch therefore, for ye know neither the day nor the hour wherein the Son of man cometh" (Matthew 25:13). In short, Scripture presents a *known day* and an *unknown day*.

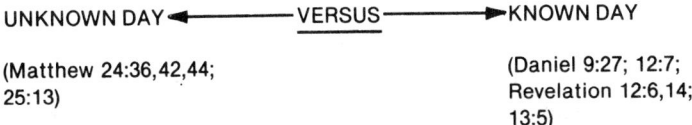

UNKNOWN DAY ◄─────── VERSUS ───────► KNOWN DAY

(Matthew 24:36,42,44; 25:13)

(Daniel 9:27; 12:7; Revelation 12:6,14; 13:5)

Is this a contradiction? You well know that the Bible never contradicts itself. My point is this: *two different days* must be in view. Christ comes, not once, but *twice*. This is the only way I know of to harmonize the pieces of the puzzle without any contradiction. With two different days, we get a picture that looks something like this:

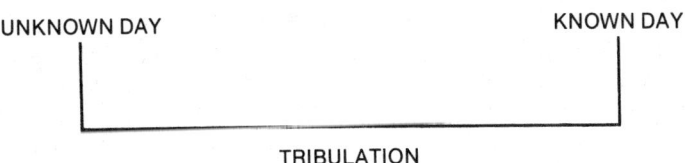

UNKNOWN DAY   KNOWN DAY

TRIBULATION

The unknown day refers to Christ's coming *before* the tribulation while the known day refers to Christ's coming *after* the tribulation. These are *two different days.* Herein lies our first evidence against a post-tribulation rapture.

ANSWERING OBJECTIONS

Post-tribulationism tries to harmonize the known day and unknown day into one day. The two are totally irreconcilable.

THE PRE-TRIBULATION RAPTURE

They are as opposite as Christ's suffering and glory.

We have seen the positive side of this question. We have gone directly to Scripture and looked at the evidence of the known day and the unknown day, evidence that points to Christ's return on *two different days*. We now come to a time of answering possible objections. We will try to anticipate any questions or objections that might be brought up.

Objection Number 1: The Context of Matthew 24. Some may raise an objection because of the context of Matthew 24. I can hear them saying: It is impossible for believers during the tribulation to know the day because Matthew 24:36 clearly says, "But of that day and hour knoweth no man, no, not the angels of heaven, but my Father only." And furthermore, this is talking about the coming *after* the tribulation, not some coming before the tribulation. Doesn't Matthew 24:29 plainly say *"after* the tribulation"? Therefore, to take the unknown day and apply it to a pre-tribulational coming is to jerk it out of context.

I appreciate this objection because I struggled with the context of Matthew 24 for quite some time myself. I felt the force of the context saying to me: The unknown day has to be *after* the tribulation. On the other hand I felt the force of the other Scriptures saying: The end of the tribulation *can* be known. I was in a dilemma. What was I to do?

Anyone can come along and pick the Scriptures on one side and sweep the others under the rug. But my conscience wouldn't let me do that. I couldn't just pick and choose the parts I liked and ignore the rest. I had to account for all the facts. Whenever I put a puzzle together, I don't like to leave any missing pieces under the rug; I want to have the complete picture, don't you?

So what is the solution to the context of Matthew 24? After I discovered the answer it was so simple that I laughed at myself for not knowing it all along. I won't take space to fully explain it now, but at the end of the book we dedicate an entire chapter

Will Believers Know the Day?

to Matthew 24. I guarantee you one thing, you will see that nothing in the explanation is strained, twisted, or distorted at all. It all will fit as naturally as a baby in a cradle.

You'd be surprised. Would you believe it if I told you that evidence for the known day lies in Matthew 24 itself? It's true. I won't explain all the details now, but I will give you a one-word clue to the interpretation of Matthew 24: *double-reference*. Instead of being a thorn in my side, Matthew 24 is the icing on the cake for my whole argument.

Objection Number 2: The Day Is Unknown to Unbelievers Only. Some may object: A known day and an unknown day does not necessarily mean there are two different *days*. It may merely mean *two different groups of people*, namely believers and unbelievers. Believers will know, and unbelievers will not know.

It is true that believers will know and unbelievers will not know at the end of the tribulation. But there is more to it. There remains a day *unknown to believers*. Read it for yourself: "Watch therefore: for *ye* know not . . . in such an hour as *ye* think not . . . for *ye* know neither the day nor the hour . . . " (Matthew 24:42, 44; 25:13).

Jesus addressed the disciples and said *you* . . . believers . . . know not the day.

The conclusion is unavoidable. Since Scripture tells of a known day and an unknown day *for believers*, then there must be *two different days*.

Objection Number 3: What About the 1290 Days? Some may object because Daniel 12:11 says, "And from the time that the daily sacrifice shall be taken away, and [from] the abomination that maketh desolate set up, there shall be a thousand two hundred and ninety days."

Why do I say 1260 days when Daniel 12:11 says 1290 days? Why the thirty-day discrepancy? Where do the extra thirty days come in? Here are two possible solutions:

THE PRE-TRIBULATION RAPTURE

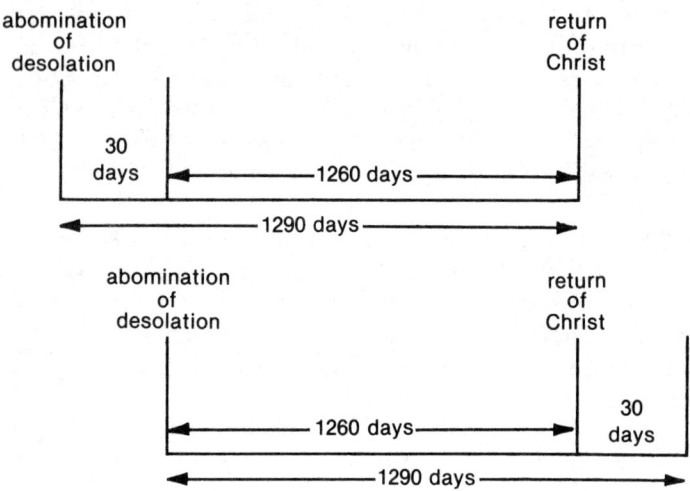

One solution puts the extra thirty days *before* the return of Christ. This is incorrect as we shall see later. The correct solution puts the extra thirty days *after* the return of Christ.

Actually Daniel 12 gives not just one nor two dates, but *three* dates. They diagram out this way:

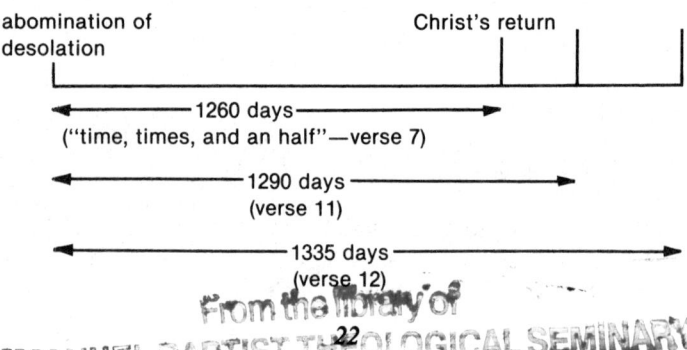

Will Believers Know the Day?

The important thing to remember about these three dates is that they all are counted from the abomination. Daniel 12:11 makes the abomination the beginning point for the 1290 days. This implies that the other two dates share the same beginning point. They begin at the same point, but they end at different points. On day 1260 Christ returns. On day 1290 something else happens. On day 1335 something else happens. What happens? Scripture doesn't spell it out, but we can make some good guesses. This, however, will have to wait until a later chapter.

Right now, though, I want to show from Scripture that it *cannot* be 1290 days from the abomination to the return of Christ. Just for a minute let's suppose that there are not 1260, but 1290 days from the abomination of desolation to the return of Christ. Remember, at the abomination of desolation the man of sin sports a blasphemous mouth against God (2 Thessalonians 2:4) and believers immediately flee for their lives (Matthew 24:15-21). Got the picture?

Now, how does this fit the time frame? Revelation 13:5 says the beast is given "persecution power" for *only forty-two months!* Then why are the saints fleeing persecution thirty days prematurely? They can't spare five minutes to go back into their house, but the persecution doesn't begin until 30 days later? It doesn't fit. Revelation 13:5 also times the beast's "mouth power" for *only forty-two months.* How can the beast be exercising his "mouth power" thirty days prematurely? Impossible! You see, the abomination *cannot* come thirty days early. The time-span from the abomination until the return of Christ cannot be one day longer than 1260 days.

Objection Number 4: The Time Is "Rounded Off." Some may evade the precise day by supposing the time is rounded off. Can this be so?

If all we had to go on was "three and one-half years," I might believe it was rounded off. If all we had to go on was "forty-two months," I might believe it. But when the Bible gives the exact day, I can't believe it.

The number 1260 is not a rounded off figure. For rounding off we would expect 1000 or 2000. Even 1250 would be better if rounding off were intended. But the number 1260 itself shows that exactness is intended. (This fits in with Daniel's 1290 and 1335 which also are not rounded-off-looking numbers.)

By the way, Sir Robert Anderson, in *The Coming Prince,* calculated the *very day* which ended Daniel's 69 weeks (see Daniel 9:24-27 and Luke 19:41-44). If so for the first 69 weeks, we would expect the end of the 70th week to be no less precise.

Objection Number 5: The Days Are "Shortened." Some may ask a question about Matthew 24:22, "And except those days should be shortened, there should no flesh be saved: but for the elect's sake those days shall be shortened." Does this mean that the three-and-one-half years predicted by Daniel will not run their full course? Does this mean that Jesus shortened Daniel's prophecy cutting it to *less than* three-and-one-half years? Does this explain why the day is unknown?

Whatever Jesus meant, I am sure that He did not mean to change prophecy. Even God cannot change God's Word. Jesus said,

> Think not that I am come to destroy the law, or the prophets: I am not come to destroy, but to fulfill. For verily I say unto you, Till heaven and earth pass, one jot or one tittle shall in no wise pass from the law, till all be fulfilled (Matthew 5:17-18).

By the way, reducing the 1260 days would also reduce the 1290 days and the 1335 days. That is quite a few jots and tittles to erase from our Bibles.

How can we be sure that Jesus did not reduce the number of days? Because Revelation confirms Daniel. About sixty years after Jesus spoke of shortening the days, the apostle John wrote of this same period of time. According to him the full 1260 days or 3½ years or 42 months is *still intact* (Revelation 12:6, 14; 13:5). Any interpretation of Matthew 24:22 which ignores these verses in Revelation is like trying to put a puzzle

Will Believers Know the Day?

together with only one piece while ignoring the rest of the pieces still in the box.

If Jesus did not mean to reduce the number of days in Matthew 24:22, then what did Jesus mean? The Bible does not say much about this, but it does give us some possible clues. Amos 8:9 says:

> And it shall come to pass in that day, saith the Lord God, that I will cause the sun to go down at noon, and I will darken the earth in the clear day.

If the sun goes down at noon, what do you have? You have a pretty short day, don't you?

There's more. Revelation 8:12 says:

> And the fourth angel sounded, and the third part of the sun was smitten, and the third part of the moon, and the third part of the stars; so as the third part of them was darkened, and the day shone not for a third part of it, and the night likewise.

From this passage we notice an astonishing thing. If the day is shorter we would expect the night to be longer. Not so here. The day is shorter and the night is shorter too! In other words, instead of a twenty-four-hour day we have a sixteen-hour day. Could this be what Jesus meant when He said, "And except those days be shortened . . ."?

Can the word "shortened" really take on this interpretation? Of course it can. We can test this by applying it to a different time measure. Suppose I were a mighty king and went about to change the calendar, and suppose I said, "I have shortened the months." Most naturally it would mean that I decreased the number of days in each month rather than changing the calendar from twelve to eleven months.

Suppose I am holding a bunch of candles in my hand and I say to you, "I have shortened these candles." Naturally you would understand me to mean that I chopped off the candles to make each one shorter rather than reducing the number of candles by throwing some away. Even if I chopped off the candles *collectively*—with a sharp knife taking one swift slice through the whole bunch—the result is that *each* candle is shortened *individually*.

Yes, the word "shortened" easily and naturally expresses shorter days. "Shortened" in the original language has the connotation of "amputated." "Amputated days" expresses the idea perfectly. In other Greek literature the word is used of "mutilated stones." (Does this mean *fewer* stones? No.) A related word is used of "short-horned" animals. (Does this mean *fewer* horns? No.) Also, "a spear broken off short." (Does this mean *fewer* spears? No.) Another related word means "an undervest with shortened sleeves." (Does this mean *fewer* sleeves? No.) Another related word means "dwarf." (Do ten "dwarfs" equal nine men? No. "Dwarf" does not reduce the number. It merely reduces the size.) Another related word means "the stumpfingered." (Does this mean *fewer* fingers? No, each finger is shorter, precisely the interpretation we suggest for ' shortened days.") These examples show that I am not suggesting anything different than what normal language would suggest.

One might object that the days *collectively* are shortened, not individually. The *time* is shortened, but the days are not. In response to this, let's ponder a similar phrase in 1 Corinthians 7:29, "the time has been shortened." Another word for "shortened" is used here, but the meaning is the same as some propose for our troublesome phrase in Matthew 24. Now in Matthew 24:22, the Holy Spirit could easily have written the word "time" just as He did in 1 Corinthians 7:29. If He *meant* "time," why did He not say so? "Time" is general, but "days" is specific. He did not say the "time" is shortened, or the "years" or the "months," but He did say the "days" were shortened. All the evidence of normal language leads me to believe that the object of shortening is the *days*.

Let's review. Evidence abounds that believers in the tribulation can know the day of Christ's return. Against this Matthew 24:22 is only one little problem passage. In light of the evidence

Will Believers Know the Day?

that the day *is known*, all I need to do is to demonstrate the *possibility* of the "shorter-days" interpretation in order to keep intact the consistency of the total system. Hard evidence has demonstrated not only its *possibility*, but its probability. It doesn't need it, but the shorter-days interpretation certainly enjoys the preponderance of the evidence.

In the court of logic, if I am holding forth a possibility, the burden of proof rests on the other side to disprove the possibility. Unless such proof arises, no one can rest on one little obscure phrase to overthrow a host of other Scriptures which clearly reveal the known day. It's not sound exegesis, is it? At least one interpretation is *possible* because it harmonizes with Scripture; whereas the other interpretation is *impossible* because it contradicts Scripture.

What if the "shorter-days" possibility is wrong? If you prefer, consider an alternate possibility. As another has expressed it, the days are "shorter than they normally would have been in terms of the purpose and power of the oppressors." In other words, if Satan and antichrist had their way, they would remain in power indefinitely. But God intervenes to cut their plans short and to keep the human race from annihilating itself. This interpretation reduces Satan's days but not God's days.

If the "shorter-days" possibility is correct, we see the mercy and judgment of God mingled together. Mercy, because if each day is one-third shorter, then men have one-third better chance of surviving each terrible day. "And except those days should be shortened, there should no flesh be saved."

Not only mercy, but judgment. If you have a scientific mind, perhaps you have noticed a problem. If each day is shortened, then the earth has to rotate faster. If the earth rotates faster, then it would have more rotations each time it revolves around the sun. The result would be more days in a year. How can this be when God has decreed that 1260 days still come out to three and one-half years? Well, if God can change the rotation of the earth, He can surely change the orbit of the earth also in order to make the number of days in each year remain the same. A shorter orbit would compensate for a shorter day. A passage in Revelation suggests such a change in the relation of the earth and the sun. This is where judgment comes in:

> And the fourth angel poured out his vial upon the sun; and power was given unto him to scorch men with fire. And men were scorched with great heat, and blasphemed the name of God which hath power over these plagues: and they repented not to give him glory (Revelation 16:8, 9).

Comparing this passage with the one previously quoted, Revelation 8:12, shows the involvement in both cases of a *fourth angel*. This forms additional confirmation that there is some relationship between the length of the day and the heat of the day.

Judgment and mercy mingled. The time will come when God will vent His judgment, no longer mingled with mercy. "For he shall have judgment without mercy" (James 2:13). "The same shall drink of the wine of the wrath of God, which is poured out *without mixture* into the cup of his indignation; and he shall be tormented with fire and brimstone in the presence of the holy angels, and in the presence of the Lamb" (Revelation 14:10). If you are not saved, then believe in the Lord Jesus Christ and His shed blood today, while there is still mercy.

Objection Number 6: Is the Abomination a Datable event? Some may object: Perhaps the abomination of desolation is not such a clear-cut event as you make it out to be. How do you know it is so noticeable that everyone will be aware of it? What about people on the other side of the world? How will they hear of it? Maybe the abomination isn't a one-day incident either. Perhaps it is an episode spread over several days or more. All these things would fuzzy the picture and make it difficult to date the return of Christ.

I reply: The abomination is a sharply-defined one-day crisis which everyone can easily recognize. It is a natural signpost from which to date the return of Christ. How do I know this? I

Will Believers Know the Day?

know it from reading Matthew 24:15-18:

> When ye therefore shall see the abomination of desolation, spoken of by Daniel the prophet, stand in the holy place, (whoso readeth, let him understand:) Then let them which be in Judaea flee into the mountains: Let him which is on the housetop not come down to take any thing out of his house: Neither let him which is in the field return back to take his clothes.

By the way, some teach that Christ returns in the middle of the tribulation. However, believers flee into the mountains at this point (and are preserved there for 1260 days) instead of meeting Christ in the air.

Now, if you were out in the field, as this passage says, how long would it take you to run into your house and grab your coat? Two or three minutes? If you were on the top of your house, how long would it take you to dash inside and snatch a loaf of bread? Sixty seconds? The abomination is a quite sharply defined crisis, I'd say.

If I didn't know it from Matthew 24:15-18, I'd know it from 2 Thessalonians 2:3-4. In this passage Paul describes the abomination because it is the signpost marking the grand entrance of the man of sin onto the world's scene. If Paul's purpose is to give a recognizable signpost, would he give something fuzzy? No, a fuzzy signpost would make Paul's whole argument meaningless in 2 Thessalonians 2. Remember, this is the only sign he gives us by which we can tell whether the day of the Lord is at hand or not.

Now let us read Paul's signpost in 2 Thessalonians 2:3-4:

> Let no man deceive you by any means: for that day shall not come, except there come a falling away first, and that man of sin be revealed, the son of perdition; who opposeth and exalteth himself above all that is called God, or that is worshipped; so that he as God sitteth in the temple of God, showing himself that he is God.

How long will it take the man to sit down in the temple? If he sits very slowly it might take about five seconds. Yes, I'd say the abomination is quite sharply defined.

THE PRE-TRIBULATION RAPTURE

(Matthew 24:15 talks about the abomination "standing" instead of "sitting." Here are three possible explanations for this. When the man of sin walks into the temple he obviously has to stand before he sits. This standing may be what Jesus refers to. Or "standing" may refer to the sitting itself. In Greek "stand" does not necessarily mean "to stand upright." It could also mean "to be set in place." The third possibility is an image standing in the holy place.)

If I didn't know it from Matthew 24 or from 2 Thessalonians 2, I'd still know it from Daniel 12:11. In this verse God expressly pinpoints the abomination as the beginning of the countdown.

> And from the time that the daily sacrifice shall be taken away, and the abomination that maketh desolate set up, there shall be a thousand two hundred and ninety days.

If believers can use the abomination to count 1290 days, then they can easily use it to count 1260 days also.

The date of the abomination of desolation is not so fuzzy after all. It is God's appointed signpost so that anyone can tell the time. So what if the abomination lasts several days or has a prolonged effect? Even if this were true it would not destroy God's signpost at the *first day* of the episode. Extended action does not rule out a precise beginning. So what if some people don't hear about it right away? Sooner or later everybody will know about it, and when they learn of it they will also learn on what day it occurred. I suppose that even a President's assassination slips by the notice of some people. But when they finally grasp the news of it I am sure the day of occurrence is included in the news.

My point is this. The abomination of desolation is a dead giveaway. Once you know its date, you know the date of Christ's return.

Objection Number 7: The Abomination Is Past. Some may be thinking: The abomination is not a future event. It has

Will Believers Know the Day?

already occurred in past history. Therefore, we cannot use it to date the return of Christ.

It is true that precursory fulfillments have already occurred, but when Jesus places the abomination in connection with the tribulation immediately preceding His coming (Matthew 24), then we know there remains a future and final fulfillment.

But for the sake of argument, let's throw the abomination out the window altogether. Can we throw the abomination out the window and *still* date the return of Christ?

As we mentioned, the man of sin reveals himself by sitting in the temple claiming to be God (2 Thessalonians 2:3-4). Call this event what you may. Instead of "abomination" call it a "carnation." The fact remains, if you link 2 Thessalonians 2:3-4 with Revelation 13:5, then you can count 42 months. It is 42 months from the time the man of sin sits in the temple until the time he is cast into the lake of fire.

Objection Number 8: A Gap Before the Tribulation. Some may theorize this way: The date is unknown because there is a gap before the tribulation. In other words, Christ comes sometime before the tribulation, but the seven-year tribulation does not begin immediately. There is a gap of unknown duration between Christ's coming and the onset of the tribulation. So if you don't know how long the gap is, then you won't know when the seven-year tribulation begins, and then you won't be able to calculate the date of Christ's return at the end of the tribulation.

If you have been reading this chapter, then you know that this objection misses my point altogether. My point is not a seven-year countdown, but a three-and-one-half-year countdown. A person can be completely oblivious to the beginning of the seven years, but he can still catch God's signpost at the beginning of the three-and-one-half years.

By the way, I suspect that you can calculate Christ's return seven years ahead of time, but since the Bible does not say much about this, I do not stress it. Personally, I do not happen

THE PRE-TRIBULATION RAPTURE

to believe in the gap theory, since it would serve no purpose and since Scripture gives no hint of it.

Objection Number 9: A Gap After the Tribulation. Others may try to get around the possibility of knowing the day with a gap on the other end of the tribulation by saying: After the tribulation Christ does not return immediately. A gap of unknown duration follows the end of the tribulation before the return of Christ. This unknown gap makes it impossible to predict the return of Christ.

I find this theory unworkable because Matthew 24:29-30 puts His coming *"immediately* after the tribulation." Also, if Christ does not return on schedule to terminate the forty-two-month power of the beast, then who is the one casting the beast into the lake of fire in Revelation 19? If a certain group of people is nourished for only 1260 days according to Revelation 12:6 and 14, then do they go hungry afterwards for an indefinite time awaiting the return of Christ? No, this delayed-return theory just doesn't fit. Christ has to return on schedule in order to fulfill Scripture.

Objection Number 10: They Can But Won't. Some may ask this question: It is one thing to prove that tribulation saints *can* know the day, but it is another thing to prove that they *will* know. How do you know they will be counting the days? In the turbulent tribulation times, and in the confusion of fleeing for their lives, who will have the presence of mind to mark their calendar?

This objection assumes that God reveals the day and then turns right around and says you can't know it. What He gives with one hand He takes away with the other. Well, you can count on one thing, if I were going through the tribulation, here's one person who would be counting the days, along with my wife and children.

Now the Biblical evidence, not only that they can, but that *they actually will know* the day of Christ's return. The angel said to Daniel, "The wise shall understand" (Daniel 12:10). Understand what? What was the very thing Daniel was asking the angel about? *The time.* It's in the context. Read it for yourself:

> How long shall it be to the end of these wonders? . . . a time, times, and an half . . . And I heard, but I understood not: then said I, O my Lord, what shall be the end of these things? And he said, Go thy way, Daniel: for the words are closed up and sealed till the time of the end . . . but the wise *shall understand* (verses 6-10).

Of course, the wise shall understand other things too, but the *time* is prominent in this context. Yes, believers not only can, but they will understand the time.

In addition to Daniel we can go to the words of Jesus. Jesus said:

> When ye therefore shall see the abomination of desolation spoken of by Daniel the prophet, stand in the holy place, (whoso readeth, *let him understand:)* (Matthew 24:15).

Understand what? Understand what Daniel says about the abomination. If they do what Jesus commands, and if they study all that Daniel writes about the abomination, can they avoid knowing the time? When Daniel talks about the abomination, he gives the time. Therefore, obeying the words of Jesus results in knowing the time. Out of all possible things, the one thing Jesus commanded understanding about was God's three-and-one-half-year signpost. Yes, they will know.

They will know not only by reading Daniel, but also by reading Revelation. Maybe Jesus commanded them to understand Daniel, but how do I know that anyone will read and understand Revelation during that time? Well, if Revelation is a prophecy of that time period, what Christian wouldn't be reading it? Some will read and understand Revelation because Revelation 13:18 is written for those during that time:

> Here is wisdom. Let him that hath understanding count the number of the

> beast: for it is the number of a man; and his number is Six hundred threescore and six.

Anyone wise enough to understand the number of the beast would most likely be wise enough to perceive his duration of power also, because both facts are revealed in the same chapter in Revelation. For a wise student of Revelation, or at least a person who reads the entire thirteenth chapter, to know the number of the beast is to know also when his number is up.

"Only 1260 Days to Go." Now for a minute, put yourself in the shoes of a believer during the tribulation. As a tribulation saint, you are fleeing for your very life from that dreadful beast, the blasphemous antichrist. He has killed many already. What are you thinking now? You want to know how soon this will end. So you rivet your attention on those passages of Scripture which reveal the time. As you eagerly search the Scriptures you find not just one or two, but several passages, all pointing to one day.

You see that Day One is the abomination and you start counting from that. "And from the time that the daily sacrifice shall be taken away, and the abomination that maketh desolate set up . . ." (Daniel 12:11). "When ye therefore shall see the abomination of desolation spoken of by Daniel the prophet . . ." (Matthew 24:15).

As the suspense of day-to-day existence continues you find comfort and hope in those passages which reveal the time in several different ways so that there is no mistaking it. "In the midst of the week" (Daniel 9:27). "A time, times, and an half" (Daniel 12:7). "A thousand two hundred and threescore days" (Revelation 12:6). "Forty and two months" (Revelation 13:5).

As you watch many of your loved ones beheaded at the hands of the cruel beast, you begin to wonder, "Is the revealed day really correct? Will Christ really come on the appointed day?" You reread the passages to assure yourself. Yes, He cannot delay His coming past the 1260th day. Neither can He come before the 1260 days are up. It's true after all, and you have

Will Believers Know the Day?

hope.

Put yourself in their shoes. If in these days some have tried to calculate the time of Christ's pre-trib return from one or two verses and with skimpy evidence, how much more will you, a tribulation saint, with a whole fistful of plain and solid verses be anxious to calculate the day of relief from persecution. This is not idle eschatological curiosity; you are counting the days dearly as if your life depended on it. Judging from the Scriptures God has put into your hand, I cannot blame you for pinning your life hopes on one day. After God gave you these Scriptures and after allowing you to get your hopes up, how cruel it would be if He would let you down and not come on that day. Such a debacle would be more than an honest misinterpretation of Scripture, it would be an outright deception by God, and that is impossible. What He has put into print He means to fulfill in actuality.

Put yourself into their shoes. How would you feel?

I believe the battle cry of believers during that time will be, "Only 1260 days to go. Keep the faith . . . . Only 1259 days to go. Stand fast in the Lord . . . . Only 1258 days to go. Be patient . . . ."

They can know.

They will know.

THE UMBRELLA

I believe this chapter presents an airtight case, but in case anyone suspects a leak in the above evidence, I also believe there is an umbrella to cover even that. We have been talking about the difference between the known day and the unknown day. Church saints do not know the day but tribulation saints will know the day. Several Scriptures line up on both sides showing the difference. This difference is acutely brought to focus in our umbrella verse, Matthew 24:44, "Therefore be ye also ready: for in such an hour as ye think not the Son of man cometh."

THE PRE-TRIBULATION RAPTURE

Be Ready Now. All possible objections and arguments come under this umbrella, for even the best possible objection must admit a general time period when Christ must return, somewhere in the neighborhood of seven years after the tribulation begins. Anyone who reads Revelation 16 and 19 knows that certain events converge at the end of the tribulation. The armies of the world, led by the beast, gather at Armageddon. When you see these events coming to a point, you just know the end is near. It's so obvious. Ask a post-trib how much time expires between the gathering of the armies and the gathering of the saints. Is it enough time to create the unexpectancy of Matthew 24:44? Not hardly. Once the final events start whirling down the vortex, no one will even have time to write a book about it.

This general expectation is a far cry from our umbrella verse, "In such an hour as ye think not the Son of man cometh." The force of Matthew 24:44 is even stronger in the original Greek because of the progressive present tense which implies, "When you are not thinking or expecting Him to come, He will." This carries the issue beyond a certain day, for it militates against even an approximate period of expectation. The whole point that Jesus is trying to get across in this passage is the total surprise for those involved.

The entire tone of surprise in Matthew 24:44 is incompatible with what transpires toward the end of the tribulation when saints are commanded, "And when these things begin to come to pass, then look up, and lift up your heads; for your redemption draweth nigh" (Luke 21:28). The one requires looking that is perpetual and unconditional, but the other is postponed and conditional. The difference is expectancy versus unexpectancy, awareness versus surprise. The one needs only *momentary* looking, but the other demands *continual* looking. *There is a difference.* Forget the 1260 days if you want to. We still have the quandary of general expectation versus total surprise. This difference is why I conclude that *there are two aspects of His coming.* For His coming after the tribulation believers *will*

Will Believers Know the Day?

know the time; for His coming before the tribulation believers will *not* know the time.

Christ's next coming will be when we least expect it. Are you ready? Will His coming be a pleasant surprise or an unpleasant surprise? You can be ready by getting your heart right with God. Do it now before it is too late.

You cannot get ready by your own efforts. That's not good enough. God will not accept your own efforts. He will only accept the blood of Christ shed on your behalf. Admit before God that you are sinful and unworthy, and trust in Christ as your only means of salvation.

Surrender your life to God. Then trust Him every day and every hour.

Don't Throw Up Your Hands. Maybe you have no special question or objection like the ten we have listed, but maybe you are thinking: Theologians have debated this topic for years and they haven't come to an agreement yet. If scholars can't solve the problem, then how can I ever expect to know what's right? I give up even trying to understand. I'll just wait and see if Christ returns before the tribulation or not; then we'll know.

To you I say: Don't throw up your hands. You *can* know. Yes, you can. God wrote the Bible for *you,* not just for scholars.

Let's talk about this for a minute. How can you know what is right? When you read one theologian and he says one thing, and you read another and he says a different thing, how do you decide between the two? Here's how. You let the Bible decide between the two. You can read the Bible just as well as they can. Maybe you don't know Greek, but if you are Christ's you have the Holy Spirit to help you understand it. Don't let a few mere men take the Bible out of your hands.

Scrutinize the arguments given by men. See if they square with Scripture. See if they explain *some* verses but leave others *un*explained. See if they put *part* of the puzzle together but leave gaping holes. The one who puts together the most pieces is the one with the most beautiful picture. That is how you can tell.

I am sure that other interpreters have done their best to harmonize the picture for you, just as I am doing my best. I think we can help each other as we work together. If you see any gaping holes in my picture, please point them out to me. You won't be the first to do me that favor. But whatever you do, don't throw up your hands.

Icing on the Cake. Let's return to the main point of this chapter. Scripture presents a *known* day and an *unknown* day. However I slice it, dice it, dissect it, bisect it, I keep coming up with only one conclusion: *two different days.* This definitely rules out only *one* coming.

But how can that be? I still hear some questioning. Doesn't Matthew 24 place the unknown day *after* the tribulation? I mentioned earlier that Matthew 24 is the icing on the cake to my whole argument. But I want you to enjoy the rest of the meal before I serve you dessert.

"And they shall not escape" (1 Thessalonians 5:3).

3
Who Will Populate the Millennium?

When I talk with post-tribs, I like to ask them another question. The question is: Who will populate the millennium?

Why is this question so difficult for post-tribs to answer? Let me explain the situation. When Christ returns to earth after the tribulation He will rule with a rod of iron. He will bring peace and prosperity at last. Every wrong will be righted. The curse will be partially lifted so that crops will grow more abundantly. Because this time lasts for 1000 years we call this the *millennium* (Revelation 20:1-7).

Some do not believe in the millennium. If you are one of these, then I suggest that you read carefully the closing sections of the Old Testament prophetic books. There you will encounter numerous details, specific details, which can be fulfilled in no other way than in a literal millennium. Also read Jeremiah 32:42 and Amos 9:11 to find out how literally the promises will be fulfilled.

today	7 years	1000 years
church age	tribulation	millennium

THE PRE-TRIBULATION RAPTURE

Who will populate the millennium? Watch closely. Isaiah 65 describes this time of better conditions. Verse 20 says,

> There shall be no more thence an infant of days, nor an old man that hath not filled his days: for the child shall die an hundred years old; but the sinner being an hundred years old shall be accursed.

From this verse we see that people live longer, of course. But some still die. Death is not yet erased. This is important to notice. During the millennium people will be walking around on the face of this planet with *natural bodies,* subject to decay and death which we all inherited from Adam. Where do these people come from?

THE PEOPLE IN NATURAL BODIES

Are they present-day Christians? No, these people cannot be present-day Christians. The split-second that Christ returns we Christians will lose our natural bodies and gain immortal bodies.

> Behold, I show you a mystery; We shall not all sleep, but we shall all be changed, in a moment, in the twinkling of an eye, at the last trump: for the trumpet shall sound, and the dead shall be raised incorruptible, and we shall be changed. For this corruptible must put on incorruption, and this mortal must put on immortality (1 Corinthians 15:51-53).

This tranformation occurs at the *rapture.* The rapture is described in 1 Thessalonians 4:16-17:

> For the Lord himself shall descend from heaven with a shout, with the voice of the archangel, and with the trump of God: and the dead in Christ shall rise first: then we which are alive and remain shall be caught up together with them in the clouds, to meet the Lord in the air: and so shall we ever be with the Lord.

Our term "rapture" comes from the Latin translation of "caught up" in this passage. At the rapture we Christians are caught up into the clouds to meet Christ and at the same moment He transforms our bodies. So if people are still walking

Who Will Populate the Millennium?

around on the earth with *natural bodies* after the return of Christ, where do they come from?

Are they present-day non-Christians? Absolutely not, they cannot be present-day *non*-Christians! Here is a long list of verses which prove that no unbeliever will enter the millennium.

> Psalm 2:12: Kiss the Son, lest he be angry, and ye perish from the way, when his wrath is kindled but a little.

> Zephaniah 3:9: For then will I turn to the people a pure language, that they may *all* call upon the name of the Lord, to serve him with *one consent*.

> Malachi 4:1: For, behold, the day cometh, that shall burn as an oven; and *all* the proud, yea, and *all* that do wickedly, shall be stubble: and the day that cometh shall burn them up, saith the Lord of hosts, that it shall leave them *neither root nor branch*.

> Matthew 13:41: The Son of man shall send forth his angels, and they shall gather out of his kingdom *all* things that offend, and them which do iniquity.

> Matthew 24:51: [The Lord of the evil servant] shall cut him asunder, and appoint him his portion with the hypocrites: there shall be weeping and gnashing of teeth.

> Matthew 25:12: [To the foolish virgins] He answered and said, Verily I say unto you, I know you not.

> Matthew 25:30: And cast ye the unprofitable servant into outer darkness: there shall be weeping and gnashing of teeth.

> Luke 17:29: But the same day that Lot went out of Sodom it rained fire and brimstone from heaven, and destroyed them *all*.

> Luke 17:27b: [Noah] entered into the ark, and the flood came, and destroyed them *all*.

> Luke 17:32-33: Remember Lot's wife. *Whosoever* shall seek to save his life shall lose it; and whosoever shall lose his life shall preserve it.

THE PRE-TRIBULATION RAPTURE

> 1 Thessalonians 5:3: For when they shall say, Peace and safety; then sudden destruction cometh upon them, as travail upon a woman with child; and *they shall not escape* [strong dual negative in the Greek].
>
> 2 Thessalonians 1:7b-8; 2:12: When the Lord Jesus shall be revealed from heaven with his mighty angels, in flaming fire taking vengeance on them that know not God, and that obey not the gospel of our Lord Jesus Christ . . . That they *all* might be damned who believed not the truth, but had pleasure in unrighteousness.

Others could be added to this list. The Bible is full of it. For example, many of the Psalms open up with new light when viewed with this rooting out of the wicked in mind. But these listed are sufficient to prove that no unbeliever stands a chance of entering the millennium.

All will be destroyed. The little word "all" is too wide to get around. Some might wish that "all" doesn't mean "all," that it is only a figure of speech. This is only wishful thinking, though, without support from the contexts. The contexts of these verses support a literal and full meaning for "all." Check it out and see for yourself.

In the above list of verses I included a few about Noah and Lot. There is a reason for that. Jesus expressly made Noah and Lot types of the end times. Jesus compared the destruction by the flood to the destruction at the end. He also compared the destruction of Sodom to the end-time destruction. Is anyone still wondering if "all" means "all"? *All* unbelievers were destroyed by the flood *literally*. *All* unbelievers in Sodom were destroyed by fire and brimstone *literally*. If this is true in the antetypes, then how much more true it is of the day of the Lord, which is "very dark, and no brightness in it" (Amos 5:20).

Of course, I don't rely on types alone to prove my doctrine. But taken together with the other passages which clearly and explicitly say that all unbelievers will be destroyed, the examples of Noah and Lot powerfully illustrate the meaning. The contexts of the other verses in the above list also support a literal and full meaning for "all," but these examples of Noah

Who Will Populate the Millennium?

and Lot are an extra bonus.

The parables also in the above list illustrate the meaning. Suppose one of the five foolish virgins continued pounding on the door even though it was too late. And suppose the bridegroom answered that one, "All right. Come in, come in. I'll make an exception for you. But don't let it happen again." Can you imagine that? You see, if there were only one exception, it would make Jesus' parable untrue.

"Oh, but you can't make a parable teach anything you want to," some say. "The purpose of a parable is to teach only one central truth." Fine, fine, I agree. Is not the central thrust of the parable of the virgins to teach *advance preparation?* Those unprepared do not enter. It's that simple. If this is not the central thrust of the parable, then what is?

The same is true of the other parables in Matthew. Whether it be tares, bad fish, evil servant, foolish virgins, or unprofitable servant, *all* of that class suffer the *same fate.* There are only two classes of people; none of one class can cross over to receive the fate of the other class. Without exception each person receives the fate of his own class.

We cannot get around it by moving the destiny of the wicked to the end of the millennium, for this separation takes place when the Lord returns and specifically "in the time of harvest" (Matthew 13:30) which is at the end of the tribulation (Revelation 14:15).

We are surrounded by many passages. Explicit passages, illustrations, and parables all agree that no unbeliever can enter the millennium. Couple this with the fact that all present-day believers will receive new bodies at the rapture, and this leaves us with the question, "Who will populate the millennium with natural bodies?" A puzzling dilemma.

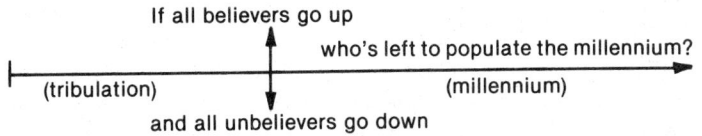

THE PRE-TRIBULATION RAPTURE

The above diagram is oversimplified because after believers go up into the air they will come back down again to rule and reign with Christ on the earth. But it illustrates my point: where do the natural-bodied people come from? Or, to put it another way, if we are the rulers during the millennium, then who are the subjects?

Could they be people saved after the rapture? Pre-tribulationists have a simple solution for the problem. By putting the rapture *before* the tribulation, this allows a *new group* of believers to spring up who will populate the millennium. After the rapture and during the tribulation many people will believe and be saved. These tribulation saints will be saved by the same means that people today are saved. The identical gospel and the identical salvation will apply during that time. The only difference is that they will be saved *after* the rapture, too late to gain a new body. If they survive the tribulation they will enter the millennium in their natural bodies.

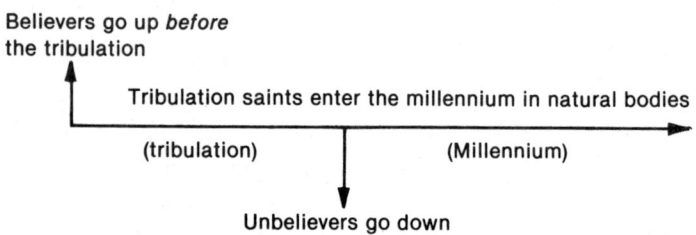

What about tribulation saints who do *not* survive the tribulation? What happens to them? They will join the resurrection after the tribulation and they will gain new immortal bodies at that time (Revelation 20:4). If you are reading this after the rapture, this fact will encourage you. Don't be afraid to die at the hands of antichrist. If he kills you, you will have a new body very shortly. If he doesn't kill you, you will be stuck with your natural body for another 1000 years. At the end of the 1000 years all will receive immortal bodies, because "flesh and blood cannot inherit the kingdom of God" (1 Corinthians 15:50).

How do post-tribs respond to this question of who will populate the millennium? Many ignore this question altogether as if it didn't exist. I don't blame them. A few make an honest attempt to answer it. We will examine some of these attempts to answer this question.

OTHER ATTEMPTED ANSWERS

Attempt Number 1: Unbelievers Enter the Millennium. One attempt to answer the question says that some unbelievers will survive the tribulation and enter the millennium. This would not be according to God's previous pattern. God destroyed the wicked old world with the flood and began afresh with righteous Noah. A fresh beginning in the millennium would follow the pattern. What proof is offered to offset this pattern? Only one passage as far as I can tell. We gave a long list of passages proving that no unbeliever can enter the millennium. If one passage appears to say the opposite, we ought to examine it very closely. The passage is Zechariah 14:16-19:

> 16. And it shall come to pass, that every one that is left of all the nations which came against Jerusalem shall even go up from year to year to worship the King, the Lord of hosts, and to keep the feast of tabernacles.
> 17. And it shall be, that whoso will not come up of all the families of the earth unto Jerusalem to worship the King, the Lord of hosts, even upon them shall be no rain.
> 18. And if the family of Egypt go not up, and come not, that have no rain; there shall be the plague, wherewith the Lord will smite the heathen that come not up to keep the feast of tabernacles.
> 19. This shall be the punishment of Egypt, and the punishment of all nations that come not up to keep the feast of tabernacles.

It is true that this passage speaks of unbelievers during the millennium. Where do they come from? If only believers enter the millennium, how do unbelievers slip into the picture? During the millennium, of course, people will have children. And since these children inherit the sin nature from Adam, some of them will turn out to be unbelievers. In fact, at the end of the millennium these unbelievers will stage a rebellion, a last-ditch attempt to overthrow Christ.

The point is this: unbelievers come *later* in the millennium, *not at the beginning.* Yes, this passage in Zechariah talks about unbelievers in the millennium, but it proves nothing about unbelievers *entering the millennium at the beginning.* That is the crucial point.

Now, this very same passage in Zechariah gives hints that *all* will believe at the beginning. Look at verse 16. It says "every one" worships. These who worship are those left over after the destruction of the armies who come against Jerusalem. These did not participate in the attack against Jerusalem. (All those who do participate in this attack are slain according to Revelation 19:21.) These left over ones, these believing worshipers, encompass "every one" at the beginning.

The next verse, verse 17, fits unbelievers who are born later in the 1000-year period. This passage does not say that these unbelievers are present at the beginning. You can make it say that if you want to, but then what will you do with the long list of passages above which say the opposite?

Now look at verses 18 and 19 which give the example of Egypt. Egypt is a seal of confirmation upon our interpretation of this passage. True, this passage indicates that Egypt might not believe at some point during the millennium. But at the beginning, at the beginning, I say, Egypt will undoubtedly believe. We know from Isaiah 19 that they, speaking of Egypt, "shall know the Lord in that day, and shall do sacrifice . . ." (Isaiah 19:21).

Zechariah 14 is an honest attempt to solve the problem, but does it really prove that unbelievers enter the millennium? What is really the clear teaching of the Bible? Set this lone passage alongside the long list of passages above and then decide for yourself what the clear teaching really is.

Attempt Number 2: A Remnant of Israel is Saved After the

Who Will Populate the Millennium?

Tribulation. A second attempt by post-tribulationists to answer the question of who will populate the millennium goes as follows: "A remnant of Israel, such as the 144,000, will believe when they see Christ descending in the clouds at the end of the tribulation. Since they are converted the instant He returns to earth, it will be too late for them to be raptured. Therefore, this believing remnant of Israel will remain on earth in natural bodies to populate the millennium."

If this were true, what would happen to the long list of passages above? Will the Lord say, "You foolish virgins should have made *advance preparation;* it's too late to let you in unless you are one of the 144,000"? Will He say, "Cast the unprofitable servant into outer darkness unless he is an Israelite"? Is Israel any exception? Do they have a deferred chance to believe which no one else has? The long list of passages above allow no room for that. No matter who you are; no matter where you're from; no matter what color, race, creed, you must believe *before* Christ returns or else you can throw away the long list of passages above.

But do not Matthew 24:30 and Revelation 1:7 say that all tribes of the earth mourn when they see Christ coming? Yes, it's true. All mourn. But do they mourn in repentance? Or do they mourn because they missed salvation? Or might there be a third reason for mourning?

For the sake of argument, let's suppose that all tribes mourn in repentance. And we'll suppose that Israel gets saved just *after* a post-trib rapture and just *as* Christ descends. We'll forget that this supposition is impossible according to our long list of verses at the beginning of this chapter. For now we'll just suppose it *could* happen this way. But in order for it to happen this way the *timing* would have to be precise. Repentance could not come before the rapture (otherwise they would be raptured), and repentance cannot come after Christ returns (otherwise they would be destroyed with the rest of the wicked). Repentance has to come precisely *after* the rapture and *before* the destruction in order for them squeak by.

THE PRE-TRIBULATION RAPTURE

Let's test this timing in Matthew 24:30-31 (assuming that Revelation 1:7 refers to the same event):

> 30. And then shall appear the sign of the Son of man in heaven: and then shall all the tribes of the earth mourn, and they shall see the Son of man coming in the clouds of heaven with power and great glory.
> 31. And he shall send his angels with a great sound of a trumpet, and they shall gather together his elect from the four winds, from one end of heaven to the other.

Now post-tribs see the rapture in verse 31. But the mourning already happened in verse 30. Therefore, the timing doesn't work out. Anyone who repents in verse 30 will be raptured in verse 31, and if raptured they will not have natural bodies for the millennium. (More about the order of events here in chapter eight.)

If the timing doesn't work out in Matthew 24:30, then what about Zechariah 12:10? Does not Zechariah 12:10 show that Israel gets saved the moment Christ descends?

> And I will pour upon the house of David, and upon the inhabitants of Jerusalem, the spirit of grace and of supplications: and they shall look upon me whom they have pierced, and they shall mourn for him, as one mourneth for his only son, and shall be in bitterness for him, as one that is in bitterness for his firstborn.

Is this verse talking about the moment Christ descends? Well, it doesn't say so. Is this verse talking about repentance and salvation? Well, it doesn't say so. Taking the verse alone we can make it mean anything we want to. But to find out what it really means we need to check other Scriptures as well as the immediate context.

A STORY ABOUT ISRAEL

As I tell you this story about Israel it will explain why a remnant of Israel repents and turns to Christ *before* His return, and it will explain why she mourns and sorrows *after* His return. Several scattered passages harmonize to tell one

Who Will Populate the Millennium?

beautiful story.

Israel Repents Before Christ Returns

To introduce our story we have two verses showing the time of Israel's repentance: "I will go and return to my place, till they acknowledge their offence, and seek my face; in their affliction they will seek me early" (Hosea 5:15). "For I say unto you, Ye shall not see me henceforth, till ye shall say, Blessed is he that cometh in the name of the Lord" (Matthew 23:39). From these verses we know that Christ will not leave heaven, Israel will not see Him descend, until they *first* repent.

How does God bring about her repentance? Let us go back to Zechariah 12, not verse 10 this time, but back to the beginning of the chapter. This part of the chapter describes the end of the tribulation period when "all the people [nations] of the earth be gathered together" against Jerusalem and "when they shall be in the siege both against Judah and against Jerusalem" (verses 3 and 2). At that critical moment extermination seems certain. Then "the governors of Judah shall say in their heart, The inhabitants of Jerusalem shall be my strength in the Lord of hosts their God" (verse 5). That cry to God at that critical moment, as they recognize that their strength is in the Lord instead of in themselves, is the salvation prayer for Israel. You see, Israel's spiritual conversion occurs in verse 5, not verse 10, of Zechariah 12.

Think of all the events which will lead up to her conversion. These days the nation Israel is victorious and proud. They feel no need to return to God, their pride will continue through the beginning of the tribulation period when they will be riding high on the coattails of antichrist. But when antichrist betrays them at the middle of the tribulation (Daniel 9:27), when he abolishes their precious religious system, and when their beloved city Jerusalem is overrun (Zechariah 14:2; Revelation 11:2), this begins their travail which ends in the spiritual birth of the nation (Jeremiah 30:6-7; Isaiah 66:8). During this travail they will undergo intense tribulation in which God will sift them as wheat (Amos 9:9) and two-thirds of the Israelites will be killed (Zechariah 13:8-9). The climax comes at the end of the tribulation, when God gathers the nations of the world against Jerusalem. By this time Jerusalem is already overrun and desolate; only half of the population remains (Zechariah 14:2). So for them to see all the nations gathered against her to exterminate her completely is a hopeless sight. And when Israel finally realizes that her national ambition is beyond recovery, when her last hope in this world is dashed to the ground, it is then that she turns her eyes upward.

Through these events God brings about the repentance of Israel. Her time of trouble is her spiritual travail (Jeremiah 30:6-7, Isaiah 26:16-17). Her spiritual birth comes as a result of *her travail,* not as a result of seeing Christ when He returns.

It is amazing to find a prophecy of Israel's repentance way back in Moses' time but we read in Deuteronomy 4:30-31: "When thou art in tribulation, and all these things are come upon thee, even in the latter days, if thou turn to the Lord thy God, and shalt be obedient unto his voice . . . he will not forsake thee, neither destroy thee . . ." This is the very first prophecy in the Bible of the tribulation, and it shows Israel repenting *during the tribulation.*

The actual prayer of repentance is prophesied by Isaiah. Part of the prayer reads as follows:

> Oh that thou wouldest rend the heavens, that thou wouldest come down . . . We are all as an unclean thing, and all our righteousnesses are as filthy rags; and we all do fade as a leaf; and our iniquities, like the wind, have taken us away (Isaiah 64:1,6).

We quote and apply these verses to other situations, which is fine. But the primary meaning, according to the context, refers to Israel during the tribulation. The context of Isaiah 60-66 gives the general time setting for Isaiah 64. Notice the prayer that God "wouldst rend the heavens." This phrase shows that God did not yet rend the heavens, and so it pinpoints the time of the prayer to *before* Christ's return from heaven.

Therefore, we discover a blend of several passages which tell

Who Will Populate the Millennium?

one harmonious story about the time of Israel's conversion.

Hosea 5:15:	I will go and return to my place, till they acknowledge their offense . . . .
Matthew 23:39:	Ye shall not see me henceforth, till ye shall say . . . .
Deuteronomy 4:30:	When thou art in tribulation . . . .
Isaiah 64:1:	Oh, that thou wouldest rend the heavens . . .
Zechariah 12:2:	When they shall be in the siege both against Judah and against Jerusalem . . . .

These verses show that Israel is converted *not* as she sees Him return in the clouds. It has to be *before*.

Christ Returns

We now continue our story. In direct answer to Israel's prayer that God would "rend the heavens," He does exactly that. He has been waiting for precisely this moment, for His chosen people to return to Him. They have turned to Him in hopeless moments before and He has miraculously saved them before. Now He saves them again. He saves them spiritually, and He also rescues them from their enemies. In response to their prayer of repentance He rends the heavens as He breaks through the clouds and "in that day shall the Lord defend the inhabitants of Jerusalem . . . and it shall come to pass in that day, that I will seek to destroy all the nations that come against Jerusalem" (Zechariah 12:8-9).

Does the return of Christ occasion the repentance of Israel? No, it is the other way around. The repentance of Israel occasions the return of Christ.

Israel Mourns After Christ Returns

The story I have been telling you so far has been about the repentance of Israel *before* the return of Christ. But I still haven't explained Zechariah 12:10 which happens *after* the return of Christ. If this verse is not talking about Israel's initial post-salvation experience, then what is it talking about?

> And I will pour upon the house of David, and upon the inhabitants of Jerusalem, the spirit of grace and of supplications: and they shall look upon me whom they have pierced, and they shall mourn for him, as one mourneth for his only son, and shall be in bitterness for him as one that is in bitterness for his firstborn.

In the context of Zechariah 12, verse 10 comes *after* the return of Christ. We have seen that Israel's cry of repentance occurs in verse 5. We have seen that Christ returns to rescue Jerusalem from her enemies in verses 8-9. Verse 10 follows. Verse 10 happens after Christ defeats the enemies, not while He is still in the clouds. Verse 11 confirms the time:

> In that day shall there be a great mourning in Jerusalem.

Where does this mourning take place? In *Jerusalem.* Why not the world over? Why only in Jerusalem? This tells me that Christ has already gathered His people from the four corners of the earth, and by this time He has brought them to Jerusalem. The time is after His coming and after His gathering.

When do they look upon Him whom they have pierced? While He is in the clouds? The text does not say so. The text says "in Jerusalem." After Christ has gathered the Israelites from the four corners of the world, after they arrive in Jerusalem, then they see Him there in Jerusalem. They see the One whom they as a nation have crucified, and they mourn over what they have done.

They may also see Him as He descends with clouds. But that's not what this verse is talking about. They may also mourn earlier. But that's not what this verse is talking about. Not this verse, nor any other verse, teaches that Israel gets saved when Christ descends.

Why Do They Mourn?

Why does Israel mourn? Are they mourning in repentance in

Who Will Populate the Millennium?

order to be saved?

The words "mourning" and "supplication" both are used in cases where the person is *already* a believer (Genesis 23:2; 1 Kings 8:30; 13:29; Psalm 130:2; 143:1; Ecclesiastes 3:4). The use of these words, therefore, in Zechariah 12:10 in no way proves that Israel becomes saved at this point. (A concordance will be helpful here.)

If not for salvation, then why does Israel mourn? Remorse and regret. Perhaps you have had this experience. When you get especially close to God you feel an acute awareness of your sinfulness. You feel a deep remorse for your past, more so than when you were first saved. This is what many Israelites will experience as they look back on their long rejection of their Messiah. Ezekiel indicates this reason for mourning (Ezekiel 20:38-43; 36:24-31).

Jeremiah indicates their supplications may be in view of a new covenant to be made in Jerusalem (Jeremiah 50:4-5).

My point is this: Scripture gives good solid reasons for the mourning that is mentioned in Zechariah 12:10. In light of this no one can positively claim that Zechariah 12:10 is talking about last-minute repentance as Christ descends with the clouds. That moment is too late for salvation.

Cleansing Is Not Repentance

In addition to Zechariah 12:10, other passages have been used to "prove" that Israel is saved at the return of Christ (such as Zephaniah 3:8-13; Zechariah 3:8-9; Malachi 3:1-5). But just like Zechariah 12:10, these passages properly fall into place *after* the return of Christ. And like Zechariah 12:10 they refer not to Israel's salvation experience, but to a post-salvation experience.

What kind of post-salvation experience is this? Joel 2:28-32 speaks of those who call upon the name of the Lord for salvation *before* the day of the Lord, and these receive a pouring out of the Spirit *afterward* (similar to the apostles in Acts 2 who received a pouring out of the Spirit *after* they were saved). You see, these tribulation saints will receive a special cleansing, a special purifying, that is distinct from the divine forgiveness they receive at salvation.

I believe this special cleansing is the prophetic fulfillment of the ancient Day of Atonement (Leviticus 16:29-30). The Day of Atonement was one of seven feasts which Israel observed. On this day Israel afflicted their souls in memory of their past sins, and on this day the entire nation was officially cleansed. It is generally agreed that the feasts of Israel have prophetic significance. In a later chapter we will show how all seven feasts find fulfillment in prophecy in order, according to the dates on the calendar. But for now we will just mention that the Day of Atonement is prophetically fulfilled *after* Christ returns and *after* He gathers His people. On this future day Israel will once again afflict their souls as they remember their past sins. And on this future day God will once and for all remove the iniquity of the nation.

This is why I say that repentance is not the same as cleansing. These are two different things. They happen at two different times. Israel repents and is saved and is forgiven *before* Christ returns. But she receives a special cleansing *after* Christ returns.

Repentance Before	*Christ Returns*	*Cleansing After*
Hosea 5:15		Joel 2:28
Matthew 32:39		Leviticus 16:29-30
Zechariah 12:5		Zechariah 12:10
Isaiah 64		Ezekiel 36:24-31
Deuteronomy 4:30-31	▼	Ezekiel 20:38-43

In other words, the verses used to prove the salvation of Israel at the return of Christ are referring instead to her post-salvation experience of official cleansing. Once Christ returns, it's too late to be saved.

What if I'm wrong about the time of Israel's salvation? What if the Lord will say to the foolish virgins, "All right, I'll let you in if you are an Israelite"? What if the Lord will say to

Who Will Populate the Millennium?

the unprofitable servant, "I'll make a special case for you if you are one of the 144,000"? What if I'm wrong and Israel does sneak into the millennium in this way?

Post-tribs would still have the problem of Gentile nations in the millennium. Zechariah 14:16-19 and Revelation 20:8 show that *many* nations, not just one nation, will populate the millennium. Furthermore, these passages show that the offspring of these nations are *natural-bodied* people (because they sin).

So post-tribs have to put *both* Israel *and* Gentiles into the millennium in order to save their case. Where will they get them from?

We come back to the main question of this chapter: "Who will populate the millennium in natural bodies?" It cannot be the church because it will be raptured and gain new bodies. It cannot be unbelievers because they will *all* be destroyed when Christ returns to earth. We cannot make an exception for Israel, because any Israelite, just like any Gentile, must be saved *before* Christ returns to earth or else they will be destroyed with the rest of the unbelievers. Who will enter the millennium with natural bodies? Only one answer remains. It has to be tribulation saints. Tribulation saints are saved during the tribulation *after* the rapture. Since they miss the rapture they remain in their natural bodies to enter the millennium.

Attempt Number 3: Ignore the Problem. Another way that I have seen post-tribs try to answer the problem of who will populate the millennium goes something like this: We don't have to answer all the problems. Some questions we can leave hanging in the air. To derive a pre-trib rapture from the question of who will populate the millennium is only an implication anyway. It is only an argument that is far from clear teaching, and so we don't have to answer it.

I agree that we don't have to answer every problem in the Bible. Since God is so far above us and since man is so puny, we cannot expect to understand everything. In this case, however, there is a difference. I'll show you what it is.

There are two kinds of implications. Some implications you can get around and some you can't get around. One day the telephone rang at our house and when I answered it I heard a voice on the other end say, "Your cat is up our tree."

I said, "What?"

"Your cat is up our tree."

For a second I was speechless (how often does this happen to you?). But as I glanced around it hit me. I responded with assurance, "I see our cat right here in the kitchen."

My neighbor on the phone simply said, "Oh," and hung up. That was the end of that.

Do you see my point? I answered my neighbor with an implication she couldn't get around. I never once came right out and plainly said, "Our cat is not up your tree." I didn't have to. I didn't go outside and look up the tree. I didn't have to find out whose cat was up the tree. All I had to do was see our own cat in the kitchen and that was answer enough. I didn't even tell my neighbor that our cat's front leg was broken and that it was in a cast and that it was not able to climb a tree. All this was true, but one simple answer was sufficient. One little implication settled the matter because it was an implication she couldn't get around.

It doesn't impress me when someone comes along and says, "Aw, that's just an implication." It doesn't impress me a bit, because there are two types of implications, implications you can get around and implications you can't get around.

Some questions regarding the Bible you can leave hanging in the air. You recognize that there are possible ways to get around those problems even though you might not happen to know what they are. But this matter of who will populate the millennium has no other possible way to get around it. *This type of implication you cannot ignore.*

I know that pre-tribs in years past have used some implications you can get around. To say that Christ comes to the air one time and to the earth the next time is a weak implication.

Who Will Populate the Millennium?

You can get around that by saying that *both* may happen on the same day. To say that Christ comes *for* His saints one time and *with* His saints the next is no proof. You can get around that by supposing that *both* happen on the same day. But pretribulationists have also used this question of who will populate the millennium. I like this question because you can't get around it. You can't ignore it.

The previous chapter also presented an implication. The known day and the unknown day *cannot* be the same day. They must be *different days*. This type of implication you can't get around.

If anyone says to you that these two chapters are only implications, simply smile and ask them: How do you get around these implications?

The next chapter will present a third implication of this type.

"Return from the wedding" (Luke 12:36).

4
When Is the Wedding?

"Pre-tribulationists have not one verse in the whole Bible which proves that the rapture comes before the tribulation. They come with arguments and implications, but where is just one little verse? Show me one verse."

Challenges like this one I have read in post-trib literature, and such a challenge deserves to be answered. Can we meet the challenge? Do we have one verse that proves pre-tribulationism?

THE ONE VERSE

Before I tell you what verse I have in mind, I want to ask you a question: When is the wedding? We know that the church is the bride and Christ is the bridegroom and someday we will be married. Earthly marriage is just a foretaste of the ultimate joy and fulfillment which we will experience at the heavenly marriage. And it will be without all the problems that earthly marriage has. An earthly wedding is beautiful to watch. But just think of the thrill and excitement we will experience at our heavenly wedding!

My question is: When is it? I think we can all agree that it is at Christ's return. Paul wrote, "For I am jealous over you with

When Is the Wedding?

godly jealousy: for I have espoused you to one husband, that I may present you as a chaste virgin to Christ'' (2 Corinthians 11:2). Right now, according to Paul, we are "espoused." This means we are betrothed or engaged. This means we are not married yet. As long as we are in the church age we are in the engagement period, not the marriage period. So I think we can all agree that *the wedding cannot take place until the rapture.* Not one minute before. Agreed?

Now, how about that challenge? Can we prove pre-tribulationism from one verse? I think we can. The verse is Luke 12:36:

> And ye yourselves like unto men that wait for their lord, when he will *return from the wedding;* that when he cometh and knocketh, they may open unto him immediately.

Read it closely. Did you notice the phrase "return from the wedding"? What does that tell you? That one little phrase gives away the whole secret. You see, if the wedding occurred before this return, then the rapture occurred before this return. A prior wedding necessitates a prior coming. It's so simple. If this one verse does not set up a chronology, then my Bible is written in riddles instead of plain words.

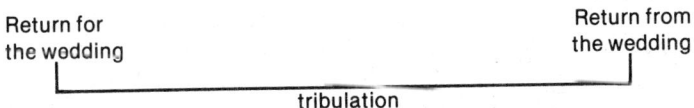

EXAMINING OBJECTIONS

Nothing more needs to be said, but lest there be any doubt about this, I'll take time now to examine possible objections.

Objection Number 1: The Post-Trib Rapture Is the Wedding. A post-trib may reason that the post-trib rapture is the wedding. In other words, as we go up we are married, and as we come down moments later this is His *return from the wedding.*

THE PRE-TRIBULATION RAPTURE

I do not object to the rapture being the wedding. But I do have one little question about this scheme.

Who's waiting?

Yes, who's waiting?

The verse says to be like men who wait for their lord's return from the wedding. If all are raptured at this time, no one is left who will be waiting.

The rapture does not fit at the end of the tribulation.

Objection Number 2: It's Only a Parable. Some may object to getting a chronology out of Luke 12:36 by saying: It is only a parable. It's not talking about the real Lord or the real wedding. It's just an earthly illustration, that's all.

Think now. What is a parable, after all? It is an earthly illustration with a heavenly meaning. Any other parable would be accepted as illustrating a heavenly meaning. Why not this one? Any other parable that talks about a wedding is commonly accepted as applying to the heavenly wedding. Any other parable that talks about a lord is commonly interpreted to apply to *the* Lord. Isn't that the purpose of a parable, to illustrate *heavenly* meaning?

Want proof? Look at the following verse:

> Blessed are those servants, whom the lord when he cometh shall find watching: verily I say unto you, that he shall gird himself, and make them to sit down to meat, and will come forth and serve them (Luke 12:37).

What earthly lord does that, reversing the expected roles? Obviously, this earthly lord illustrates the heavenly Lord. Furthermore, verse 40 clearly applies this to the coming of the Son of man.

The strength of the pre-trib position is that it can accept the chronology of Luke 12:36 at face value. The weakness of the post-trib position is that it cannot accept the implications of the chronology.

We know that God inspired every word of the Bible; so we can trust the chronology in Luke 12:36. Would Jesus use an un-

When Is the Wedding?

truth to teach a truth? Of course not. Jesus is a better teacher than that. Out of all possible parables that He could have chosen or invented, He gave this one. Why? Why not another one? He gave us this particular parable because it teaches accurately concerning the second coming, and I cannot imagine Him choosing a parable that would be misleading in any way. Yes, we can trust the chronology.

ANOTHER VERSE TO CONFIRM IT

I am sure that some are thinking: you cannot prove doctrine from a parable. A parable can only be used to illustrate doctrine which is clearly taught elsewhere in Scripture.

I agree with this wholeheartedly. I merely used this one verse, Luke 12:36, because some post-tribs have asked for one verse, and so I gave it to them. But having done that, let us go to another passage in Revelation which confirms the illustration we have seen in Luke.

> Let us be glad and rejoice, and give honour to him: for the marriage of the Lamb is come, and his wife hath made herself ready. And to her was granted that she should be arrayed in fine linen, clean and white: for the fine linen is the righteousnesses of saints (Revelation 19:7-8).

This passage also sets up a chronology, the identical chronology as Luke 12:36. Notice, "His wife hath made herself ready (past tense)." Notice also, "And to her was granted (past tense) that she should be arrayed in fine linen." Now if the wife, which is the church, is robed and readied, then she must also be raptured. Even without assuming that the wife is the church only, the implications remain valid. There is no way for her to be robed and readied unless she were in heaven, and there is no way for all believers who make up the wife to be in heaven without the rapture.

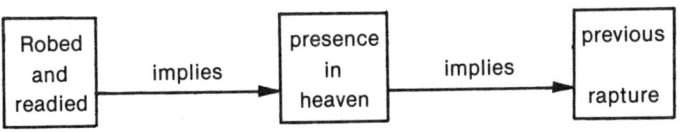

If the rapture occurred previously, this would rule out a post-trib rapture, because at this point in Revelation 19 Christ has not yet left heaven to begin His descent to earth after the tribulation.

To set Luke 12:36 and Revelation 19 in perspective, think of a shopping trip. Suppose my wife came in the door and said to me, "I just *returned from* the grocery store."

"I'm glad you're home now, but where did you go?

"I just said. I *returned from* the grocery store. A trip *from* the store implies a *previous* trip *to* the store."

"Good point. That settles the chronology, but what other evidence do you have?"

"Evidence? Just look at the bags of groceries in my arms! Doesn't that tell you where I've been?"

Just as my wife brought the groceries safely home, so Christ has brought His bride safely home to heaven by Revelation 19. The bride, robed and readied, are the "groceries," proving a previous trip to earth by Christ.

The chronology of Revelation 19 does not fit post-tribulationism. It's that simple.

But it's not that simple, really, because I am sure some will raise objections. So let's take time now to answer possible objections to our chronology in Revelation 19.

Objection Number 1: The Wife Is Readied on Earth. Some may object that the wife may not wait until the rapture to be robed and readied. Why couldn't she receive robes *on earth* and be readied for the marriage while *on earth?*

It is true that Revelation 3:18 speaks of being clothed in white raiment now. But being clothed spiritually is different from being clothed physically. Revelation 3:4-5 points up the difference:

> Thou hast a few names even in Sardis which have not defiled their garments; and they shall walk with me in white: for they are worthy. He that overcometh, the same *shall be clothed* in white raiment; and I will not blot out his name out of the book of life, but I will confess his name before

my Father, and before his angels.

Yes, we now have garments in a spiritual sense. But we await the actual moment when we will be arrayed physically. This happens only in heaven.

Let me give you a real live example of this. Do you remember the souls under the altar in Revelation 6:9-11? When did they receive their white robes?

> And when he had opened the fifth seal, I saw under the altar the souls of them that were slain for the word of God, and for the testimony which they held: And they cried with a loud voice saying, How long, O Lord, holy and true, dost thou not judge and avenge our blood on them that dwell on the earth? And white robes were given unto every one of them; and it was said unto them, that they should rest yet for a little season, until their fellowservants also and their brethren, that should be killed as they were, should be fulfilled.

As faithful as these souls were on earth, even unto death, they did not receive their robes on earth. They had to await heaven. Yes, this happened before their resurrection. But resurrection has nothing to do with my argument. My point is they had to await heaven. Yes, they are not church saints, but that is irrelevant to my argument because post-tribulationists believe they are church saints anyway. My point is they had to await heaven.

I know of only one exception, and the exception proves the rule. Jesus was seen in dazzling white on the mount (Mark 9:1-3), but He was in a heavenly transfigured state at the time. You and I won't be arrayed like that until we get to heaven.

Not only do these other Scriptures demand arrival in heaven, but the very definition of "fine linen" demands arrival in heaven. "Fine linen is the righteousnesses of saints" (Revelation 19:8). "Righteousnesses" is plural in the Greek; so we know it is talking about the various righteous deeds we do in the power of the Holy Spirit. If my robe is made up of the deeds I do, then my righteousness is not complete until my life on earth is complete. As long as I have more righteous deeds to do, my robe is not finished. Can you imagine going to a wedding, and here comes the bride down the aisle in a half completed wedding dress? A bride with holes in her dress not sewn up yet is not quite ready for the wedding.

But the wife of the Lamb in Revelation 19 is ready. Her dress has no holes; all the sewing is done. She has no more righteous acts to perform; they are all done. She has no more deeds to do because her life on earth is complete. The very definition of "fine linen" will not allow the bride to be ready on earth.

If the wife, which is the church, has arrived in heaven by Revelation 19, this not only disproves post-tribulationism but it also militates against the partial rapture theory which says that part of the church is raptured before the tribulation and the rest are left behind. This passage informs us that no segment of the bride is left straggling upon the earth. She is *all* in heaven. If she were not all in heaven, how could she be robed and ready?

(Also against the partial-rapture theory, 1 Corinthians 15:51 says "we shall *all* be changed," not *some* of us. First Thessalonians 4:17 says "we which are alive" shall be raptured, not some of us).

The attempt to robe the wife on earth has failed. Other Scriptures forbid it, and the definition of "fine linen" forbids it. The wife has left earth and she has arrived in heaven by Revelation 19, and she had to get there somehow. She must have gotten there either by rocket or by rapture.

Objection Number 2: The Marriage Is After the Tribulation. In order to get around the idea of a rapture before Revelation 19 others may object that the marriage occurs *after* the tribulation. The marriage is *mentioned* before Christ's return, but it actually *takes place* after Christ's return.

I agree that the marriage is after, but this objection misses my point altogether. My argument is based, not on the wife's marriage, but on her robing and readiness. The marriage may be future, but her *preparation* for the marriage is *past*. That's

When Is the Wedding?

the point.

This does raise a problem of a different nature, though. If Revelation 19 places the marriage *after* the tribulation, then why does Luke 12:36 place the wedding *before* the end of the tribulation? As you recall, Luke 12:36 says,

> And ye yourselves [be] like unto men that wait for their lord, when he will return from the wedding.

Can *both* Luke 12:36 and Revelation 19 be correct? Is the wedding before or after Christ's return? Will the real wedding please stand up?

This seems a problem only because of our English culture. Remember, the writers of the Bible did not live in our country. They didn't know anything about our weddings. They wrote from a background of their own wedding customs. According to Eastern marriage customs the marriage has *three phases*. Walvoord explains it this way:

> Though marriage customs varied in the ancient world, usually there were three major aspects: (1) The marriage contract was often consummated by the parents when the parties to the marriage were still children and not ready to assume adult responsibility. The payment of a suitable dowry was often a feature of the contract. When consummated, the contract meant that the couple were legally married. (2) At a later time when a couple had reached a suitable age, the second step in the wedding took place. This was a ceremony in which the bridegroom accompanied by his friends would go to the house of the bride and escort her to his home. This is the background of the parable of the virgins in Matthew 25:1-13. (3) Then the bridegroom would bring his bride to his home and the marriage supper, to which guests were invited, would take place. It was such a wedding feast that Christ attended at Cana as recorded in John 2:1-12.
>
> The marriage symbolism is beautifully fulfilled in the relationship of Christ to His church. The wedding contract is consummated at the time the church is redeemed. Every true Christian is joined to Christ in a legal marriage. When Christ comes for His church at the rapture, the second phase of the wedding is fulfilled, namely, the Bridegroom goes to receive His bride. The third phase then follows, that is, the wedding feast.[1]

So the marriage of the Bible has three phases, the betrothal, the processional, and the feast. We are in the betrothal stage now, the rapture-processional is what Luke 12:36 refers to ("return from the wedding"), and the feast is what Revelation 19 refers to. Therefore, we find no contradiction at all between Luke 12:36 and Revelation 19. They merely refer to different aspects of the marriage.

(I am not disputing that Israel also is the bride, or part of the bride. She had an earlier marriage, divorce, and will be remarried. See Jeremiah 3:1,8,14,20. The marriage of Israel need not correspond in time with the marriage of the church, or at least I know of no Scripture which says so. Revelation 21:9-14 portrays a unity of the bride that does not wipe out distinctions.)

There is also the matter of a feast to prepare for. Some people are under the impression that the marriage feast transpires *during* the tribulation instead of after the tribulation as we have said. But what is a feast without guests? If I invited people over to my house for dinner, I would not begin the meal until all the guests arrived. Who are the guests at the marriage supper of the Lamb? It couldn't be the church because the church is the bride. No one sends the bride an invitation to her own wedding. If not the church, then that leaves Old Testament saints and tribulation saints. These are the guests. If the feast took place in heaven during the tribulation, then the tribulation saints would miss the supper. And you and I would miss their company too.

No, tribulation saints will not miss out on the wedding invitation. "And he saith unto me, Write, Blessed are they which are called unto the marriage supper of the Lamb" (Revelation 19:9). The mention of invited guests at this point tells me that the feast is anticipated instead of dissipated. Invited guests look *forward* to a feast. If the feast were almost over what would be the purpose of mentioning invited guests at this point?

A second indication of a future feast is this: the wife is ready. Ready for what? Ready to attend the marriage feast, of course. Suppose you are invited out to dinner and you get all

When Is the Wedding?

ready and go. You enjoy a delicious feast of fried chicken and all the trimmings. After you finish the main course out comes your favorite dessert, strawberry pie. You relish every bite of it, and just as you are about to take the last bite, your host exclaims, "Are you ready for dinner?" Quite out of place, isn't it? You see, the mention of the wife being "ready" at this point tells me the feast is future.

A third indication of a future feast is the usage of the word "come" in the phrase "the marriage of the Lamb is come" (Revelation 19:7). In other words, it is about to begin. In Greek "is come" is in the past tense, but I understand it to be a *dramatic past*. The dramatic usage of a verb indicates that something is on the verge of happening. This usage of "come" is common in Revelation. It occurs, not once, nor twice, but it forms a striking pattern as you can see from checking out Revelation 6:17; 11:18; 14:7, 15. Let me show you one of these passages as an example:

> And the kings of the earth, and the great men, and the rich men, and the chief captains, and the mighty men, and every bondman, and every free man, hid themselves in the dens and in the rocks of the mountains; and said to the mountains and rocks, Fall on us, and hide us from the face of him that sitteth on the throne, and from the wrath of the Lamb: for the great day of his wrath *is come;* and who shall be able to stand? (Revelation 6:15-17).

As you can see, the people are terrified of wrath on the verge of breaking forth. If God's wrath had already vented itself, then it would be a little late for the people to cry for the mountains and rocks to fall on them. They yearn to hide, not from wrath past, but from wrath future. Their cry is, "Who *shall* be able [not who *was* able] to stand?" This illustrates the dramatic usage of "is come" as it is used consistently throughout Revelation. I believe Revelation 19:7 is no exception to the pattern, because in the context are the "ready wife" and the "invited guests" which point to a future feast.

Evidence of a feast after the tribulation comes not only from this context, but also from other Scriptures. Matthew 25:10, from the parable of the virgins, is a fourth indication. The setting of this parable is *after the tribulation* as you can see by following the flow of thought from Matthew 24 onwards. At the conclusion of the parable, Jesus says that the wise virgins "went in with him *to the marriage.*" Therefore, the marriage—that is, the marriage feast— is *after* the tribulation.

A fifth indication of the time of the feast is what Jesus said to His disciples at the last supper. "But I say unto you, I will not drink henceforth of this fruit of the vine, until that day when I drink it new with you in my Father's kingdom" (Matthew 26:29). This places the time at the commencement of the millennial kingdom after the tribulation.

A wonderful celebration will be the marriage feast. I look forward to it very much. I will relish that meal more than I have relished any meal in my life. I hope to see you there too. If you are reading this book before the rapture, then you can be there as part of the bride, the wife of the King of the universe. If you are reading this after the rapture, then you can share in the celebration too as royal guests. Here is your invitation: "The Spirit and the bride say, Come. And let him that heareth say, Come. And let him that is athirst come. And whosoever will, let him take the water of life freely" (Revelation 22:17).

You have the opportunity, however, to choose your feast. Everyone alive at the end of the tribulation will attend a feast. If not the marriage feast, it will be another feast. What is this other feast?

> And I saw an angel standing in the sun; and he cried with a loud voice, saying to all the fowls that fly in the midst of heaven, Come and gather yourselves together unto *the supper of the great God;* that ye may eat the flesh of kings, and the flesh of captains, and the flesh of mighty men, and the flesh of horses, and of them that sit on them, and the flesh of all men, both free and bond, both small and great (Revelation 19:17-18).

Choose your feast. Will you enjoy the marriage feast? Or will you be enjoyed at the Supper of the Great God, not as

When Is the Wedding?

guests, but as food?

Pointing out the contrast between these two feasts is intended when John was instructed to write, "Blessed are they which are called unto the marriage supper of the Lamb" (Revelation 19:9). Our English translation loses something, but the Greek emphasizes the marriage feast by changing the word order so that it reads something like this: "Blessed are they which to the marriage supper of the Lamb are called." In other words, the language implies, "Blessed is he that is called to *this* feast *rather than to that other feast.*"

What a contrast!

The future feast rests on past preparation. I happen to believe that the marriage feast is celebrated after the tribulation for the five reasons given above. So when a post-tribulationist objects that the feast is after, I fully agree with him. My argument is not based on the feast, but on the preparation. The wife is robed and readied—that is my point. To be entirely ready she must be entirely in heaven, and if she is entirely in heaven she must be raptured.

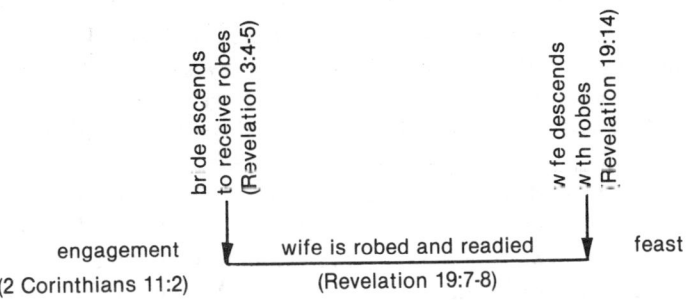

Objection Number 3: The Time Is Reversed. Some post-tribs may agree that a ready wife necessitates a raptured wife, and so they may try to get around the problem in another way. They may try to say that Revelation 19 is not written in order—the chronology is reversed. By switching the passage around, they manage to place the readiness of the wife *after* the return of

THE PRE-TRIBULATION RAPTURE

Christ to earth.

Here are three reasons why the chronology in Revelation 19 cannot be reversed. The first and obvious reason is that it is written in this order. If it was written in this order it must be in this order. I realize that parts of Revelation are not in order because the seals, trumpets, and vials backtrack and amplify each other instead of following consecutively. But even there the order is not random; it follows a pattern of cycles. And the pattern of cycles is made obvious enough so that we can perceive them, as we shall see in a later chapter. There is nothing wrong with an orderly pattern like that, but to play hopscotch chronology is a different story. To reverse the time in Revelation 19 follows no pattern. This reminds me of the proud mother watching her son in a marching band. "Look," she said, "my boy is the only one in step!"

The book of Revelation has nothing out of step, but everything falls into place. The cycles of seals, trumpets, and vials take place in chapters 6 through 18. These chapters backtrack and amplify one another in an orderly patterned way. But by chapter 19 these cycles are over. From 19 on everything is chronological. Everything is in order. Therefore, to reverse the time in Revelation 19 not only is *un*patterned, but also it goes *contrary* to the pattern of Revelation 19-22!

It is written that the wife is ready *before* Christ's coming to earth. If it is written that way, then let's leave it that way.

The second reason for leaving the order as it stands is the context immediately following. Notice verse 14: "And the armies which were in heaven followed him upon white horses, clothed in fine linen, white and clean." Who are these armies clothed in fine linen? Where did they come from? And why are they wearing fine linen? These questions are easy to answer because it has just been explained to us about the wife of the Lamb being arrayed in fine linen. It is like a play; one scene prepares us for the next. As the drama of Revelation unfolds we first see the wife arrayed, and next we watch her in her new garments ride down from the sky on white horses. The two

When Is the Wedding?

segments are hinged together in such a way that one has to follow the other and to invert the order would ruin the whole thing.

The third reason for leaving the order intact is the context preceding. The first part of the chapter contains "Alleluia's" occasioned by the destruction of the great whore, Babylon. This is a tip-off regarding the time. When is Babylon destroyed? It has to be sometime before the end of the tribulation because of its aftereffects described in Revelation 18.

> And the kings of the earth, who have committed fornication and lived deliciously with her, shall bewail her, and lament for her, when they shall see the smoke of her burning (Revelation 18:9).

When Christ returns to earth He will terminate all overt wickedness. Therefore, for these wicked kings to lament the sinful city, instead of rejoicing, shows me that the time is before Christ's return.

Here is another aftereffect of Babylon's destruction:

> Rejoice over her, thou heaven, and ye holy apostles and prophets; for God hath avenged you on her (Revelation 18:20).

This sounds like the apostles and prophets are still in heaven. If Christ had returned they would have returned to earth with Him.

Therefore, there is some time—I don't know how long—between the destruction of Babylon and the coming of Christ to earth. This is where the "Alleluia's" come in. In Revelation 19 the "Alleluia's" come in response to the destruction of Babylon. This tells me that the time is yet *before* Christ's coming. If Christ had come, it seems to me that the "Alleluia's" would be in response to the victory of Armageddon instead of the victory over Babylon. In a football game, as soon as a player makes a great play, everyone stands up and cheers. To stand up and cheer the play previous to that, or two plays ago, is a little late and out of place.

THE PRE-TRIBULATION RAPTURE

Therefore, the "Alleluia's" in response to Babylon's destruction place the time before Christ's return. And as one "Alleluia" flows into the next one, and that one into the next one, and that one into the next one, before you know it the wife is ready. (How fitting it is, because Babylon the harlot, decked in purple and scarlet, gives way to the wife of the Lamb, arrayed in fine linen, clean and white.) The readiness of the wife is hopelessly enmeshed in a context which puts the time before Christ's return.

Another item from the context preceding is "a great voice of much people in heaven" (verse 1). If these people are still in heaven then the time has to be before Christ's return, because when Christ returns to earth He brings all the saints to earth with Him.

In light of the context, how can anyone invert the time? Well, I suppose someone could say that the first part of Revelation 19 happens *before* Christ's return, the middle part skips to *after* Christ's return, and the last part *reverts back* to Christ's return itself. Hopscotch chronology does not appeal to me, especially when the passage reads so smoothly and orderly as it is written.

In light of the three reasons given above for leaving the order intact, what evidence is offered to the contrary? Only one word as far as I know. The word is "reigneth" in verse 6 of Revelation 19.

> And I heard as it were the voice of a great multitude, and as the voice of many waters, and as the voice of mighty thunderings, saying, Alleluia: for the Lord God omnipotent *reigneth*.

The point is made that "reigneth" is in the *present tense*, and therefore, the time must be during the reign of Christ *after* His return. It is fine to base an argument on one word if that word carries insurmountable implications. But in this case the argument tries to squeeze too much out of the one word "reigneth."

When Is the Wedding?

For one thing, the tense of a verb in Greek does not always tell the time. Usually, but not always. In this context, "reigneth" could very well be what grammarians call the *futuristic present*. Dana and Mantey define the futuristic present this way:

> This use of the present tense denotes an event which has not yet occurred, but which is regarded as so certain that in thought it may be contemplated as already coming to pass.[2]

They then cite the example of Matthew 26:2, "Ye know that after two days is the feast of the passover, and the Son of man *is betrayed* to be crucified."

Therefore, a present tense can denote a future event if the context so dictates. And since the context of Revelation 19 is before Christ's return, a futuristic present for "reigneth" is a good possibility.

Another possibility is that "reigneth" refers to the reign of Christ in the broad sense not limited in time to His millennial reign. This possibility, too, comes from the context. In the preceding context we find the destruction of Babylon (chapters 17 and 18), and the "Alleluia's" which open chapter 19 are occasioned by the destruction of Babylon. It is in light of Babylon's destruction that praise arises for His present reign. By destroying Babylon Christ demonstrates that He is reigning, and this happens *during the tribulation rather than during the millennium*. I look forward to Christ's reign in a special sense during the millennium, but I know that Christ reigns in the broad sense throughout all ages. The mere use of the word "reign," therefore, does not prove millennium to me.

With these two possibilities for the meaning of "reigneth" in the present tense—and both of these possibilities come straight from the context—I see no reason to make the tense of the verb invert the natural order of Revelation 19 making the chronology come unglued, especially in light of the three reasons given earlier which glue the passage together in such a

THE PRE-TRIBULATION RAPTURE

way that the chronology has to remain the way it is.

Objection Number 4: The Past Tense Is Not Past. I can think of only one more way that post-tribs may try to dodge the idea of a wife robed and readied by Revelation 19, namely, to claim that the tenses of the key verbs are not a simple past tense. "His wife *hath made herself ready.* And to her *was granted* that she should be arrayed in fine linen, clean and white." Although "hath made ready" and "was granted" are past tense, some may claim that these verbs grammatically are "dramatic past" which speaks of a *future* event rather than a past event. Can this be so? Not without support from the context. Always the context determines such matters.

As I examine the context I find no support for making it future but abundant support for leaving it past. Let's look at the evidence.

According to the context the wife has to be already robed and readied (*past* tense). Why? Because the marriage feast is about to begin. We can chart the flow of thought this way:

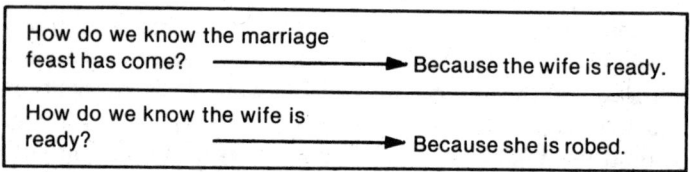

It follows a logical sequence. Since she is robed she is ready. Since she is ready the marriage feast can now proceed. One event depends on the other. By this reasoning, if the wife were not yet robed and readied, it would seem premature for John to write that the time for the marriage has come. The future feast awaits past preparation.

You see, it is not the *past tense alone,* but it is the *whole force of the context* which places the wife's readiness *prior* to Christ's return to earth.

Besides, so far as I have been able to determine, the verbs

When Is the Wedding?

"made ready" and "granted" are nowhere else used in a "dramatic past" sense. Contrariwise, the verb "come" has consistent dramatic usage in Revelation. Likewise, "reign" is used in this way (Revelation 11:17). But where else in the entire New Testament is the *past* tense for "made ready" and "granted" used to denote a *future* event? It is without precedent and without contextual support.

If God intended to denote a future event, He could easily have worded it, "The wife is about to make herself ready," or "The time has come for the wife to make herself ready." Why didn't He put it that way if that is what He meant? (He *did* use similar wording in Revelation 11:18.) If this book is a "revelation" then God's inspired words ought to reveal instead of conceal. His words (and tenses) lead *toward* the truth instead of saying the *opposite* of truth.

All four objections fail to get around Revelation 19. The wife cannot be robed and readied while on earth, the time of the feast is irrelevant because it is the time of readiness that counts, the chronology cannot be reversed, and the past tenses are simple past. Revelation 19 is too high, we can't get over it; too wide, we can't get around it; too low, we can't get under it.

Therefore, since the wife is robed and readied by Revelation 19, she must have been raptured by Revelation 19. This rules out a post-trib rapture.

We have looked at Luke 12:36 and Revelation 19:7-8, both presenting a certain order of wedding events. Now I would like to show you a third passage. Once you hit on the truth you find that the Bible harmonizes all over. Psalm 45 prophesies about the marriage of the King. Verse 14 says,

> She shall be brought unto the king in raiment of needlework: the virgins her companions that follow her shall be brought unto thee.

The virgins *follow*. What does that tell you? If the wife is the church, and if the virgins are tribulation saints (as they are in Matthew 25:1-13), then tribulation saints *follow* church saints.

THE PRE-TRIBULATION RAPTURE

The church age is completed at the rapture, and the tribulation period *follows*.

Now I don't use this passage for proof, you understand. I just throw it in to show you how the Bible harmonizes. This Psalm takes the literal marriage customs of the day, the literal wedding processional, and applies it to the marriage of the King. As a pre-tribulationist I can enjoy the luxury of how it all fits together.

Objection Number 5: These Are Only Implications. I've read enough post-trib literature to guess what a sharp post-trib is probably thinking now. "All you've given us is *implications*. One implication after another. Don't you have even one *outright statement* from the Bible declaring plainly that the rapture comes before the tribulation?"

Well, if I have given implications, then all I am asking for is some answers to these implications. That's fair enough, isn't it?

I could say the same thing about post-trib arguments if I wanted to. I could say that all they have is implications; they have not one single Scripture which says outright, "The rapture is after the tribulation." Sure, Matthew 24:29-31 places a "gathering" after the tribulation. But is this gathering the rapture? That's implication. Sure, 1 Corinthians 15:52 places the rapture at the "last trumpet." But is the last trumpet the seventh trumpet of Revelation? That's implication. Sure, Revelation 20:5-6 places the "first resurrection" after the tribulation. But is the first resurrection the rapture resurrection? That's implication. Sure, 2 Thessalonians 1:7 places "rest" after the tribulation. But is rest identical to rapture? That's implication. Sure, 2 Thessalonians 2:1 mentions the gathering of the church. But does this occur after the tribulation? That's implication.

I could toss aside all post-trib arguments in this manner if I wanted to. I could ignore them all and say, "Where is one *outright statement* from Scripture?" But I don't. I think it only

When Is the Wedding?

fair that I examine each implication on its own merits. In the following chapters I will scrutinize each implication, one by one, to see if it will stand or fall.

As I said before, implications come in two sizes. Some you can get around and some you can't get around. All I am asking is that you scrutinize my implications to see if you can get around them or not.

Did you know that some Bible writers used implications? Let me show you a few.

One obvious implication in the Bible is the Trinity. Nowhere in the Bible does it say in so many words, "There is one God who exists in three persons." We have put this doctrine together by implications. Does this mean the Trinity is a weak doctrine? By no means. The doctrine is strong because the implications are strong. If implications are sufficient to prove the Trinity, are they not sufficient to prove the time of the rapture?

Another implication is one that Jesus gave concerning Himself:

> Then came the Jews round about him, and said unto him, How long dost thou make us to doubt? If thou be the Christ, tell us plainly. Jesus answered them, I told you, and ye believed not: the works that I do in my Father's name, they bear witness of me (John 10:24-25).

Jesus expected them to believe the implications from His works. These implications were so strong that an outright statement was unnecessary. He was not offering anything less; He was offering something just as strong or stronger. Does it make sense to accept these implications concerning Christ and reject implications concerning the rapture? Jesus held the Jews accountable on the basis of implications alone. Does the manner of His second coming demand more proof than the manner of His first coming?

Of course, not everything in the Bible is implication. Most of it is not. Especially so for the way of salvation. The plan of salvation is spelled out so clearly in Romans and in Galatians and elsewhere that no one can accuse God of not clearly telling

THE PRE-TRIBULATION RAPTURE

us how to be saved. For deeper Bible study, though, some treasures lie beneath the surface in order to hide them from unbelievers and in order to prod believers to study the Word more.

Resurrection in the Old Testament is another implication. If you were going to prove resurrection from the Old Testament, how would you do it? Here is how Jesus did it:

> Then came unto him the Sadducees, which say there is no resurrection . . . And Jesus answering said unto them, Do ye not therefore err, because ye know not the scriptures, neither the power of God? . . . As touching the dead that they rise: have ye not read in the book of Moses, how in the bush God spake unto him, saying, I am the God of Abraham, and the God of Isaac, and the God of Jacob? He is not the God of the dead, but the God of the living: ye therefore do greatly err (Mark 12:18-27, excerpts).

Did Jesus offer a plain statement? No, He offered an implication, pure and simple. And the listeners were in error for not knowing and believing this implication. Does God expect us to understand implications about the rapture? Of course He does.

Peter proved Christ's resurrection from a different passage, but it was still an implication. Before Christ rose from the dead, it is said of Peter that he "knew not the Scripture, that he must rise again from the dead" (John 20:9). What Scripture? It says that Peter knew not the Scripture. What Scripture? Does the Old Testament say in plain words that Christ must rise again? Is there such a Scripture?

A few days later Peter knew the Scripture. He was preaching; so he had to know it. What Scripture was it? It was Psalm 16. Here is Peter as he is preaching from Psalm 16:

> For David speaketh concerning him, I foresaw the Lord always before my face, for he is on my right hand, that I should not be moved: therefore did my heart rejoice, and my tongue was glad; moreover also my flesh shall rest in hope: because thou wilt not leave my soul in hell, neither wilt thou suffer thine Holy One to see corruption. Thou has made known to me the ways of life; thou shalt make me full of joy with thy countenance. Men and

When Is the Wedding?

brethren, let me freely speak unto you of the patriarch David, that he is both dead and buried, and his sepulchre is with us unto this day. Therefore being a prophet, and knowing that God had sworn with an oath to him, that of the fruit of his loins, according to the flesh, he would raise up Christ to sit on his throne; he seeing this before spake of the resurrection of Christ, that his soul was not left in hell, neither his flesh did see corruption (Act 2:25-31).

Does Psalm 16 say in plain words that Christ must rise from the dead? No, it doesn't. But Peter drew an implication from it that was strong enough to face a potentially hostile crowd. Now, does anyone expect me to come up with a stronger statement for the rapture than Peter did for the resurrection?

I could show you others, but I'll stop here. My point is this: let's be consistent, let's be fair. If Bible writers use implications, if the entire post-trib case rests on implications, then why demand more out of pre-tribulationists? We all have to accept the Bible the way it is written, not the way we want it to be.

We are down to this. Are my rapture implications strong or weak? Can you get around them or can you not get around them?

As much as possible I have tried to stay away from weak implications. I could have argued that Christ returns to the *air* one time and to the *earth* the next time. But I have avoided that argument because theoretically Christ could return to the air and to the earth all in one motion.

I could have argued that Christ returns *for* His saints one time and *with* His saints the next time. But I have avoided that argument, because theoretically He could come for His saints and with His saints all on the same day.

Post-tribs have been asking for something stronger, and so I have tried to give strong arguments. The argument of the known day versus the unknown day is strong because the only possible answer is two different days. The question of who will populate the millennium is strong because somebody with a natural body has to populate the millennium. If not the unsaved, if not those raptured, then who? It has to be somebody.

THE PRE-TRIBULATION RAPTURE

The timing of the wedding is strong because the order of events can run only one way. I invite all to scrutinize these implications, and more to follow later. Are they not just as strong as an outright statement?

I too might wish for the Bible to state the time of the rapture differently, but I cannot wish for it to state the time more clearly, for it is already as clear as can be. All I need do is to accept the way the Bible is written and believe it.

If you were alive in Jesus' day, would you join the others in saying, "If thou be the Christ, tell us plainly. These implications you are giving us are not what we asked for at all. You want us to settle for something less, and we won't settle for anything less than an outright statement." Would you press such demands? No, I'm sure you wouldn't.

Some post-tribulationists have asked for one verse, just one verse, that proves pre-tribulationism. In this chapter I offer Luke 12:36. Will you believe it?

1. John F. Walvoord, *The Revelation of Jesus Christ* (Chicago: Moody Press, 1966), p. 271.

2. Dana and Mantey, *A Manual Grammar of the Greek New Testament* (Riverside, NJ: Macmillan Publishing Co., 1955), p. 185.

"Therefore . . . watch" (1 Thessalonians 5:6).

5
First Thessalonians: Salvation

"The apostle Paul was a post-trib and I can prove it from First and Second Thessalonians."

"No, no, Paul was a pre-trib and I can prove it from First and Second Thessalonians."

Why is there so much disagreement about First and Second Thessalonians? Why do some people find Paul teaching post-trib and others find him teaching pre-trib? Could it be that Paul taught *neither*? Could it be that all this disagreement is over nothing? Yes, strange as it may seem, I believe that Paul was *neither* pre-trib *nor* post-trib, and . . . I can prove it from First and Second Thessalonians.

LOOKING BACKWARD

Does this mean that there is no evidence whatsoever for pre-tribulationism in the Thessalonian epistle? Not really. Because looking back from our perspective of fuller revelation we can see little clues.

Suppose you go shopping to buy your son a surprise birthday

present. When you arrive home your son knows you went somewhere and so he asks questions about where you were. You do not believe in lying, but you do not want to reveal the secret yet. So what do you do? You answer his questions vaguely with the truth carefully concealed. Then surprised on his birthday he exclaims, "Ah! Now I know why you answered me that way! If I were thinking I should have known all along that you had something up your sleeve."

In First and Second Thessalonians we can see clues as we look back, but we cannot establish a clear-cut pre-trib or post-trib teaching.

A Pre-trib Clue? Here is one of my favorite pre-trib clues in the Thessalonian epistles. First Thessalonians 3:3-4 says, "That no man should be moved by these afflictions: for yourselves know that we are appointed thereunto. For verily, when we were with you, we told you before that we should suffer tribulation; even as it came to pass, and ye know."

Notice carefully how the Holy Spirit guarded Paul's words. Notice that Paul speaks of tribulation which *already* came to pass. He mentions nothing about the great tribulation yet future. Why is this a clue?

You see, Paul's main subject in this epistle is the events surrounding the great tribulation. If he were writing about something else I wouldn't expect him to mention the great tribulation, but when this is a major point, the omission is highly significant.

Now if Paul were a post-tributionist, or if the Holy Spirit didn't guard his words, I think he would have written 1 Thessalonians 3:3-4 differently. Remember, Paul is leading up to his main point, events surrounding the great tribulation. Remember, he is known for making his arguments as strong as possible, like a lawyer. How natural, then, would it be for him to jump at this golden opportunity to cap off his exhortation by saying, "Be patient in present tribulation, even as we will need ultimate patience in the ultimate tribulation. Present

First Thessalonians: Salvation

tribulation is preparation for the future tribulation. Learn patience now because you will need it even more when the great tribulation comes."

Why didn't you state it like that, Paul? Don't you know that your exhortation concerning present tribulation does me no good if a greater tribulation is coming for which I have no exhortation? If I really had to go through the great tribulation, you passed up your perfect opportunity to tell me to have patience for it. I thought your arguments were sharp and strong. What happened to your lawyer-like mind?

Did Paul's lawyer-like mind really slip? Or did the Holy Spirit prevent him from mentioning the great tribulation because we will not go through the great tribulation?

The Rapture Described. Let's quickly move on to Paul's description of the rapture in 1 Thessalonians 4:13-18. Paul gives a detailed account, but the one thing he omits is the *time.* Read this passage and see if you can tell whether Paul is a pre-trib or a post-trib:

> But I would not have you to be ignorant, brethren, concerning them which are asleep, that ye sorrow not, even as others which have no hope. For if we believe that Jesus died and rose again, even so them also which sleep in Jesus will God bring with him. For this we say unto you by the word of the Lord, that we which are alive and remain unto the coming of the Lord shall not prevent [precede] them which are asleep. For the Lord himself shall descend from heaven with a shout, with the voice of the archangel, and with the trump of God: and the dead in Christ shall rise first: Then we which are alive and remain shall be caught up together with them in the clouds, to meet the Lord in the air: and so shall we ever be with the Lord. Wherefore comfort one another with these words (1 Thessalonians 4:13-18).

Instead of teaching pre-trib or post-trib in this passage, Paul has a more basic and practical purpose in mind: hope and comfort concerning the dead. He is not concerned with the time. So Paul has the Lord descending from heaven, believers ascending from the earth, and he leaves all of us hanging in the air. The secret is clouded.

THE PRE-TRIBULATION RAPTURE

However, as we examine this passage with our detective cap on, we might uncover some revealing clues.

Of What Were They Ignorant? Let's begin examining this passage by looking at Paul's introduction:

> But I would not have you to be ignorant, brethren, concerning them which are asleep, that ye sorrow not, even as others which have no hope. For if we believe that Jesus died and rose again, even so them also which sleep in Jesus will God bring with him (1 Thessalonians 4:13-14).

Of what were they ignorant that was causing so much sorrow? If we knew exactly what the Thessalonians were ignorant of, we could better understand Paul's answer. Were they merely ignorant of the *time* of the resurrection in relation to other end-time events? Or were they entirely ignorant of the *fact* of the resurrection? Let's find out.

One theory suggests that the Thessalonians were ignorant about the resurrection at the pre-trib rapture. They mistakenly thought that their Christian loved ones who had died would miss the rapture and would not be resurrected until after the tribulation. They didn't know there was a resurrection at the rapture.

Against this theory I object that Paul did not teach a pre-trib rapture as we will prove later. Also against this theory, I would agree with Gundry that the delay of resurrection for a mere seven years is little ground for sorrow. Remember, these Thessalonians were sorrowing "even as others which have no hope."

Another theory suggests that the Thessalonians were ignorant about the resurrection at a *post*-trib rapture. They mistakenly thought that the resurrection was not until after the millennium. If departed loved ones were to miss that blessed one-thousand years, this would be sufficient ground for sorrow, according to this theory.

Against this theory I object that it still leaves the Thessalonians *some hope*. Keep in mind, they were sorrowing as those

First Thessalonians: Salvation

who have "no hope." *No* hope—this is the key. Also, the one-thousand-year length of the millennium was not revealed until years later (Revelation 20:1-7), and so the Thessalonians could not have known how long this period of time was. Consider also, that if the Thessalonians were sharp enough to discern the millennium, then they would also have been sharp enough to discern the correct time of the resurrection before the millennium as given in Daniel 12:2 and in Isaiah 26:19.

I believe, contrary to the above theories, that the Thessalonians were entirely ignorant of the fact of the resurrection. I find no reason to assume they had *some hope,* when the text plainly states they had "no hope." They had no hope *even as unbelievers.* Unbelievers do not believe in a resurrection at all!

But these are Christians, you say, not unbelievers. They obviously believed in a resurrection of some kind, didn't they? I reply, this assumes too much. Keep in mind that Paul spent only a few short weeks in Thessalonica; his teaching was unexpectedly interrupted. And at the date of Paul's writing, the Thessalonians were still only a few months old in the faith, raw converts fresh from paganism (Acts 17:1-10). If there is proof that they all knew of a resurrection, where is it? Before making assumptions, why not consider the evidence on the other side?

Consider the evidence from 1 Corinthians 15 that even *believers* did not believe in a resurrection! "How say some *among you* that there is *no resurrection* of the dead? . . . the dead rise *not at all*" (excerpts from 1 Corinthians 15:12,29). The Corinthians had the benefit of an entire year and a half of Paul's teaching, not just a few weeks as did the Thessalonians (Acts 18:11). So if it is possible for the Corinthians to be so mistaken—and Corinth is not far from Thessalonica; the same Greek culture and the same type of people were in both cities—then how much more easily could the Thessalonians likewise be mistaken? It is true, after all, that the Thessalonians had "*no* hope" of a resurrection. You see, there is Biblical precedent for Christians being mistaken about the *fact* of resurrection, but there is *no* Biblical precedent for Christians being mistaken about the *order* of resurrection. If there is any assuming to be done, let us assume *with* the evidence instead of *against* the evidence. When you toss a piece of wood into a stream do you assume it will float with the current or against the current?

To make the evidence even stronger, Paul uses the identical argument to combat the error both in 1 Thessalonians 4 and in 1 Corinthians 15. His argument rests on Christ's resurrection. If Christ was raised, he says, then those who belong to Christ will also be raised. Now if merely the *order* of resurrection were the question, then there would be no point in Paul's basing his answer on the resurrection of Christ. Christ's resurrection proves the *fact,* but it proves nothing about the *order.* Paul's identical answer in both chapters implies an identical question. A common solution, without evidence to the contrary, implies an identical problem. The problem was not believing in a resurrection at all.

But there is evidence, some will say, that the Thessalonians were merely ignorant of the order of resurrection. Does not Paul stress the *order* as he describes the rapture? How do we explain that?

> For this we say unto you by the word of the Lord, that we which are alive and remain unto the coming of the Lord shall not prevent [precede] them which are asleep. For the Lord himself shall descend from heaven with a shout, with the voice of the archangel, and with the trump of God: and the dead in Christ shall rise first (1 Thessalonians 4:15-16).

I reply that Paul's stress of the order is to further emphasize the *fact* of resurrection. You can see this in the grammatical structure of the passage. Notice the word "for" which begins verse 15. That word "for" introduces the reason or the explanation for what precedes. *The fact* of resurrection precedes the "for"; the *order* of resurrection follows. The order, then, *explains* and further emphasizes the fact. The little word "for" links the two together in this relationship.

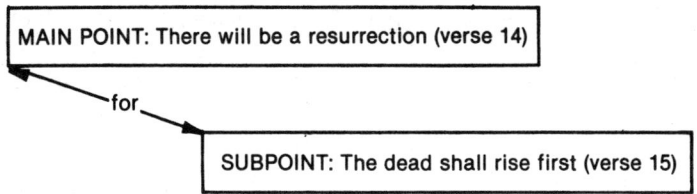

Verse 14 similarly reveals the intended relationship. The emphasis is on "those who sleep" rather than "bring with Him" (because of the reversal of the normal verb-object order). This grammatical emphasis stresses the fact that the dead *will* rise instead of *when* they will rise.

Two literary keys in interpreting a passage are the introduction and conclusion. They are better than any commentary, because God's own commentary on the middle of a passage is the beginning and ending. We have just seen how the introduction (verses 13-14) speaks of the *fact* of resurrection rather than the order. Likewise the conclusion (verse 17) is directed at the *fact,* not the order, of resurrection: "And so shall we ever be with the Lord." As if this were not enough, there is *another* divine commentary (i.e., conclusion) in the next chapter (5:10) which is also directed at the *fact* of resurrection: "Who died for us, that, whether we wake or sleep, we should live together with him." The fact is primary; the order merely strengthens the fact.

Of what were the Thessalonians ignorant? I believe they were entirely ignorant of the fact of the resurrection, because they were sorrowing as those who had "no hope," because better trained Christians like those in Corinth made the same mistake; and because the grammatical and literary structure of 1 Thessalonians 4 subordinates the order and lays stress on the fact.

Another Pre-trib Clue? Why is it so important to know what the Thessalonians were ignorant of? Fact or order, what difference does it make? What does it prove?

It is important, because if we understand their ignorance,

then we can better understand Paul's answer. The way Paul answers is very interesting. Do you notice anything unusual about it? Put your detective cap on. Do you see clues you never noticed before?

If you were a Bible teacher in Paul's day, how would you answer the Thessalonians? Remember, we have to prove to the Thessalonians the *fact* of resurrection, not the order primarily; so let us concentrate on that aspect. If you wanted to teach the Thessalonians the fact of the resurrection, how would you do it?

If I were doing it, I would go to the Scriptures, and I would give them a verse like Daniel 12:2 which plainly teaches a resurrection. I would say, "See, the Scripture teaches a resurrection; therefore, there *is* a resurrection." But strangely Paul did *not* refer to a Scripture like Daniel 12:2. Instead he shared a word that he received directly from the Lord. Why? Is this a clue that Paul's resurrection is *different* than Daniel's resurrection? A different resurrection at a *different time*?

Well, maybe. Let us look closer and see if the difference is real or apparent. Read Daniel 12 and look for the answer to the question, "*When* is the resurrection of Daniel's body?" If you have a Bible handy, set this book aside and do it now.

Did you find the answer? The answer is in the last verse, "For thou shalt rest, and stand in thy lot at the end of the days" (Daniel 12:13). Daniel's resurrection is at *the end of the days*. When is that? Daniel gives three sets of days in this chapter. Verse 7 gives 1260 days (a time, times, and an half) which is the day that Christ returns as we saw in Chapter 2. Verse 11 gives 1290 days. Verse 12 gives 1335 days. Three sets of days. When is Daniel's resurrection? Daniel's resurrection is at the *end of the days*. Which day is that? The 1335th day!

Day 1260 is the return of Christ and day 1335 is the resurrection of Daniel. Therefore, Daniel's resurrection comes *75 days after* Christ's return. Yes, the difference between Paul's resurrection and Daniel's resurrection is very real. In Paul's resurrection the dead are raised *first,* the moment Christ descends in

First Thessalonians: Salvation

the clouds. In Daniel's resurrection, the dead are raised *later,* 75 days after Christ returns. These two men are talking about *two different resurrections,* different resurrections at *different times.*

No wonder Paul did not give the Thessalonians a Scripture like Daniel 12:2 in order to prove the resurrection to them. It wouldn't fit the resurrection he was about to reveal. And no wonder the Holy Spirit guided Paul to mention the *order* of resurrection. Church saints will not be raised at some later time as are Old Testament saints, and God wanted us to know that our departed loved ones will be raised first.

A New Revelation. We have noticed that the Holy Spirit guided Paul not to refer to the Old Testament to prove the resurrection of the church. Now keep your detective cap on. Do you notice anything else unusual?

A striking characteristic of 1 and 2 Thessalonians is that Paul is constantly referring to previous teaching or previous experience. At every chance he gets he repeats the refrain "you know" or "you remember" or "I told you before" or "you are witnesses." The lone exception to this pattern—the contrast is as striking as black and white—is Paul's description of the rapture!

Other Topics	Rapture
"as ye know" (1 Thess. 1:5)	
"For yourselves, brethren, know" (1 Thess. 2:1)	
"as ye know" (1 Thess. 2:5)	
"for ye remember" (1 Thess. 2:9)	"But I would not have you to be ignorant...for this we say unto you" (1 Thess. 4:13,15).
"ye are witnesses" (1 Thess. 2:10)	
"as ye know" (1 Thess. 2:11)	
"for yourselves know" (1 Thess. 3:3)	

THE PRE-TRIBULATION RAPTURE

"we told you before" (1 Thess. 3:4)

"and ye know" (1 Thess. 3:4)

"For ye know" (1 Thess. 4:2)

"we also have forewarned you" (1 Thess. 4:6)

"For yourselves know perfectly" (1 Thess. 5:2)

"Remember ye not, that, when I was yet with you, I told you these things?" (2 Thess. 2:5)

"ye know" (2 Thess. 2:6)

"for yourselves know" (2 Thess. 3:7)

Now the rapture is an important subject. If Paul had taught them about the rapture previously while he was with them, don't you think he would have "reminded" them of his teaching, or said "You know this" or "I told you before"? This was Paul's pattern; he surely would have *if* he could have. Instead of saying "I told you before" he says "I tell you now," as if this were the very first time he was telling them this. Instead of saying "you know this well," as he does everywhere else he gets a chance, he says "you are ignorant." Unique!

Here is the evidence we have been looking for. If we let the epistle speak for itself, letting the facts fall where they may, we arrive at the conclusion that Paul never taught the rapture previously to the Thessalonians. The rapture is a brand new revelation, not a repetition of an old one. To assume otherwise is to swim against the river of evidence.

WHAT WAS PAUL'S POSITION?

This evidence has led me to believe that this epistle was the *first occasion* that Paul taught the rapture to the Thessalonians. Now, what is so significant about this and why is it important? Keep your detective cap on. Do you notice a significant omission?

First Thessalonians: Salvation

The time! Paul omits the time! Paul, are you pre-trib or post-trib? You didn't tell us which!

Why didn't Paul reveal the time? Well, maybe he didn't know the time. As far as we know Paul was neither pre-trib nor post-trib.

Now if Paul had previously taught the Thessalonians the time of the rapture, then there would be no reason for him to repeat it here. But since the weight of evidence tells us he did *not* teach the rapture previously, then it is highly significant that he omits the time. He omitted the time because he had no time to reveal at this point. Paul was neither pre-trib nor post-trib.

EVIDENCE	CONCLUSION
They were "ignorant" of a resurrection instead of "knowing" about it. Paul said, "This I [now] say" instead of "This I remind you of."	This was a first-time revelation of the rapture.
In his first revelation of the rapture, Paul omits the time.	Paul taught neither pre-trib nor post-trib.

I think we need to take a fresh look at the Thessalonian epistles and read them anew as if we had never read them before. This is what I tried to do. I tried to shove all bias out of my mind, all preconceived notions, all assumptions, and I tried to follow strictly the evidence that is given.

Do you see the problem that we have gotten ourselves into by assuming too much when we read Thessalonians? It causes problems in three areas. First, it causes problems among ourselves. Pre-tribs assume Paul taught pre-tribulationism previously to the Thessalonians, and post-tribs assume he taught post-tribulationism previously. As a result we disagree when we come to interpreting the Thessalonian epistles because we assume that Paul had to be either pre-trib or post-trib, and it never dawns on most of us that he might be neither. I think many of us are disagreeing over nothing and there is no reason for it.

Assuming too much in the Thessalonian epistles causes a second problem. It not only causes needless controversy among ourselves, it also leads to interpretations that contradict Scripture. In some cases when a post-trib derives his post-trib implications from these epistles, he feels that he doesn't have to explain other parts of the Bible. The question of the known day versus the unknown day he can leave hanging in the air. It doesn't matter who will populate the millennium. The question about the time of the wedding can be safely passed over as long as he has his post-trib implications from the Thessalonian epistles. In this way assuming too much in Thessalonians leads into a dilemma with other Scripture.

A third problem caused by assuming too much in Thessalonians is that we miss some of the meaning in the Thessalonian epistles themselves. If we are looking for pre-trib or post-trib, then we miss what he is *really* talking about. When Paul sat down to write these epistles, he had a certain point in mind that he wanted to get across. Today when I read the epistles, I want to put myself into Paul's shoes, to get inside his mind, to understand exactly what he was getting at in each passage. I have discovered that when I cast aside my preconceived notions I appreciate these epistles more than ever before. I have discovered that Paul really has something valuable to say, and if I push aside ideas of pre-trib or post-trib I can then see the passages clearly enough to catch the fuller impact of Paul's main point. Try it and see. As we discuss these passages I think you will see what I mean.

It's Only Natural. A natural reading of 1 Thessalonians has led me to believe that Paul was neither pre-trib nor post-trib. He did not teach the time of the rapture to the Thessalonians, either in person or by letter, as the above evidence indicates. Is

First Thessalonians: Salvation

this surprising? Or shocking? If you know anything about progressive revelation, this shouldn't be surprising at all.

Progressive revelation means that God reveals truths progressively or gradually, not all at once, but step by step. This is God's *normal pattern,* nothing unusual at all. This is the pattern of the Old Testament which gradually unfolds before us the prophecies of Christ's first coming. The same pattern holds true for the New Testament as it reveals step by step the truths concerning Christ's second coming. Paul's place in the steps of revelation is to give a *description* of the rapture. Through him God revealed the description, but *not the time.* That comes later in the steps of revelation. If Paul *did* reveal the time, it would be unusual; it would be a deviation from God's pattern of progressive revelation. (A worse deviation from the principle of progressive revelation is to inject the description *and* time of the rapture into Matthew 24.)

"But Paul was an apostle! How could the great apostle Paul not know the time of the rapture?" I reply that the Old Testament prophets did not always understand what they wrote.

> Of which salvation the prophets have enquired and searched diligently, who prophesied of the grace that should come unto you: Searching what, or what manner of time the Spirit of Christ which was in them did signify, when it testified beforehand the sufferings of Christ, and the glory that should follow" (1 Peter 1:10-11).

The Old Testament prophets understood the two aspects of the coming of Christ, but the *time* they did not understand. If this was true for Old Testament prophets, I am not surprised at all if the same was true for the apostle Paul.

Where Did Paul Get His Revelation? We have pointed out that Paul did not appeal to the Old Testament for his revelation of the resurrection and rapture. If not the Old Testament, from where did Paul get his revelation? Could it be from the Olivet Discourse (Matthew 24)? Could it be from those words which Jesus spoke on the mount of Olives saying, "And he shall send his angels with a great sound of a trumpet, and they shall gather together his elect from the four winds, from one end of heaven to the other" (Matthew 24:31)?

No, Paul could not have received his revelation from these words of Jesus. First, these words of Jesus are not about the rapture. The gathering He speaks of is not a gathering into the air, but a gathering into an entirely different place as we will demonstrate in a later chapter.

A second reason for Paul's not receiving his revelation from the Olivet Discourse is Galatians 1:12: "For I neither received it of man, neither was I taught it, but by the revelation of Jesus Christ." God normally gave revelation *directly* to Paul instead of through the mediation of men. Now the Olivet Discourse was spoken by Jesus and was later passed on by men, both orally and in written form. Paul was not there to hear Jesus speak on the mount of Olives; so if Paul learned of the rapture from the Olivet Discourse, he would have learned of it through men. If it really happened this way, then it would be an exception to Galatians 1:12.

The available evidence indicates that Paul did not receive his revelation of the rapture and resurrection from the Old Testament, nor from the Olivet Discourse, but he received this brand new revelation directly from the Lord Himself.

Why Does Paul Speak of Comfort? Paul concludes his description of the rapture with comfort. Why? Does he offer comfort because the church will not go through the tribulation? No, he says nothing about the tribulation or the time of the rapture.

It is comfort regarding the *fact* of resurrection, not the *time* of resurrection. "Be comforted in that your believing loved ones will live again." That is all Paul is saying. A post-trib, just as much as a pre-trib, can be comforted in that his loved ones will live again. Such comfort has nothing to do with the time of the rapture.

Suppose for a minute that you had to go through the tribulation. You would still have the comforting thought that your believing loved ones will live again, wouldn't you? You see, even going through the tribulation does not wipe out this comfort that Paul is talking about. To derive a pre-trib implication from this comfort is as unrelated as grabbing for an apple in a bag of oranges.

As you can see, I am trying to take a fresh look at 1 Thessalonians, assuming nothing, but letting the evidence speak for itself. I have found this approach to be the most satisfying as well as the most revealing.

THE PROBLEM OF THE "LAST TRUMPET"

A powerful argument in the hands of post-tribs has been the "last trumpet." The "trump of God" which signals the rapture in 1 Thessalonians 4:16 is identified as the "last trump" in 1 Corinthians 15:52.

For the Lord himself shall descend from heaven with a shout, with the voice of the archangel, and with the *trump of God:* and the dead in Christ shall rise first (1 Thessalonians 4:16).	In a moment, in the twinkling of an eye, at the *last trump:* for the trumpet shall sound, and the dead shall be raised incorruptible, and we shall be changed (1 Corinthians 15:52).

What makes this the *last* trumpet? If this is the last trumpet, then what were the *first* trumpets? Post-tribs take us to the book of Revelation which tells of seven angels blowing seven trumpets during the tribulation. They reason that the rapture trumpet must be the seventh trumpet or after these seven tribulation trumpets in order to be last. This would clearly place the rapture at the *end* of the tribulation instead of at the beginning. Logical, isn't it?

How do we answer this argument? What does the "last trumpet" really mean? Before identifying what I believe to be the first trumpet, will you observe with me that the word "last" is a *relative* word. It does not necessarily mean there are none to follow. Your best friend, your concordance, can show you that. For example, Paul was the "last" to see Christ although John saw Him and we shall see Him later (1 Corinthians 15:8). Last is relative.

Surely, post-tribs agree on this point. Are there not trumpets used during the millennium? Or are trumpets banished forever? Certainly, "last" trumpet does not rule out any trumpets following; it merely tells us to seek a trumpet preceding.

With this in mind, let us ask the question, "When Paul spoke of the last trumpet, did he have in mind the seven trumpets of Revelation as the first trumpets?" When you think about it, you can see the discrepancy at once. Revelation was not even written by Paul's time! The book was not around for Paul to read. Nor for the Corinthians to read.

If you lived in Corinth and received a letter from Paul speaking of the "last trumpet," how would you understand it? Where would you go to seek the first trumpet? To a book not yet written? No, you would go to the Old Testament, of course. That was their Bible at the time.

If you were a faithful Corinthian trying to understand the "last trumpet" you would read in your Old Testament until you came to Leviticus 23. Then your eyes would light up and you would jump up from your chair and say, "This is it! The feast of trumpets!"

The Feast of Trumpets. The feast of trumpets is one of seven feasts described in Leviticus 23. It is no secret that these feasts have *prophetic significance.* Although Israel first celebrated the feasts, the church now benefits in their prophetic fulfillment:

The Passover Feast (Leviticus 23:4-5) finds its fulfillment in 1 Corinthians 5:7, "Christ, our passover, is sacrificed for us."

The Feast of Unleavened Bread (Leviticus 23:6-8) finds fulfillment in 1 Corinthians 5:8, "Therefore let us keep the feast, not with old leaven, neither with the leaven of malice and wickedness; but with the unleavened bread of sincerity and truth."

The Feast of Firstfruits (Leviticus 23:9-14) pictures the resurrection of Christ according to 1 Corinthians 15:20: "But now is Christ risen from the dead, and become the firstfruits of them that slept."

The Feast of Weeks, or Pentecost (Leviticus 23:15-22) is fulfilled in Acts 2 by the coming of the Holy Spirit on the day of Pentecost.

The Day of Atonement (Leviticus 23:20-32) pictures Christ's atonement for us (Hebrews 9-10).

The Feast of Tabernacles (Leviticus 23:34-44) prefigures the time of blessing (Deuteronomy 16:14) during the millennium (Revelation 21:3), during which the church will participate as rulers (Revelation 20:4).

The Feast of Trumpets (Leviticus 23:23-25) finds its fulfillment—where? We have seen that each of the other feasts has prophetic significance for the church. Can you see any church-related event to which we could point the fulfillment of this feast? Maybe the Feast of Trumpets is the only feast that has no fulfillment in the church. Or could it be that the first trumpet is fulfilled in the "last trumpet"? Is this not the answer that we have been looking for?

Where Is the Fulfillment? It is noteworthy that of the seven feasts, four of them find fulfillment in 1 Corinthians. Even more noteworthy is that the "last trumpet" shares the *same chapter* as the "firstfruits"! These are partners because both deal with the resurrection and second coming. We read, "Christ the firstfruits; afterward they that are Christ's at his coming" (1 Corinthians 15:23). The resurrection of Christ is the "firstfruits," and the resurrection of believers is at the "last trumpet" (verse 52). If "firstfruits" alludes to the feasts of Leviticus 23, then its partner in the same chapter, the "last trumpet," does too.

Why does Paul use the "firstfruits" and the "last trumpet"

together in 1 Corinthians 15? Because they represent the first and the last of the ingathering. If you were a Jewish farmer your holiday schedule would go like this: The Feast of Firstfruits celebrated the first of the barley harvest. Fifty days later the Feast of Weeks (also called the Feast of Harvest or Pentecost) observed the end of barley harvest and the beginning of wheat harvest (Exodus 23:16; Deuteronomy 16:16). About a half a year later the Feast of Trumpets occurred near the end of the summer's ingathering. Fifteen days later the Feast of Tabernacles celebrated the completion of the ingathering (Leviticus 23:39; Deuteronomy 16:13).

As it was with the feasts, so it is in the prophetic fulfillment. The resurrection of Christ signaled the beginning of the harvest of men's souls into the church. The day of Pentecost was truly a day of harvest as Peter preached and 3000 souls were added to the church. The time of harvest continues even now. But it will end for us when we hear the "trump of God" at the rapture, and we will celebrate all our labors for Him during the millennium.

(Be aware that the dates of the feasts can not be used to predict the day of the rapture. It is true that the first four feasts were fulfilled on their respective days. The last three feasts, however, form a separate group on the calendar, and their dates do not correspond with the time intervals of the end-time events.)

Not only does the typology fit, but the chronology also fits. The one-half year between the Feast of Pentecost and the Feast of Trumpets represents this long period of time known as the church age. We are now in that summer of harvest. The last major church event to occur was the outpouring of the Holy Spirit on the day of Pentecost. The next main event to occur is the "trump of God" at the rapture.

First Thessalonians: Salvation

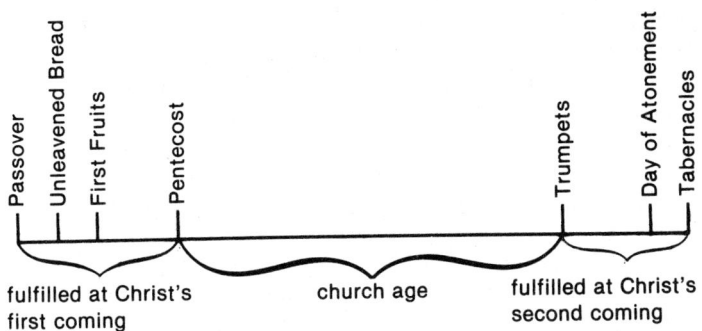

The prophetic view of the feasts is not new. Even post-tribs would agree in general, but some might object, "Does not the Feast of Trumpets typify the *gathering of Israel* rather than the rapture of the church? Does not Isaiah 27:12-13 link the trumpet with the gathering of Israel to her land after the tribulation?"

I reply, the trumpet applies to *both* Israel *and* the church, a concept with which even post-tribs agree as I will show in a minute. It is true that Isaiah 27 applies the trumpet to Israel, but 1 Corinthians 15 applies it also to the church. It has *double reference*. The church partakes some way or another in the fulfillment of *each of the other feasts*. Why should the Feast of Trumpets be the lone exception?

In addition to 1 Corinthians 15 which applies the trumpet to the church, indication of double reference comes from Numbers 10:1-10. The Lord told Moses to make *two trumpets* of silver. Why two trumpets? We know from Isaiah 27:12-13 that one is fulfilled in Israel and we know from 1 Corinthians 15:52 that one is fulfilled in the church. The trumpets were blown to "gather" the people (Numbers 10:2-3,7) just as God will blow the trumpet to gather the church and to gather Israel on separate occasions. But how do we know that these two silver trumpets were the same ones blown at the Feast of

Trumpets? Because Numbers 10:10 says that these should be blown "in the beginnings of your months," and the Feast of Trumpets was the beginning of the seventh month.

Even post-tribulationists will agree with me that the "last trumpet" has double reference. They identify the trumpet of Matthew 24:31 as the rapture trumpet and "last trumpet." Also, does not a comparison of Matthew 24:31 with Isaiah 27:12-13 show that the gathering of Israel is in view?

And ye shall be gathered one by one, O ye children of Israel. And it shall come to pass in that day, that the great trumpet shall be blown, and they shall come which were ready to perish in the land of Assyria, and the outcasts in the land of Egypt, and shall worship the Lord in the holy mount at Jerusalem (Isaiah 27:12b-13).	And he shall send his angels with a great sound of a trumpet, and they shall gather together his elect from the four winds, from one end of heaven to the other. (Matthew 24:31)

Unless post-tribs divorce Matthew 24:31 from Isaiah 27:12-13 to which it obviously alludes, they must conclude that Matthew 24:31 refers to *both* the gathering of Israel and the gathering of the church (as Gundry does). So even in the post-trib view, the last trumpet has *double* reference. Carrying it further, if the church looks back to the same first trumpet as Israel does, then even a post-trib can safely identify the Feast of Trumpets as the first trumpet. Therefore, there is no compelling need, either Biblically or theologically, to resort to the seven trumpets of Revelation in order to explain the "last trumpet."

All I need to demonstrate here is the *possibility*. As long as this interpretation of the "last trumpet" remains possible, any post-trib proof from the "last trumpet" falls short.

We have demonstrated that the Corinthians, as they read about the "last trumpet" from Paul, could easily identify the

First Thessalonians: Salvation

first trumpet in their own Scripture, and there was no need for them to resort to trumpets not yet written about in Revelation. Paul alludes to the feasts four times in 1 Corinthians, and twice in the fifteenth chapter; so it would be perfectly natural for the Corinthians to catch the allusion to the feasts. This they could understand; a non-existent book they could not understand.

THE PRE-TRIBULATION RAPTURE

THE SEVEN FEASTS OF ISRAEL
(See Leviticus 23; Numbers 28:16—29:40; Deuteronomy 16; Numbers 10:1-10)

Old Testament Feasts		Prophetic Significance	New Testament Reference
The Passover	1st month, 14th day	sacrifice of Christ	1 Cor. 5:7
Unleavened Bread	1st month, 15th - 22nd days	communion with Christ (sinlessness)	1 Cor. 5:8
Firstfruits	1st month, 16th day	resurrection of Christ	1 Cor. 15:20
Pentecost (Feast of Weeks)	50 days after Firstfruits	formation of church	Acts 2:1-4
Feast of Trumpets	7th month, 1st day	1. *rapture trumpet* 2. gathering of Israel (Isa. 27:12-13)	1 Cor. 15:52
Day of Atonement	7th month, 10th day	1. Christ's blood 2. Israel's cleansing (Zech. 12:10—13:1)	Heb. 9—10
Feast of Tabernacles	7th month, 15th - 22nd days	millennium	Rev. 21:3

First Thessalonians: Salvation

THE RELATION BETWEEN CHAPTERS FOUR AND FIVE

The main thrust of chapters four and five of First Thessalonians is tucked away in one little verse, 1 Thessalonians 1:10. Paul likes to give introductory previews or built-in outlines like this. In 1 Thessalonians 1:10 he previews chapters four and five this way: "And to wait for his Son from heaven, whom he raised from the dead, even Jesus which delivered us from the wrath to come."

The phrase "to wait for his Son from heaven, whom he raised from the dead" anticipates chapter four where the resurrection of Jesus is the basis for the resurrection of our loved ones. The second phrase of 1 Thessalonians 1:10, "who delivered us from the wrath to come," previews chapter five where deliverance from wrath is the basis for watchful living. Reading 1 Thessalonians 1:10 helps us to understand the heart of the matter in chapters four and five.

Chapter four, then, speaks of deliverance from death while chapter five speaks of deliverance from wrath. Chapter four promises life while chapter five promises salvation.

Comparing the chapters further we find an interesting and ironic play on the word "sleep." In chapter four believers sleep in death while in chapter five unbelievers sleep while alive. This presents some contrasts:

CHAPTER FOUR: dead believers ⟶ appointed to life ⟶ have hope
CHAPTER FIVE: living believers ⟶ appointed to death ⟶ have no hope

From chapter four we learn not to sorrow as unbelievers (verse 13); from chapter five we learn not to sleep as unbelievers (verse 6).

We see, then, that chapters four and five are as two halves forming the whole. These halves are linked together in thought, but not necessarily in time as we shall see later.

When Is the Day of the Lord? The subject of 1 Thessalo-

THE PRE-TRIBULATION RAPTURE

nians 5:1-11 is the day of the Lord. When is the day of the Lord? Does it begin with the tribulation or *after* the tribulation?

At this point I must part company with most pre-tribulationists and agree with Gundry's evidence that the day of the Lord begins *after* the tribulation.[1] Pre-tribulationists have been afraid to admit that the day of the Lord begins after the tribulation, because they thought that would be the same as admitting the *rapture* is after the tribulation. Such is not the case as we shall see. If a painter stretched his canvas as much as we sometimes stretch our interpretation to fit our theological framework, he would end up with a distorted picture. But if we let the Bible speak for itself and patiently let the interpretations come naturally, then we will see a more beautiful and harmonious picture in the end.

Let's look at some evidence on the day of the Lord. What does the phrase "the times and the seasons" bring to your mind?

> But of the times and the seasons, brethren, ye have no need that I write unto you. For yourselves know perfectly that the day of the Lord so cometh as a thief in the night (1 Thessalonians 5:1-2).

According to popular usage today "times and seasons" might bring to mind signs of the times which indicate the rapture is near. Find a verse to support that usage. The only other verse I know of which uses "times and seasons" brings to mind, not pre-tribulational signs, but the Messianic kingdom which comes *after* the tribulation (Acts 1:6-7).

By the way, what did the Thessalonians "know perfectly"? Did they know perfectly signs of the coming rapture? No, they knew, not signs, but surprise. They knew perfectly of the day's *surprise upon unbelievers.* It says nothing of their knowing *signs* for believers to watch for. Does this passage say that we can know the time of the rapture? No, it is not talking about that at all.

Let's return to evidence concerning the time of the day of the

First Thessalonians: Salvation

Lord. The day of the Lord comes "as a thief in the night" (1 Thessalonians 5:2). It may surprise you, but nowhere in the Bible does this figure of the thief occur in a pre-tribulational context. This is a post-tribulational figure (see Revelation 16:15).

The day of the Lord involves "sudden destruction" (1 Thessalonians 5:3). The tribulation, on the other hand, is not "sudden" destruction but gradual destruction. Also the day of the Lord is *total* destruction ("and they shall not escape"), but the tribulation is only *partial* destruction.

Elijah the prophet must come *before* the day of the Lord (Malachi 4:5). Although this was partially fulfilled in John the Baptist, it will be finally fulfilled in one of the two witnesses during the tribulation (Matthew 11:14; 17:11-13; Luke 1:17; Revelation 11:1-13). The day of the Lord, therefore, must come after the tribulation.

The sun and moon must be turned to darkness and blood *before* the day of the Lord (Joel 2:31; Acts 2:20). From Matthew 24:29 we learn that this occurs *after* the tribulation. (There is no distinction between the "day" of the Lord and the "great day" of the Lord. "Great" is merely a description of the day, as a comparison of Joel 2:11 and 2:31 will show.)

Joel 3:14 pinpoints the time. It says, "The day of the Lord is near in the valley of decision." This points to Armageddon at the *end* of the tribulation.

Evidence abounds, but even if there were no evidence, common sense would tell us that the tribulation is the day of *man,* not the day of the Lord. Not Christ, but antichrist is on the throne. Men all over the world shake their fist at God, raise their blasphemies to an unprecedented pitch, and cling more tenaciously to their idols. How different from the time when, "The Lord alone shall be exalted in that day" (Isaiah 2:11,17). The tribulation surely is not the day of the Lord.

If it is true that the day of the Lord begins after the tribulation, then what about this puzzling question: "How can anyone say 'peace and safety' at the end of the tribulation?"

THE PRE-TRIBULATION RAPTURE

This sounds like before the tribulation.

> For when they shall say, Peace and safety; then sudden destruction cometh upon them, as travail upon a woman with child; and they shall not escape (1 Thessalonians 5:3).

Here are some possible reasons for people saying "peace and safety" at the end of the tribulation. First, the death of the two witnesses occurs shortly before the end (Revelation 11:14). "And they that dwell upon the earth shall rejoice over them, and make merry, and shall send gifts one to another; because these two prophets tormented them that dwelt on the earth" (Revelation 11:10). The extermination of these two tormenters may be one reason for saying "peace and safety."

Also, the world's armies are preparing for Armageddon at this time. The world could be saying, "We will once and for all exterminate that troublesome Jerusalem, and when we do we will have peace and safety at last. This will be the war to end all wars." This is another possible reason for saying "peace and safety" at the end of the tribulation. There doesn't have to *be* peace and safety, as Gundry points out, but the people *say* "peace and safety."

The opposite seems to be true now. Right now instead of saying "peace and safety" people are fearfully saying "war and danger." Prospects of peace will not be in sight until antichrist deceives the world and promises peace for all.

The "travail" of 1 Thessalonians 5:3 pictures the close of the tribulation rather than the tribulation itself. "Travail" in the Bible pictures several different things, as your concordance will reveal. The "travail" of Israel during the tribulation brings life (Jeremiah 30:4-7); whereas this travail at the end of the tribulation brings death to the unrepentant (Isaiah 13:6-9).

When is the day of the Lord? The day of the Lord begins with the sudden and total destruction of the wicked *after* the tribulation (1 Thessalonians 5:3), and it continues through the millennium until the new heavens and new earth (2 Peter 3:10-13).

First Thessalonians: Salvation

Not Appointed to Wrath. Understanding the day of the Lord in 1 Thessalonians 5 sheds light on verse nine: "For God hath not appointed us to wrath, but to obtain salvation by our Lord Jesus Christ." Pre-tribs have used this verse to "prove" that God has not appointed us to go through the tribulation. Yes, some wrath does come during the tribulation, but the "wrath" spoken of here refers not to the wrath of the tribulation, but to the wrath of the *day of the Lord after* the tribulation. Now you see why post-tribs do not believe us when we try to "prove" pre-tribulationism from 1 Thessalonians 5:9. We have plenty of proof elsewhere. We're not hurting for evidence; so I'm content to let the Bible speak for itself. And to the post-tribs we say a hearty "thank you" for forcing us to dig and find out what the Bible really says.

More evidence concerning the time of the day of the Lord will come to light in 2 Thessalonians. That we will save until the next chapter.

Why Watch? Have I backed myself into a corner? If the day of the Lord begins seven years after the rapture, if the church will not even be around to meet the day of the Lord, then the question is thrown at me, "Why are we exhorted to watch in 1 Thessalonians 5? How can we watch for the day of the Lord if we will be raptured seven years prior to that day?"

Well, let me encourage you to read 1 Thessalonians 5 very carefully:

> But of the times and the seasons, brethren, ye have no need that I write unto you. For yourselves know perfectly that the day of the Lord so cometh as a thief in the night. For when they shall say, Peace and safety; then sudden destruction cometh upon them, as travail upon a woman with child; and they shall not escape. But ye, brethren, are not in darkness, that that day should overtake you as a thief. Ye are all the children of light, and the children of the day: we are not of the night nor of darkness. Therefore let us not sleep, as do others; but let us watch and be sober. For they that sleep sleep in the night; and they that be drunken are drunken in the night. But let us who are of the day, be sober, putting on the breastplate of faith and love; and for an helmet, the hope of salvation. For God hath not appointed

THE PRE-TRIBULATION RAPTURE

us to wrath, but to obtain salvation by our Lord Jesus Christ, who died for us, that, whether we wake or sleep, we should live together with him. Wherefore comfort yourselves together, and edify one another, even as also ye do (1 Thessalonians 5:1-11).

Did you catch it? Not once does Paul say to watch *for* the day of the Lord. So to ask me the question, "Why should we watch for the day of the Lord?" is to ask me a loaded question. Paul never says to watch *for* the day of the Lord. In fact, he says the opposite.

Watch closely: "But ye, brethren, are not in darkness . . . ye are all the children of light . . . *Therefore* let us watch . . . *For* [because] God hath not appointed us to wrath" (excerpts from 1 Thessalonians 5:4-9). We do not watch *in order to be delivered* from that day; rather we watch because we have *already been delivered.* Read it again. Paul says, "We are delivered; *therefore* watch," not "Watch *in order to* be delivered." Do you see the difference? Watching is not the cause of deliverance, but deliverance is the cause of watching!

Paul's reasoning is consistent with everything else in the Christian life. Good works are not *in order to* be saved, but they follow *because* we are saved. God *has* called us with a heavenly calling, and then we live up to that. He *has* sanctified us, and then we live out that holiness. He *has* given victory over sin, and then we believe and claim that victory. Likewise, we *have* been delivered from the wrath of the day of the Lord; *therefore* we watch. Isn't this the highest motive to please God? You watch, *not* to prove yourself, but out of *gratitude* for what God has *already* done for you. How wonderful is God's way!

When I was in seminary I was taught to take a red pencil and circle all inferential conjunctions such as "therefore," "for," "in order that," etc. It is a simple thing that anyone can do, and it helps you to see at a glance the reasoning and the flow of thought. It is significant that Paul says "therefore" watch instead of watch "in order that." And it is all the more significant when everyone *expects* him to say, "Watch *for* the day." Humanly speaking, Paul could easily have made such a slip of

First Thessalonians: Salvation

the pen, but the Holy Spirit was guiding and guarding His Word so that it would come out just right.

By Paul's reasoning in this context, being children of the light refers to our *spiritual position* and destiny, *not* to *intellectual* enlightenment regarding signs and events. It has to do with the way we *live* rather than what we know and watch for.

What Does "Watch" Mean? If we do not watch "for" the day of the Lord, then what does "watch" mean? Does not the word "watch" imply looking *for* something?

Well, in modern English it does. But, remember, the New Testament was written in Greek. In Greek, as well as in the old English into which our King James Version was translated, the word simply means "to be alertly awake." In fact, the identical word is translated "wake" in verse 10 of 1 Thessalonians 5.

You can prove the meaning of "watch" to yourself without even knowing Greek. Notice that it is the opposite of "sleep" in 1 Thessalonians 5:6. The opposite of "sleep" is "awake." In the garden of Gethsemane Jesus was praying while Peter, James and John fell asleep. When Jesus found them He said to Peter, "Sleepest thou? Couldest not thou *watch* one hour?" What did He mean? Watch for the soldiers? No, Jesus simply meant, "Stay awake and pray" (Mark 14:37-38).

If all our Bibles said "be awake" instead of "watch" for every occurrence of the word in 1 Thessalonians 5, then maybe this misunderstanding would never have come up. Maybe no one would have ever thought that we were supposed to watch for the day of the Lord. Maybe everyone would know what Paul really meant: "You are delivered; you are children of light; so *wake up* and live as a Christian should."

How Do We Stay Awake? What is involved in staying awake? How do we apply this to Christian living? I am amazed at how often the Bible explains itself. The Bible is its own best commentary. First Thessalonians 5:6-8 explains the meaning of "watch" in this context so that we know exactly what Paul means by it. The pattern of parallels reveals the meaning.

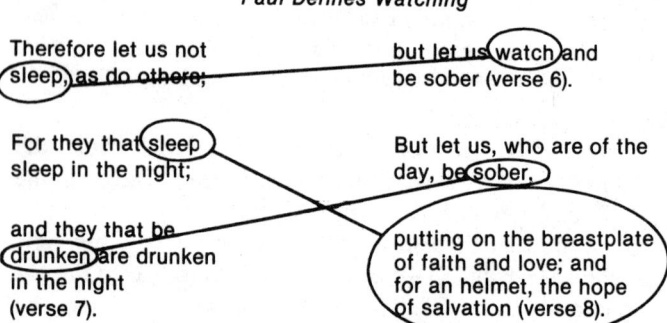

Notice that the two columns are opposites. "Sleep" opposes "watch," and "drunken" opposes "sober." The parallel is perfect except for one thing. Instead of using the word "watch," verse 8 substitutes a *definition* for the word. Watching means "putting on the breastplate of faith and love; and for an helmet, the hope of salvation." Faith, love, and hope. Exercise these virtues in your Christian life, and you will be a watchful Christian, or should I say, a Christian who is alertly awake. Thank you, Paul, for giving us your own definition of watching.

This kind of watching *anyone* can do. It is not limited to those with an intellectual grasp of world events. Those with the poorest minds can concentrate on their personal Christian character. Those also with pockets too poor to afford a newspaper are not stopped from this kind of watching. The lonely Christian isolated in a Communist prison cell can have a life of watching, even though he hasn't the faintest idea of "signs" happening outside of his four walls.

The Hope of Salvation. Of the three virtues involved in staying awake, faith, love, and hope, the last one is especially highlighted by Paul in this epistle. Paul stresses the hope of salvation in verse 8 because it is opposite to the fear of wrath

First Thessalonians: Salvation

which unbelievers face.

Why do we, as believers, have this hope of salvation? Here is the reason:

> For God hath not appointed us to wrath, but to obtain salvation by our Lord Jesus Christ, who died for us, that, whether we wake or sleep, we should live together with him (1 Thessalonians 5:9-10).

Why do we have hope? Because "[Jesus] died for us, that, whether we wake or sleep, we should live together with him." In other words, our hope of salvation is the *rapture*! Read verse 10 again. Verse 10 is actually a summary of Paul's description of the rapture in chapter four.

(Some would say the word "sleep" in 1 Thessalonians 5:10 is not the same as "sleep" in 1 Thessalonians 4:13-18 because a different Greek word is used. They would say it means "ungodly living," as in 1 Thessalonians 5:6-7, instead of "death." However, meaning changes as the context changes, and since 5:10 is an obvious reference to chapter 4, it is lifted into that context. To depend on the words being different in Greek is shaky in this case, because they are synonymous anyway. But to settle the matter once and for all, can you imagine the apostle Paul admitting that salvation will come to those who live ungodly! That would destroy the force of "edify" in verse 11. Would he give a big buildup for righteous living and then end by admitting that it doesn't matter anyway?)

Paul explains the hope of salvation in terms of the rapture. The rapture is our salvation from the day of wrath. The rapture is our *means of deliverance* from wrath. This is our strong hope. We look, not for wrath, but for rapture.

Now let me say that both pre- and post-tribs share the identical hope of salvation. To the post-trib the rapture comes to rescue them *immediately* before the wrath of the day of the Lord; while to the pre-trib the rapture comes *seven years* before. In either case the rapture is the means of salvation. And as we nurture this strong hope, along with faith and love, we will live as watchful Christians.

The Context. Post-tribs like to think that Paul said to watch *for* the day of the Lord, because this would mean going through the tribulation to meet the day of the Lord after the tribulation. As we have pointed out, Paul never said that.

Admitting this, post-tribs may then appeal to the context and say, "But the *context implies* watching for the day of the Lord." This is progress. By progress I mean that they now admit that Paul never said to watch for the day of the Lord. Now their argument has shifted from outright statement to implication. This is progress. I don't mind if you believe in implications; all I want for you to see is that it *is an implication.* I want you to recognize that the post-trib argument rests on nothing more than implication in 1 Thessalonians 5.

Now we mentioned previously two kinds of implications, strong ones and weak ones. Some implications you can get around and some you can't get around. With this in mind, let us examine the context in 1 Thessalonians 5. Let us see what it really implies. I don't know of one thing in the context to imply looking *for* the day of the Lord, but many things in the context imply wakeful living.

Notice the simple proximity of words. In the context "watch" has closer proximity to "daytime" than to "day of the Lord." The stronger implication, therefore, is "stay awake" rather than "look for signs."

Does mere mention of the day of the Lord imply that we should watch for it? No, not at all. That is a careless use of contextual interpretation. When we consider the context in interpretation, we must not only consider *what* is said, but *how* it is used, and *how* it fits into the flow of thought. For example, the day of the Lord is there and I am here. What is my relation to it? *That's* the question. Is it one of looking or living? Am I looking for signs of its coming so that I won't be surprised? Or am I so thankful that I am delivered from that day that I live

First Thessalonians: Salvation

now to please God?

WHICH IS THE CONTEXT?

watching to avoid its surprise

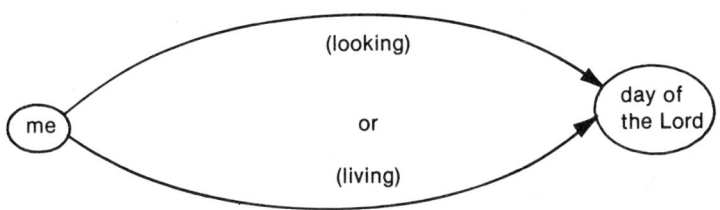

watching because I am safe from its surprise

Conjunctions Are the Key. How is the day of the Lord used in this context? What does the context really imply. Everything in the context points one way. Read 1 Thessalonians 5:1-10 carefully, and notice Paul's progression of thought:

But of the times and the seasons, brethren, ye have no need that I write unto you. For yourselves know perfectly that the day of the Lord so cometh as a thief in the night. For when they shall say, Peace and safety; then sudden destruction cometh upon them, as travail upon a woman with child; and they shall not escape (verses 1-3).

The destiny of night people is destruction,

(But) ye, brethren, are not in darkness, that that day should overtake you as a thief. Ye are all the children of light, and the children of the day: we are not of the night, nor of darkness (verses 4-5).

But we are day people;

Therefore let us not sleep, as do others; but let us watch and be sober. For they that sleep sleep in the night;

THE PRE-TRIBULATION RAPTURE

and they that be drunken are drunken in the night. But let us, who are of the day, be sober, putting on the breastplate of faith and love; and for an helmet, the hope of salvation (verses 6-8).

Therefore let us live like day people,

(For) God hath not appointed us to wrath, but to obtain salvation by our Lord Jesus Christ. Who died for us, that, whether we wake or sleep, we should live together with him (verses 9-10).

For the destiny of day people is salvation.

Notice the conjunctions: "but" . . . "therefore" . . . "for." These little words show how Paul's thoughts are connected. They are like signposts guiding us along in a smooth-flowing natural-sounding progression of thought. Misread one of these signposts and the meaning becomes disjointed like this: "We day people will not be surprised by the day of the Lord; *therefore,* so that we won't be surprised let us watch for it." It doesn't make sense. What is the "therefore" there for? Maybe Paul should have reversed it and said, "We watch; therefore, we won't be surprised." Maybe he should have said, "We watch; therefore, we won't be destroyed" instead of saying, as he did, "We won't be destroyed; therefore, watch." He should have reversed his logic; he should have made the "therefore" do an about-face, if he meant "looking" instead of "living."

The Thief and Surprise. According to Paul's logic (as revealed by the conjunctions), it is the night people who have to watch out for the thief, not day people. Day people are concerned with living, not looking. If it is daytime at your house, do you stand at the window looking for a thief to come? Of course not. Thieves generally strike at night, not in the day. In the daytime you do your job, you stay awake, you stay sober, but you don't worry about the thief. *The context deals with the life we live,* not with what we look for. What good does it do to look for the thief in the daytime?

First Thessalonians: Salvation

Not only do we have a day-night difference, but we have a destination difference. This diagram pictures the two destinations.

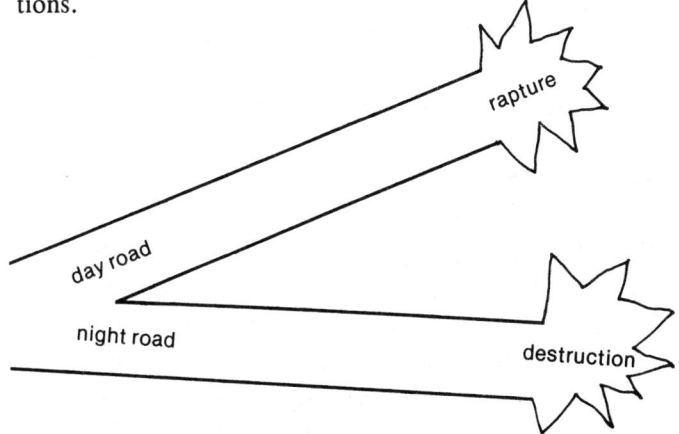

The thief lurks along the night road. To those on the day road, the thief represents no danger. We are safe. Rapture awaits us, while destruction awaits them.

The surprise of destruction cannot touch us. We are on a different road. We are careful, not to avoid its surprise (because the rapture will surprise us anyway), but we are careful to live worthy of the road we are on.

Questions and Answers About "Surprise." In the lists below notice that there are eight spaces but only seven words contrasted.

thief	no thief
night	day
destruction	salvation
surprise	

What goes in the blank space? Post-tribs would answer "*Awareness* through seeing signs." I answer, "Safety."

115

THE PRE-TRIBULATION RAPTURE

How do we know that "surprise" is not contrasted to awareness? Because Paul mentions no signs to look for or to be aware of.

How do we know that "surprise" is contrasted to safety? Because verse 3 says, "For when they shall say, Peace and safety, then sudden destruction cometh upon them as travail upon a woman with child."

How does this work out in actual experience? In actuality we will be raptured safely to heaven before the destruction hits. Even post-tribs have us being caught up to meet Christ before He descends with "sudden destruction." This is why we are *safe* while they are *surprised*.

How do we know that safety comes through rapture? Verse 10 describes our salvation in terms of rapture (compare 4:14,17).

Does not the day of the Lord include the rapture? If it does, I do not know of any Scripture which says so. All we can be certain of is that the day of the Lord brings "sudden destruction," and this comes *after* the rapture.

Does not 1 Thessalonians 5 prove that we will "meet" the day of the Lord? We will meet the rapture (whenever that is) and they will meet the destruction of the day of the Lord. The only way that we will "meet" that moment of sudden destruction is by descending with Christ from the clouds.

Does not Paul require us to be on earth until the destruction hits? If so, the first generation Thessalonians did not make it. Certainly they "watched." (The signs they could not yet see, but they could stay "awake" spiritually.) Certainly they were safe from the thief. But that did not imply remaining on earth until the thief struck. Certainly the future events remained a *valid motive* for watchful living even though their living was separated in time from the events which motivated them.

Does not verse 4 imply that we will be "overtaken" by the day of the Lord, but not "as a thief"? Not necessarily. It is not that easy to separate "overtake" and "as a thief," because they go together like bread and butter. "Overtake" in the

Greek literally means "come down upon." This is a bad connotation. God's wrath will not "come down upon" *any* believer. Even tribulation saints who "meet" the day and go through it protected will not have that day "come down upon" them at all. Therefore, "as a thief" merely reinforces the meaning of "overtake." It hardly implies that the day will overtake (come down upon) the church.

Why won't the day overtake us as a thief? Post-tribs answer, "Because we will be aware of approaching signs." Paul answers, "Because we are appointed to salvation" (in other words, we will be with Christ when the thief strikes).

Looking or Living? Does the context really imply looking? Let's think about it. Why look? Are we supposed to look *in order to avoid destruction*? That doesn't make sense because the destruction represents no danger to Christians. Even the post-trib scheme has the Christian safely raptured before destruction falls. If the destruction of the day of the Lord is no danger to us, why look for it?

Furthermore, mere looking doesn't exempt anyone from destruction. It is the *life we live,* the surrender of our wills to God, that makes us ready to meet the day of destruction. An unbeliever can fearfully look for the day of the Lord, but that won't help him when the time comes. If destruction is the reason, then living makes better sense than looking. Paul's purpose in this section is to "edify" (verse 11), to build up our *living,* to put it on a higher plane.

So why look? Are we supposed to look *in order to see signs* so that we know when the day is near? That doesn't make sense in this context because these signs have not appeared yet. In 2 Thessalonians Paul explains what these signs are and he says that since these signs have not occurred yet we should concentrate on living instead of looking. If I were a post-trib I would have no way of looking for the day of the Lord until the abomination of desolation occurred first.

So why look? Are we supposed to look so that we won't miss

THE PRE-TRIBULATION RAPTURE

the rapture? According to 1 Thessalonians 4:17 and 1 Corinthians 15:51 we all will be raptured, looking or not, ready or not. The result is the same. We will be just as raptured and they will be just as destroyed.

So why look? Yes, we have reason to look and it is Peter, not Paul in this context, who explains it:

> Looking for and hasting unto the coming of the day of God, wherein the heavens being on fire shall be dissolved, and the elements shall melt with fervent heat? Nevertheless we, according to his promise, look for new heavens and a new earth, wherein dwelleth righteousness (2 Peter 3:12-13).

In this passage Peter uses the word "look," instead of "watch" as Paul does, because Peter *means* "look." The new heavens and the new earth is what we look for. This aspect of the day of the Lord occurs, not when Christ returns, but 1000 years later (see Revelation 20-21). We look for an event 1000 years *beyond* the rapture, 1000 years *after* we get our new bodies, 1000 years *past* the time when we have gone to be with Christ. The looking that Peter talks about, therefore, proves nothing about pre-trib or post-trib, because his looking is 1000 years removed from the issue and *either* a pre-trib *or* a post-trib can look for what he looks for.

I can go one step further. As a pre-trib, I do look for the day of destruction at the *beginning* of the day of the Lord. Now as I am on earth, I look for it; and when I am raptured and in heaven I will still be looking for it. Mere looking proves nothing whatsoever about the time of the rapture. And as I look, I don't get my Scriptural support for looking from 1 Thessalonians 5—that is not what Paul is talking about. I get it from a passage like Revelation 6:9-11 where the souls under the altar, although in heaven, still look for the day of destruction. If from heaven we can look, then looking proves nothing for post-tribulationism.

In a nutshell, number one, Paul does not *say* to watch for the day of the Lord. Number two, the context does not *imply* to watch for the day of the Lord. Number three, even if Paul did say or imply to watch for the day of the Lord, looking for that day would still not prove post-tribulationism, because we can look from heaven.

Motivation for Living. My purpose has been to let the context speak for itself. I am guided by the Greek meaning of "watch" rather than being misguided by the modern English meaning. I accept Paul's own definition of "watching" in verse 8 instead of injecting my own definition. I take the natural meaning of "therefore" in verse 6 instead of reversing its meaning. I consider that the primary duty of a day person is to stay awake rather than to look. I understand that "looking" does not make sense in this context.

If these considerations from the immediate context are not enough, then let me show you one more verse earlier in the book. Remember, Paul gives previews early in the book and explains more fully later in the book. 1 Thessalonians 2:12 captures the thought of 1 Thessalonians 5 in a nutshell: "That ye would walk worthy of God, who hath called you unto his kingdom and glory." Paul's point is our *living,* walking worthy of God. A glorious destiny is ours, *therefore,* let us live up to it.

I hope and pray that we can all quit trying to prove pre-trib or post-trib from this epistle when it teaches neither. We can all agree—as the Word of God speaks for itself—that the time of the rapture is not revealed in 1 Thessalonians. We can all agree that the rapture—whenever it occurs—is the hope of salvation prior to the day of the Lord. And we can all receive comfort and edification from this epistle and live in gratitude because God has made us children of light.

1. Gundry, *The Church and the Tribulation,* p. 89ff.

"Therefore, brethren, stand fast, and hold the traditions which ye have been taught" (2 Thessalonians 2:15).

6
Second Thessalonians: Glory

After the Russian revolution of 1917, a man went up to his pre-trib pastor, tore his Bible in half and shouted, *"You lied to us!"* I read this account and similar accounts of the dangers of pre-trib teaching in a post-trib periodical. It makes my heart sink to think that pre-tribulationism has been improperly taught. Is pre-tribulationism some unrealistic escapist theology? Does it mean we won't ever have to prepare for tribulation? No, no, no, this is not the way to teach pre-tribulationism.

As long as we are in this old world we will have tribulation. We should expect it. We should prepare for it. Richard Wurmbrand suffered fourteen years of tribulation and torture in Communist prisons. He represents thousands of others who suffer for their faith. Just because I happen to believe that I will escape the last seven years of tribulation, that doesn't mean I have an easy road. In some degree I expect to suffer tribulation every day of my life for the rest of my life. That is my privilege—yes, privilege—as a Christian.

Second Thessalonians: Glory

The Thessalonians prematurely expected escape from all their troubles. They thought the Lord would come right away to destroy their enemies. Paul writes his second epistle to the Thessalonians to correct this false notion, and his theme is *God delays punishment of the wicked in order to produce patience in the believer.*

WHEN DOES "REST" COME?

A strong passage in the hands of post-tribulationists has been 2 Thessalonians 1:6-8. The following description of Christ's coming with fire and vengeance could only refer to His return after the tribulation:

> Seeing it is a righteous thing with God to recompense tribulation to them that trouble you; and to you who are troubled *rest* with us, when the Lord Jesus shall be revealed from heaven with his mighty angels, in flaming fire taking vengeance on them that know not God, and that obey not the gospel of our Lord Jesus Christ (2 Thessalonians 1:6-8).

The word "rest" in this passage is a noun, not a verb. God will recompense "rest" to us *after* the tribulation. If rest comes after the tribulation, the argument goes, then the rapture comes after the tribulation. But do rest and rapture come at the same moment? Does rest mean rapture? This is the unanswered question.

To get the picture clearly before us, look at this diagrammatical representation of the passage:

| God will recompense | { tribulation to them / rest to you } | when the Lord Jesus shall be revealed from heaven with His mighty angels |

God will recompense *two things:* "tribulation" and "rest." "Rest" for believers comes *after* the tribulation, as post-tribs are quick to point out. Ah, but what about "tribulation" for unbelievers? When does that come? Does "tribulation" also come *after* the tribulation?

Obviously we need to do some unraveling or both post-tribs and pre-tribs will get tangled up in this passage. We pull first on the one loose string which we can agree upon. We all know that "tribulation" for unbelievers *begins seven years earlier,* but it *culminates* at the end when the Lord takes fiery vengeance. You see, the word "tribulation" can be used in two ways. Usually when we say "tribulation" we mean the *period* of tribulation. But Paul in this passage uses "tribulation" to mean God's vengeance at the *end* of the period. So the answer is yes, "tribulation" (in the narrow sense) occurs *after* the "tribulation" (in the broad sense).

Now, if Paul uses "tribulation" in the narrow sense, then what about "rest"? Usually when we say "rest" we mean rest in the broad sense, relief from persecution, escape from trouble. Rapture is rest in the broad sense. Rapture is relief from persecution. Rapture is escape. But Paul has a more specific meaning in mind for "rest." For him "rest" means the glory of the Lord being revealed in the saints.

Let me explain further. Or rather let Paul himself explain further, because Paul has a habit of introducing a topic and then explaining later on and Paul's own explanations are the best commentaries that I have ever found. After introducing "tribulation" in verse 6, Paul explains in verses 8-9 what he means by "tribulation." It is vengeance and destruction. After introducing "rest" in verse 7, Paul explains in verse 10 what he means by "rest." "Rest" means glory and admiration. The Lord's glory shines forth in us, and others will behold with wonder and astonishment because they see that God is in us. That is rest in the *fullest* sense. It is not mere relief from persecution. Relief is only *half* rest. It is not mere escape from trouble. Escape is only *half* rest. It is not the rapture he is talking about. Rapture is only *half* rest.

As wonderful as the rapture is, that is not all we look for-

Second Thessalonians: Glory

ward to. After the rapture sin *still* reigns on the earth. God is *still* scorned. Neither are the raptured believers recognized and vindicated. Even though we are in heaven, no one else knows it. They might think we were taken away by UFO's.

No one who truly loves righteousness could be content with this half-rest condition. We long for that *final victory* when God reveals Himself to the whole world, when righteousness finally defeats sin, and when the whole world admires us for who we really are. When you and I come riding down from the sky on those white horses (Revelation 19:14), then those who knew us on earth will stand there with mouths gaping in astonishment. "They were not crazy after all! God is in them!" That's more than release. That's vindication.

This is not my feeling alone, because the martyrs in Revelation 6:9-11 feel the same way. These martyrs, *even though they are in heaven,* do not have full rest. "They cried with a loud voice, saying, How long, O Lord, holy and true, dost thou not judge and avenge our blood on them that dwell on the earth?" They are told to rest temporarily until the time for the full and natural rest that Paul talks about. Why are they not satisfied having full rest? Do they long for their resurrection bodies? No. They long for God's *vengeance.* Having relief for themselves does not satisfy.

My friend, as wonderful as the rapture is, it is not our final hope.

You can see from this diagram that rapture is only half the story:

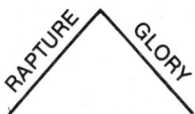

Going up is rapture. Coming down is glory (whether one second later or seven years later). Paul centers on the second part, glory, when he speaks of "rest."

So 2 Thessalonians 1:6-7 must be unraveled completely. We

cannot leave half of it still tangled. Just as "tribulation," in the full sense, comes *after* the tribulation, so "rest" in the full sense comes *after* the half-rest of the rapture. Both "tribulation" and "rest," in the broad sense, *begin* seven years earlier; but both *culminate* at the end.

Now post-tribs can assume that "rest" means rapture and thereby "prove" that the rapture comes after the tribulation. And if I wanted to I could assume that "tribulation" means the seven-year period and thereby "prove" that the rapture occurs at the identical moment the tribulation begins. But such assuming misses the point of Paul altogether. Paul is not talking about rapture. I will let Paul define his own words as he explains "tribulation" in verses 8 and 9, and as he explains "rest" in verse 10.

THE BASIS OF BESEECHING

Chapter two opens with the statement, "Now we beseech you, brethren, *by* the coming of our Lord Jesus Christ, and *by* our gathering together unto him, that ye be not soon shaken in mind, or be troubled, neither by spirit, nor by word, nor by letter as from us, as that the day of the Lord is at hand." Most commentators say the word "by" is better translated "concerning." The translation "by" makes the coming of Christ and our gathering unto Him the *basis* of Paul's beseeching (favoring pre-tribulationism). The translation "concerning" makes Christ's coming and our gathering the *object* of Paul's beseeching (favoring post-tribulationism). Which is right? Is Paul beseeching "by" our gathering or "concerning" our gathering unto Christ?

Well, if you question the majority of commentators what do you do? You check their *reasons*. Any average Bible student has a right to disagree with a commentator if he has better *reasons*.

The main reason they change "by" to "concerning" is that the Greek word was no longer commonly used in adjurations during New Testament times. In fact, they claim it is not so used even once in the New Testament. Although I respect their knowledge of the history of the Greek language, I still wanted to ask my good friend about it, my concordance. In the concordance I came across a verse which makes me wonder if this word is *never* used in adjurations without exception. Second Corinthians 5:20 uses this identical preposition: "We pray you *in* Christ's *stead,* be ye reconciled to God." He obviously is not praying "concerning" Christ, but "by" Christ or "on behalf of" Christ. Does this not prove the possibility of exception to the general rule? The word *can* mean "by" instead of "concerning" when used with a word in the same class as "beseech."

I wonder, too, if Paul wanted to say "by," which Greek word better expresses the idea than the one he used? You see, the root meaning of this word is "over." Having laid a *foundation* in First Thessalonians of our gathering unto Christ in the rapture, he now makes a plea "over" that. If the plea is "over" the foundation, the rapture is the *basis* of the plea. I know of no better Greek word Paul could have used to express this idea. He chose this word with a purpose. He easily could have used the other Greek word which more usually means "concerning," and that would have saved the commentators a lot of work in correcting Paul.

Let's evaluate the reasons further. I'm saying the best interpretation has the best reasons behind it. The decisive factor in any interpretation is the context. In this context what exactly is Paul beseeching? Is he beseeching *concerning* our gathering unto Him as post-tribs claim? Is he beseeching *concerning* the rapture? The discrepancy becomes apparent immediately. Not even once does Paul mention our gathering or the rapture in the entire rest of the book. He does not talk about it at all! It lies in the background; it forms the *foundation* for what he is talking about. But a simple reading of the epistle shows that Paul is beseeching *concerning* something entirely different.

He is beseeching the Thessalonians concerning their *attitude*. He tells them to be patient. They were "troubled" (2:2), which means they were "agitated" like a wave of water hopping around. As Gundry points out, the Thessalonians entertained wild anticipations that the day of the Lord was at hand. But Paul beseeches them to calm down and be patient a while longer. The *object* of beseeching is the *attitude* of the Thessalonians and the *disorderly conduct* it led to.

Some of the Thessalonians were in such an uproar over the idea that the Lord's coming was upon them that they quit their jobs and were running around like chickens with their heads cut off. Paul says, "Screw your heads back on, get back to work, and wait for the Lord's coming, but with *patience*." Notice Paul's command:

> And the Lord direct your hearts into the love of God, and into the patient waiting for Christ. Now we command you, brethren, in the name of our Lord Jesus Christ, that ye withdraw yourselves from every brother that walketh disorderly, and not after the tradition which he received of us (2 Thessalonians 3:5-6).

Comparing the latter half of this passage with 2 Thessalonians 2:1-2 is illuminating. One passage helps us to understand the other because they are parallel. Both contain the *object* of beseeching and both contain the *basis* of beseeching.

COMPARISON

	2:1-2	3:6
BASIS OF BESEECHING	Now we *beseech* you, brethren, by the coming of our Lord Jesus Christ, and *by* our gathering together unto Him,	Now we *command* you, brethren, *in* the name of our Lord Jesus Christ,

Second Thessalonians: Glory

OBJECT OF BESEECHING	That ye be not soon shaken in mind, or be troubled, neither by spirit, nor by word, nor by letter as from us, as that the day of Christ is at hand.	That ye withdraw yourselves from every brother that walketh disorderly, and not after the tradition which he received of us.

Notice the parallels in the two passages. "Command" is similar to "beseech," only stronger. In one passage Paul pleads for a settled attitude, in the other passage he explains that the *way* to have a settled attitude is to be patient and settled in their work. In both passages the *basis* of Paul's plea is the Lord and the *object* of his plea is their unsettled attitude evidenced in disorderly work habits.

Notice how the second passage sheds light on the first. In 3:6 would you say that Paul is commanding them *concerning* the Lord? Of course not. He commands concerning their *conduct,* but he commands them *by* or "in the name of" the Lord. If you agree that these two passages are parallel, then 3:6 is a divine commentary on 2:1-2 showing that "by" should be translated "by" instead of "concerning" as some human commentators say. If you do not agree that the two passages are parallel, then I merely used 3:6 as contextual evidence illustrating what Paul's point is in this epistle. He makes his plea *by* the Lord and *concerning* the attitude and conduct of the Thessalonians.

For the proper translation of the word "by" we have looked at evidence from the concordance, evidence from the context, and now let us look at evidence from common sense. If "concerning" were the correct translation, how could you possibly *beseech,* or ask, concerning the coming of Christ? Can you beseech Christ to come sooner? This Paul does not do. Can you beseech someone else to beseech Christ to come? This Paul does not do. Can you ask someone when Christ is going to come? This Paul does not do. I'm just showing that it doesn't make sense to beseech *concerning* the coming of Christ. Common sense tells me that Paul does not beseech, or ask, concerning the coming of Christ at all.

Instead of asking he *tells* them. Rather than beseeching he *teaches* concerning Christ's coming. Furthermore, he does not primarily teach concerning the *gathering of believers*; he teaches concerning the *destruction of unbelievers*. The whole context is overwhelmingly against the idea that the coming of Christ is the *object of beseeching*; it is rather the *object of teaching* which in turn provides the *basis for beseeching*.

DOES PAUL BESEECH "BY" OR "CONCERNING" THE COMING OF CHRIST?

The attitude of the Thessalonians	object of beseeching
The coming of Christ	object of teaching and basis of beseeching

Conclusion: He beseeches them "concerning" their attitude "by" the coming of Christ. The proper translation in 2:1 is "by" instead of "concerning."

Since Paul beseeches them "by" the coming of Christ, we then ask, *how* does Christ's coming form the basis of his beseeching? Is it based on the *time* of the rapture? Is Paul saying, "Since the rapture comes first I beseech you not to be troubled about the day of the Lord which comes later"? No, Paul says nothing about the time of the rapture in these epistles. This will become more clear as we go along.

Then how is Christ's coming the basis of Paul's beseeching? The basis is, not the time, but the *rewarded patience* at Christ's coming. Paul says, "You will gain your reward; so be patient. Because of the just recompense at Christ's coming, I beseech

Second Thessalonians: Glory

you to have a patient attitude during the delay."

What reward is Paul talking about? Reward at the rapture or reward at Christ's coming to earth? Which aspect of Christ's coming forms the basis of his beseeching? The answer is *both* aspects. Paul says, "Now we beseech you, brethren, by the coming of our Lord Jesus Christ, *and* by our gathering together unto him." In this one verse Paul mentions *both* aspects of Christ's coming and both form the basis of his beseeching. The "coming" is that aspect when Christ returns to earth after the tribulation, because that is the coming Paul primarily talks about in this epistle. The "gathering," of course, is the rapture, the other aspect.

Does it seem strange that Paul mentions both aspects in one breath when the two aspects are seven years apart? Does it seem even stranger that he would reverse the order? Even for post-tribs who place the two aspects seconds apart instead of years apart the order in this verse is reversed. Even according to them our gathering in the air occurs before the coming to destroy antichrist and his followers. But here the coming is mentioned first in order to make a smoother transition from chapter one, because chapter one talks about the coming instead of the gathering.

Why are they mingled? Well, read on to see why it is not strange at all that Paul would mingle both aspects in one verse. It is the most normal thing that he could do.

DOUBLE REWARD

The double aspect of Christ's coming brings a double reward, namely salvation and glory. Rapture brings salvation, and Christ's coming to earth brings glory. How do I know this? By comparing two passages. Study these two passages below. Read them over several times. Notice the parallels between the two. These parallels are not accidental because one passage introduces chapter two and the other passage concludes chapter two.

THE PRE-TRIBULATION RAPTURE

TWO-FOLD COMING	TWO-FOLD REWARD
2 Thess. 2:1-2 (introduction to chapter 2)	*2 Thess. 2:13-15 (conclusion to chapter 2)*
Now we beseech you, brethren,	But we are bound to give thanks alway to God for you, brethren beloved of the Lord,
(by) the *coming* of our Lord Jesus Christ,	because God hath from the beginning chosen you to *salvation* through sanctification of the Spirit and belief of the truth;
and by our *gathering* together unto Him,	whereunto he called you by our gospel, to the obtaining of the *glory* of our Lord Jesus Christ.
that ye be not soon shaken in mind,	(Therefore,) brethren, stand fast,
or be troubled, [or "agitated" from side to side]	and hold the traditions which ye have been taught,
neither by spirit, nor by word, nor by letter as from us, as that the day of Christ [the day of the Lord] is at hand.	whether by word, or our epistle.

By setting these passages side by side, all I am trying to do is to let Paul explain himself as he does so many times. The arrows show items that are reversed in the parallel (this is not unusual for Paul as you can see from the outlines in Appendix I). Now as we examine these two passages, point by point, we will better appreciate how the hope of Christ's coming produces patience in our lives.

"Coming" in one passage parallels "glory" in the other passage. I know that these are parallel because of 2 Thessalonians 1:7-10: "When the Lord Jesus shall be revealed from heaven with his mighty angels, in flaming fire taking vengeance

Second Thessalonians: Glory

on them that know not God . . . when he shall come to be *glorified* in his saints." Christ's coming to earth after the tribulation brings glory for us. Doesn't this inspire you to be patient? Every minute you wait means glory then. The longer you wait now, the more glory it will bring then. Every hardship, every trial you endure now will multiply exceedingly your glory then. So have patience.

"Our gathering together unto him" in one passage parallels "salvation" in the other passage. I know that these are parallel because of 1 Thessalonians 5:9-10:

> For God hath not appointed us to wrath, but to obtain *salvation* by our Lord Jesus Christ, who died for us, that, whether we wake or sleep, we should live together with him.

As we learned in the previous chapter, this passage alludes back to the rapture as described in 1 Thessalonians 4. We learned there that *the rapture is our means of salvation* from wrath. This salvation is ours because we have believed the truth and because we have been sanctified by the Spirit. As we are all gathered unto Christ in the clouds we will escape this old world. All its problems, all its pressure, all its heartaches will be left behind forever, and forgotten. But salvation from our problems is nothing compared to salvation from God's wrath. Such is our destiny; so have patience.

Now let us examine the two circled words in the parallel passages, namely "by" and "therefore." Both words point out the *basis* of Paul's plea. In the one passage his plea is based on the two-fold coming. In the other passage his plea is based on the two-fold reward. This forms additional evidence that "by" is properly translated "by" instead of "concerning" because the relationship of thought in both passages is identical.

We have a solid two-fold basis for patience, salvation at the rapture, and glory at His second coming. Salvation and rapture are emphasized in 1 Thessalonians. Glory after the tribulation is the keynote in 2 Thessalonians. This double aspect of His coming has nothing to do with the *time* of the rapture. All of us can be edified and encouraged by the double reward we will receive. To be taken out of the world is salvation; to be admired by the world (whether it is one second later or seven years later) is glory.

Both aspects form the *basis* of Paul's beseeching, not the *object*. Paul is saying, "Since you will be rewarded by salvation and glory at the coming of Christ you can afford to be patient." That is how Paul beseeches them "concerning" their attitude "by" the coming of Christ.

"THE FALLING AWAY"

Both pre- and post-tribs have used the following verse to "prove" the time of the rapture:

> Let no man deceive you by any means: for that day shall not come except there come a falling away first, and that man of sin be revealed, the son of perdition (2 Thessalonians 2:3).

The troublesome term has been "falling away." What does it mean? There are two common views. Some believe it is a falling away from the faith, or apostasy. Others feel it is a falling away from the earth, or rapture. Depending on their view of the time of the day of the Lord, some use the "falling away" to "prove" that the rapture comes before the man of sin while others use the same verse to "prove" that the man of sin comes before the rapture.

Which interpretation is correct? Falling away from the faith or falling away from the earth? After wavering back and forth between these two views I finally settled on a third view. Let me explain the third view now before I answer the other two views. By the way, the third view will do nothing to "prove" pre-tribulationism or post-tribulationism—disappointing to both sides, I'm sure—but it will open up the passage in new light helping us to understand it better.

Paul does here what he does so many times elsewhere. He

Second Thessalonians: Glory

first *introduces* a topic and then he *explains* it. We saw how he did this in chapter one (where he introduced and explained "tribulation" and "rest"), and he does this *consistently* throughout 2 Thessalonians as the outline in Appendix I reveals. Once again Paul's own interpretation comes to our rescue.

Verse 3 *introduces* two topics: "the falling away" and the "revealing." The following verses go on to *explain* these two topics. Verse 4 explains the "revealing" of the man of sin while verses 6-7 explain the "falling away." No better commentary sits on my shelf than the Bible itself!

	REMOVAL	REVEALING
INTRODUCTION	Let no man deceive you by any means: for that day shall not come, except there come a *falling away* first, (3a)	and that man of sin be *revealed*, (3b)
EXPLANATION	and now ye know what withholdeth that he might be revealed in his time. For the mystery of iniquity doth already work; only he who now letteth will let, until he be *taken out of the way.* (6-7)	the son of perdition; who opposeth and exalteth himself above all that is called God, or that is worshipped; so that he as God sitteth in the temple of God, showing himself that he is God. (4)

What is "the falling away"? It is none other than the taking out of the way of the One who is holding back the revealing of the man of sin. The removal of one allows the revealing of the other. Paul explains it so well. He explains "the falling away" as "taken out of the way" (verse 7). The phrases are synonymous. Both phrases are hinged to the revealing of the man of sin, because the removal and the revealing are linked

THE PRE-TRIBULATION RAPTURE

together twice in this passage:

Except there come a falling away first, and that man of sin be revealed (verse 3).	Until he be taken out of the way. And then shall that Wicked be revealed (verses 7-8).

The next question is, "Who is the one withholding who is taken out of the way?" I agree with many Bible scholars that it is the Holy Spirit. He is the one with the power to hold back the man of sin. If it is not the Holy Spirit, then I do not know of any other explanation for both the masculine and neuter which are used in verses 6 and 7. "What withholdeth" (verse 6) is neuter in accordance with the word "spirit" which is neuter in the Greek. "He who now letteth" (verse 7) is masculine in accordance with the real personality of the third person of the Godhead.

How does the Holy Spirit restrain the man of sin? Through the church? No, but by direct and personal restraint. Gundry explains it well:

> "Become out of the midst" [or, "taken out of the way"] does not demand removal from the world. "Midst" more literally means "middle." The restrainer is standing in the middle, i.e., between the *person* of the Antichrist and the *revelation* of the Antichrist. It is as though the Antichrist stands in the wings, eager to break forth onto the stage of history. But the Holy Spirit blocks entrance until the appointed moment when He will step out of the way and allow the man of lawlessness to stride onstage before the admiring eyes of mankind. Perhaps a misunderstanding of the expression "become out of the midst" as passive has aided the pre-tribulational idea of withdrawal from the world. The expression is not passive. Lenski captures the meaning exactly with his idiomatic rendering "*get* out of the way."[1]

This view does not demand the removal of the Holy Spirit from the earth during the tribulation. In this way we avoid the problem of trying to explain how evangelism and conversions take place on an unprecedented scale during that time. Second Thessalonians 2 speaks only of the Holy Spirit's relation to antichrist, not to the rest of the world.

Second Thessalonians: Glory

Is "The Falling Away" the Rapture? Perhaps the reader may agree now that "the falling away" is the moving out of the way of the Holy Spirit. However, pre-tribulationists may still insist on coupling the rapture with that. If the Holy Spirit indwells believers, some say, do not the Holy Spirit and the church depart from the earth at the same time?

If you read the passage carefully you will see that they do *not* depart at the same time. The Holy Spirit is removed and the man of sin is revealed in the *middle of the tribulation,* exactly 3½ years *after* the rapture! The revealing of the man of sin involves his sitting in the temple claiming to be God. This is the abomination of desolation which occurs in the middle of the tribulation, as we saw in chapter two. Antichrist is around before then, of course, but he is not revealed as the man of sin until the abomination of desolation.

Not only this passage places the revealing of the man of sin at the abomination of desolation, but also Revelation 13:5 is very clear that antichrist is granted power to oppose God for *only 42 months.* If he has this power for only 42 months, the last 3½ years of the tribulation, then we know that he *cannot* be revealed as the man of sin who opposes God at the *beginning* of the tribulation when the rapture occurs.

If the revelation of antichrist occurs at the middle of the tribulation, some may yet object that the removal of the Holy Spirit could still occur at the beginning of the tribulation, resulting in a 3½-year gap between the removal and the revealing. However, the text indicates no gap. Removal and revealing occur virtually simultaneously. Watch closely. Verses 7-8 say, "*Only* he who now letteth [restraineth] will let [restrain], *until* he be taken out of the way. And *then* shall that Wicked be revealed. . . ." The "only" thing standing in the way is the Holy Spirit. Once He steps aside what else is there to hold back antichrist for 3½ more years? Such a gap is unwarranted. Therefore, the removal or "the falling away" occurs at the mid-point.

If the Holy Spirit does not depart until the middle of the

THE PRE-TRIBULATION RAPTURE

tribulation, some may wonder, "Does this not prove that the rapture also occurs at the middle of the tribulation?" No, let me give you one more piece of evidence that completely disassociates this departure from the rapture. Remember in the last chapter we demonstrated that the rapture was *first* revealed in the first epistle to the Thessalonians. Paul did *not* teach the rapture while he was with them. This is the key. Now in 2 Thessalonians 2:5 Paul says, "Remember ye not, that, *when I was yet with you,* I told you these things?" This is a dead giveaway. If Paul taught the removal and the revealing while he was *with* them, then the removal could not possibly refer to the rapture which was first taught *taught* by *letter.*

"The falling away" is the removal of the Holy Spirit only. It has nothing to do with the rapture at all. The rapture and the "falling away" are totally separate, both in Paul's teaching and also in time by 3½ years.

Is "The Falling Away" Apostasy? As you can see, I am trying to let Paul speak for himself. I am satisfied to mold my theology around him rather than molding him around my theology. I find when I do that, I appreciate the Bible more as it opens up in crystal clarity.

Now let's handle another objection: If "the falling away" is not the rapture, is it a falling away from the faith, or apostasy? To believe this is to assume something Paul never says. In fact, the man of sin and his followers were *never in the faith* in the first place. If they were never *in* the faith, how could they possibly fall *away* from the faith? It doesn't fit.

Some would answer that the man of sin has a *religious appearance,* and that is why he can be tagged as falling away from the faith. It is true that he has a religious appearance in the first 3½ years as he pretends to be friends with the Jews (Daniel 9:27). However, Paul makes no mention of this and this has nothing to do with the context here. Paul's account begins at the *middle* of the tribulation when antichrist openly opposes God. In Paul's mind he comes on the scene opposing God from

Second Thessalonians: Glory

the first minute. No falling away from a previous position.

More crucial to the point, though, even if Paul could have in mind a falling away from the Jewish faith, this is not quite the same as falling away from Christianity. Apostasy to Paul meant turning away from the *truth,* namely *Christianity.* It is impossible for one *already* in error, namely Judaism, to apostatize from the faith. This makes the so-called "religious appearance" of the man of sin irrelevant to the question.

Never in all his career does the man of sin even claim to be a Christian. He puts on the cloak of Judaism in the first 3½ years, and he promotes his own religion in direct opposition to God in the last 3½ years. No room abides for a falling away from the *true* faith.

If not the apostasy of antichrist, could not "the falling away" refer to apostasy in general which is to occur sometime in the last days? First Timothy 4:1 says:

> Now the Spirit speaketh expressly, that in the latter times some shall *depart from the faith,* giving heed to seducing spirits, and doctrines of devils.

Is this departure from the faith the departure that Paul is talking about in 2 Thessalonians 2:3? The word itself is neutral. It derives meaning only from the context. Whenever the Bible *means* departure from the faith, it says so by adding a qualifying phrase like "from the faith." First Timothy 4:1 says "from the faith," but 2 Thessalonians 2:3 does not. Paul included the phrase when writing to Timothy and he could have included it in writing to the Thessalonians if that is what he meant, but he didn't. If Paul omitted "from the faith," I hesitate to insert it myself.

Furthermore, apostasy in general is too vague. Apostasy in some degree has existed ever since Paul wrote to Timothy. How would this serve as a clear-cut sign to the Thessalonians? It's too hazy.

Rather than being vague, Paul is very specific. He says "the" falling away. (We do not see the definite article in the

THE PRE-TRIBULATION RAPTURE

English, but it is in the Greek.) The article "the" in this context tells me that it is clearly identifiable in a point of time, not some nebulous thing that people would disagree about identifying. "The" refers back to that departure taught previously by Paul while he was with them, the one that they already knew about. "Remember ye not, that, when I was yet with you, I told you these things? And now ye know what withholdeth" (verses 5-6a).

Simpler Is Better. As a general rule the simpler interpretation is to be preferred over the more complicated. To take "the falling away" as the departure of the Holy Spirit who restrains antichrist is as simple as cutting cake. When you cut cake you try to cut equal pieces; you cut it symmetrically. You normally do not chop off a bite-sized sliver for one guest and large pieces for the rest.

How natural it is to take "the falling away" as introducing one piece of cake and to take "revealed" as introducing another piece of cake, and then to find the symmetrical pieces of cake explained in the verses following. If I were preaching these would be the two points of my outline, except I would alliterate them as follows: removal and revealing. Why didn't Paul alliterate them? Well, he did, as we shall see in a minute.

In contrast to the symmetrical cake, both commonly-held views of "the falling away" cut off that term as a bite-sized sliver. It stands alone with little or no explanation. If you cut off "the falling away" and say it refers to the rapture, then you are left with a passing reference, very obscure, and it is left unexplained. Nowhere else in the Bible does this word mean "rapture"; so if it is unexplained here, how does Paul expect us to get "rapture" out of it?

If you would seek its explanation back in 1 Thessalonians 4:13-18 and its description of the rapture, that too is obscure. How could the Thessalonians be sure that Paul intended a reference to something he wrote months ago, especially when he did not even use the same word? If you would seek its ex-

Second Thessalonians: Glory

planation in 2 Thessalonians 2:1 which mentions "our gathering together unto him," that too is only mentioned in passing. If we are to depend on this passing mention, this brief mention, then we are expected to understand the obscure term "the falling away" without a full explanation. It is a bite-sized sliver. (All this is not to mention that Paul is referring to something he taught *in person,* not by letter. These explanations become impossible if we accept the evidence that Paul did *not* teach the rapture while he was with them.)

Also, if you cut off "the falling away" and say it means apostasy from the faith, it still stands alone as a bite-sized sliver with no support from the context. We have no apostasy from the *true* faith mentioned or hinted in the context. If it means apostasy from the faith, then it is a bite-sized sliver.

If Paul did explain "the falling away," he would explain it according to his normal pattern, wouldn't he? Paul's normal pattern is to introduce a topic first and then explain it. He does this *consistently* in 2 Thessalonians. Why forsake his usual pattern of explanation to seek an explanation elsewhere? When Mother usually serves your cake on a dish, why look under the table for it?

When both commonly-held views cut off "the falling away" as a bite-sized sliver, what is the result? An unsymmetrical cake. Verses 6-7 which speak of the Restrainer is a lopsided piece because it carries no introduction with it. The description of the man of sin (verses 3b-4) enjoys an introductory word: "revealed." But the restraining of the Holy Spirit has to do without an introductory word.

THE PRE-TRIBULATION RAPTURE

THE UNSYMMETRICAL VIEW

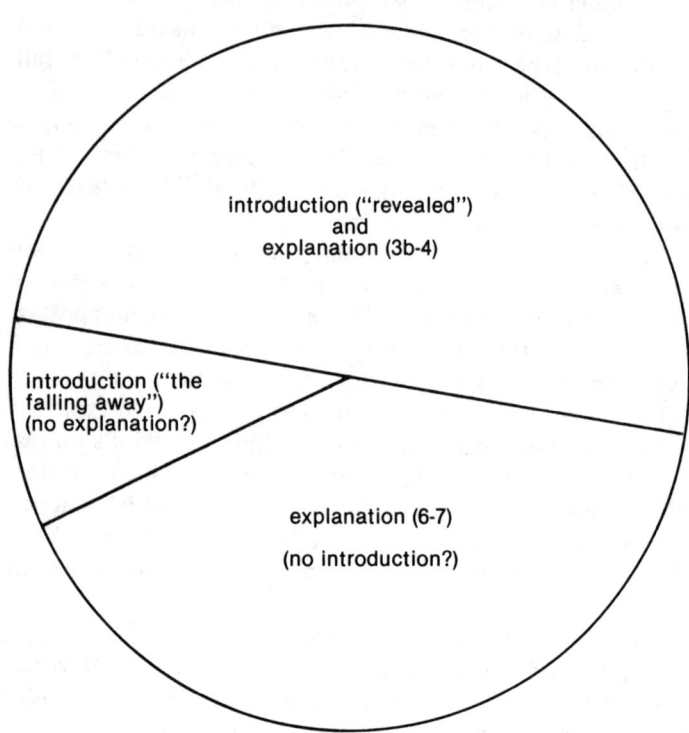

What happens if we join the misfit pieces of the cake? Beautiful symmetry. We have two introductory words, "the falling away" and "revealed" (verse 3), and then we have two explanations (verses 3b-4 and verses 6-7). It all falls into place *according to Paul's common style.* It is as simple as cutting cake.

A Double Play on Words. One question remains. Why did Paul choose this word "falling away"? If "rapture" were intended he could have chosen better, because nowhere else

Second Thessalonians: Glory

does this word mean "rapture." If falling away "from the faith" were intended, he could easily have chosen to add the words "from the faith," because this word always carries a similar qualifying phrase when that meaning is intended. But why did he choose this word as it is?

Paul makes a play on words which you can see in the Greek. In Greek this is a compound word, literally translated "standing away." Now if you look back one verse, to verse 2, you read "as that the day of the Lord is at hand." The word "is at hand" is also a compound word, literally translated "stand in." As we put the two together, we see that Paul makes this catchy statement: "That day will not 'stand in' until the Holy Spirit 'stands away.' " The Greek Thessalonians would spot this play on words and get the message at once.

There is more. The next key word after "falling away" is "revealed." These are the two key words of the entire section as we have seen, and herein lies a second play on words. When a preacher wants you to remember the key words of his outline, what does he do? He alliterates! Paul makes a nice alliteration here in the Greek. Not only do both words start with the same letter, but the first three letters in each word are identical (*a-p-o* in Greek). These words form Paul's two-fold outline on which he elaborates in the following verses.

There is more. Not only is "falling away" choice because it makes a double play on words, but it also conforms nicely in meaning to what Paul intends to say. "The falling away" matches the parallel phrase in verse 7, "taken out of the way." As we saw above, this is better translated actively instead of passively. In other words, the Holy Spirit "gets out." To "get out" and to "stand away" are very similar in meaning, and in this context they explain each other. Paul could not have chosen a better word. Of course, he couldn't miss with the Holy Spirit guiding him.

WHEN IS THE DAY OF THE LORD?

In the last chapter we learned that the day of the Lord begins *after* the tribulation. Now let's look at further evidence of this from 2 Thessalonians.

Paul mentions the "day of the Lord" in 2 Thessalonians 2:2. (The King James Version has "day of Christ," but it is generally agreed that "day of the Lord" is the correct reading. I believe the two terms are interchangeable anyway.) He mentions it but he does not define it. He acts as though he has already been talking about it in chapter one. He assumes the Thessalonians *already know* what it is from what he has been talking about. Like a good detective, then, we ask the question: What was on the minds of the Thessalonians? And: What was on the mind of Paul?

From the very first we see that *persecution* was uppermost on the minds of the Thessalonians (see 1:4 and following). If you were in their shoes you would hope for the day when the persecution would *stop*. That is exactly what the Thessalonians hoped for and that is why Paul told them about the "righteous judgment of God" (1:6). This righteous judgment comes *after* the tribulation (1:7-8). It is true that some will have "relief" from persecution by the time the tribulation *begins,* the first generation Thessalonians by death and the last generation of the church by rapture. But God does not actually *stop* persecution during the tribulation; final judgment occurs *only after the tribulation.* This is the day of the Lord.

If you were in the shoes of the Thessalonians, you not only would want persecution to stop, but you would want it to stop *soon.* If you received a supposed "letter from Paul" saying that the day of vengeance was immediately upon us, you would get all excited, and you might even quit your job as some of the Thessalonians did.

To correct this notion Paul wrote that the day is *not* yet upon us but it is *delayed* (2:2-3), and to prove the delay he reminds them of the events which lead up to the day of the Lord. These events lead up to the *final destruction* (2:8). *This* is the day of the Lord.

Therefore, permeating both chapters one and two is the em-

Second Thessalonians: Glory

phasis on the *final vengeance,* not the intervening tribulation events. Chapters one and two go together like hand in glove. One introduces the other. Chapter one explains the *fairness* of vengeance, while chapter two explains the *delay* of vengeance. Through it all, the time is *after* the tribulation.

So when Paul mentioned "the day of the Lord" without definition, assuming that the Thessalonians knew what he was talking about, we too can know what he is talking about if we keep in mind the context.

Did They Think They Missed the Rapture? Did the Thessalonians mistakenly believe that they missed the rapture? Were they afraid that this landed them right in the middle of the day of the Lord, a period of unchecked persecution?

According to 1 Thessalonians 5, they *knew perfectly* that the day of the Lord brought *sudden destruction* (not unchecked persecution). This sudden destruction had not yet hit their persecutors; so they could hardly be mistaken about it. Unless they forgot completely what they knew perfectly a few months earlier.

Did They Think They Were in the Tribulation? Suppose for a minute that the day of the Lord were the entire tribulation period. Suppose that the Thessalonians mistakenly thought they were in the tribulation because of the great persecution they were suffering. If this were the case, then how would Paul's answer in chapter one *introduce* the topic of the tribulation if he talked about vengeance only *after* the tribulation? You had better change your introduction, Paul. And if chapter two gives antichrist as a sign in the *middle* of the tribulation, then what evidence does that give that the Thessalonians were not in the *beginning* of the tribulation? You had better give a better sign, Paul.

If presence in the tribulation were the concern, then why did not Paul clearly tell the Thessalonians the rapture comes first? If the tribulation were the day of the Lord, then why does Paul, in chapter two, quickly jump to the *end* of antichrist's career and take so much time to describe his destruction and the destruction of his followers? I think you ought to rewrite chapter two, Paul, in order to fit the concept that the tribulation is the day of the Lord. You ought to write it this way: "You are mistaken that your present persecution is the tribulation. The real day of the Lord comes when antichrist initiates an unprecedented wave of persecution upon believers whom he will destroy with the blasphemy of his mouth and consume by the deceitfulness of his coming."

Did They Think They Would Yet Experience the Tribulation? Take another supposition. Suppose that Paul were trying to prove that they were not yet in the tribulation, that the real tribulation was yet future. If this were the case, how would this be of any *comfort* to the Thessalonians? This would not remedy their present persecution any, it would aggravate it. What if you were undergoing deep trouble and I said to you, "Cheer up, you ain't seen nothin' yet. Just wait until the *real* tribulation comes!" You would probably say, "What kind of a friend are you? I don't need that kind of comfort. I need some *solution* to my problems."

God, through Paul, gave exactly that. The solution to all our problems is the great day of the Lord when every wrong shall be righted, when God's enemies receive vengeance, when God's children receive glory. This is true comfort to sustain us in present trouble. This is the day of the Lord.

WHY THE TRIBULATION SIGNS?

Have I backed myself into a corner again? If the day of the Lord is *after* the tribulation, does this not imply that the church will be on earth to watch the events leading up to that day?

It is true that Paul highlights tribulation events in chapter two. Post-tribulationists suppose that the church is to watch for the day of the Lord through these signs. They ask, "Why does Paul give us tribulation signs if we will not go through the tribulation? The signs are irrelevant if we are not going to be around to see them."

This reasoning misses Paul's intent. Paul never gives these signs for us to watch. He never says that we are to watch for the approaching day of the Lord through these signs. His purpose is almost *opposite*. He gives these signs to prove that the day is *not* at hand. Paul makes his point from the *absence* of the signs, not the *presence* of the signs.

By secondary application, *tribulation saints* can look for the end of the tribulation through these signs, but for the church whom Paul is writing to, his primary purpose is entirely different. For tribulation saints the presence of the signs show the day is near, but for the church the absence of the signs show the day is far off.

To Prove the Certainty of Destruction. Let me elaborate on Paul's purpose by explaining two reasons for his outlining tribulation events in chapter two. Here are his two reasons: Paul wants to prove the *delay* of the day of the Lord and the *certainty* of it. First, verses 3-7 prove the *delay,* and Paul's purpose here is to give correction regarding the time. He says, "Do not get so excited yet hoping for vengeance on your persecutors. Let me remind you that God is waiting for the proper time to let wickedness come to a head in the man of sin first. This is why it must be delayed."

Secondly, verses 8-12 prove the *certainty* of vengeance, and his purpose here is to comfort the Thessalonians, not to give signs to watch for. Question: If these are signs to indicate the approaching day of the Lord, then wouldn't the mention of specific and telltale events be sufficient? Why does Paul take extra time to vividly describe the deceptive power of antichrist? And why does he take more time to explain the reasons for the destruction of antichrist's followers? If you insist that the "signs" have a purpose, then please tell me the purpose of Paul's getting carried away on a tangent like a preacher who forgot his main point. In verses 8-12 Paul goes *far beyond what is needed for signs.* Why?

Matthew 24 contains *genuine signs.* That is what the disciples asked for and that is what they got. Jesus lists the signposts without unnecessary explanation. Why didn't Paul do that? Why does Paul go far beyond mere signs?

Obviously Paul has more in mind than mere "signs." He wants to prove the certainty of vengeance in order to reassure the hearts of the Thessalonians. "Punishment may be delayed, but on the other hand it is still sure to happen. You may have to wait awhile, but do not give up hope completely."

To Give the Destiny of the Persecutors. In order to prove the certainty Paul lists, not mere signs, but *the events and causes leading up to* that day. He is reassuring the Thessalonians who are wondering, "How will persecutors be destroyed?" He lists the *chain of events.* First the man of sin will arise. Then God will allow him to deceive and lead astray those who are against the truth. Then when they are all fully deluded God will with full justice apparent to all give them the punishment they deserved in the first place. Verse 12 is the key: God sends antichrist to deceive in order "that they all might be damned." This purpose of God to damn the persecutors is the culmination of all that Paul has been saying, and it is the key which unlocks every "sign" in chapter two.

You see, it was not mere "signs" concerning antichrist the Thessalonians were concerned about. It's deeper. They needed to know, "What are the chain of events leading up to the damnation of our persecutors?" This is the only way to account for every word and "sign" in chapter two. It also explains why Paul begins with the persecutors in chapter one and ends with the persecutors in chapter two, because the destiny of the persecutors is what the events of chapter two are all about.

When you read through the epistle, if you will keep persecution uppermost on your mind, just as the Thessalonians did when they read the epistle, then it will all become as clear and understandable to you as it was to the Thessalonians. If it looks fuzzy to you, try their glasses.

For Correction and Comfort. As in chapter two Paul proves the delay and the certainty, more than "signs," he lists the delayed but certain *chain of events* which lead to vengeance upon unbelievers. These events are not for the purpose of watching, but for the purpose of *correction* and *comfort*. It is correction regarding the time ("it is delayed") and it is comfort regarding the certainty ("it is sure to happen"). This has nothing to do whatsoever with the church being on earth during the tribulation. The church needs only to *know* about these events in order to receive correction and comfort. Paul does not require the church to be present to *watch* these events transpire.

These signs Paul talks about have not yet occurred. Paul taught the Thessalonians to watch in the *absence* of signs. Likewise, Jesus taught the disciples to watch in the *absence* of signs. So watching is something else besides sign-gazing.

Consider this. If "signs" were the primary impact of this epistle, it would lose its relevance to most generations, including the first generation Thessalonians who were supposed to be edified by this epistle. Christians through the ages would be looking for signs they never saw. By our interpretation, this epistle is very relevant to *every generation* of believers, not just the last. The final recompense is a motive for patient living no matter how far away it is in time. If signs are required in order to watch, then all earlier generations without signs would have excuse not to watch.

How ironic it is that post-tribs, who desired to maintain the "relevance" of the signs for the church, lose their relevance to most generations of the church, while the interpretation presented maintains the relevance of these events for every Christian of every age.

This epistle is tailor-made for believers behind the Iron Curtain today. Some have been disillusioned because they have been falsely taught that the rapture would rescue them from

WHY NO MENTION OF "RAPTURE"?

In the past, the non-mention of the rapture before the tribulation in 2 Thessalonians 2 has been embarrassing for pre-tribulationists. (This has caused them to seek a questionable reference to the rapture in "the falling away" as seen above.) However, according to our interpretation, it is irrelevant for Paul to mention rapture because it does not form a direct causal link leading to the destruction of the persecutors. This chain of events is not set in motion until three and one-half years later when the man of sin comes onto the scene and draws a following after him. Since the rapture occurs a full three and one-half years before the beginning point of Paul's narration, we cannot accuse him of skipping over it, and so it forms no embarrassment to us at all.

Besides, if the question is turned around, it becomes more embarrassing for post-tribulationists. Why does Paul not mention a rapture just before the destruction of antichrist? If there is a rapture then, and if he supposedly is writing "concerning" the rapture, why does he skip right over it?

Post-tribs should expect to see the rapture mentioned in verse 8, mid-tribs should expect to see the rapture mentioned in verse 3 or 4, while pre-tribs expect it in neither place.

A Pre-Trib Clue? Second Thessalonians is full of solid teaching and comfort. Very practical. Its teaching concerning the future gives us much strength for our day-to-day problems. However, 2 Thessalonians does not prove the time of the rapture one way or another. This being the case, do we not have at least a clue?

Some might see a clue in "comfort" (2:17) just as in 1 Thessalonians. It is a comforting thought that we will not go through the tribulation, and so the word "comfort" implies a pre-tribulation rapture, according to this argument.

If you think that, do not feel badly. I used to think that way too, even well after starting to write this book. Then I discovered the true significance of this "comfort." This comfort is for *continued tribulation*! Paul is saying, "Be patient because the day of the Lord is delayed and your persecution will continue awhile longer. In the meantime, may God give you supernatural comfort to sustain you during your tribulation."

It is those in tribulation who need comfort the most, and that is why Paul offers comfort here. Of course, present tribulation does not prove that we will go through the future "great tribulation," and so this "comfort" gives us no clue one way or the other.

Why Is Work Commanded? A better clue is the command to work (2:15; 3:6-12). Have you ever thought through the *reason* for Paul's command to work? Have you ever thought about the *reason* some Thessalonians were leaving their jobs? The Thessalonians reasoned that the day of the Lord was at hand. If you knew the Lord was coming next week you probably would not go to work either. There would be no reason to, because you wouldn't get your paycheck until the week after and you would be in heaven by then. Besides, it would make better sense to use that last week to warn people to become saved and get ready.

Paul's reason for telling them to get back to work was that the day of the Lord was *not* at hand. Second Thessalonians 2:15 is the key verse: "Therefore, brethren, stand fast, and hold the traditions which ye have been taught, whether by word, or our epistle." "Traditions" in this context refers to working (see 3:6-12). The word "therefore"—this is a key word—tells me his instruction to work is *based on* what he has just said in chapter two beginning from verse one. Paul has said, "Antichrist has not appeared yet, and so the day of the Lord is still some time away. *That is why* you had better continue working." Have you considered this *reason* for working?

Now just suppose that antichrist *does* come, *then* what reason remains for working? The whole basis for Paul's command to work in this epistle disappears! He gives *no instruction regarding work in the great tribulation.* To me this is a clue. There is no need for such instruction if the church will not be in the great tribulation.

In Matthew 24 Jesus gave definite instructions to the Judeans who will be on the earth to see antichrist revealed at the abomination of desolation. He told them to flee immediately into the mountains. If the Judeans have instructions, why do the Thessalonians have none?

If I were going through the tribulation and antichrist appeared, I would want to know, "Should I continue working or should I flee into the mountains somewhere like the Judeans?" That is important to know. If the church is going through the tribulation, Paul should have said, "Continue working now because antichrist has not appeared, but *when* he comes to power *here is what to do* . . ." Paul never says, "Here is what to do."

I believe that God will in some manner make known to tribulation saints what they should do when the occasion arises. But here Paul had the occasion because he was already talking about work and he missed his golden opportunity to give tribulation instructions.

It might be objected that God knew the Thessalonians would not live until the tribulation anyway and that is why He did not give instruction regarding work in the tribulation. To be consistent, however, remember that the Thessalonians' persecutors did not live until the tribulation either. But God told what would happen to their persecutors as if they would live through the tribulation and meet the Lord when He comes to take fiery vengeance upon them. You see, the epistle is written so that it could apply to the last generation. This inspired epistle is profitable for doctrine, not only for that first generation, but also for every succeeding generation. So the question remains:

Second Thessalonians: Glory

If he explained the final outcome of the persecutors, why did he not explain the final outcome regarding work? Could it be that, whichever generation you're in, the one is profitable to know about and the other is not?

Why does Paul only give instructions regarding work based on the absence of antichrist and not his presence? Just as 1 Thessalonians is missing exhortation to patience in the tribulation, so 2 Thessalonians is missing instruction regarding work in the tribulation. These are clues, but no more.

AN ISLAND IN THE FOG

We have very meticulously gone through First and Second Thessalonians and demonstrated that the time of the rapture cannot be proved one way or the other from these epistles. This accords with God's normal pattern of revealing truths one step at a time.

Even after seeing all the evidence for a safe and sane interpretation of the Thessalonian epistles it may bother some that the two aspects of the second coming of Christ are mingled together. Both aspects are mentioned in one breath in 2 Thessalonians 2:1. Some may say, "The 'coming' and 'gathering' in 2 Thessalonians 2:1 are obviously the same. They can't be seven years apart because only an 'and' separates the two." Mingling both aspects in one verse might appear a little foggy for some, even though Peter himself admitted that some things were hard to understand (2 Peter 3:16).

Let me reassure you. We have an island in the fog, solid ground to stand upon. For Paul to mingle the two aspects is the most natural thing he could do as a writer of Scripture. Sure, it seems strange if you don't know the Old Testament. But if you know the Old Testament . . . .

The Old Testament and Christ's Coming. The following Old Testament passages unmistakably view two aspects of Christ's coming as one, just as two mountain peaks appear as one from a distance.

THE PRE-TRIBULATION RAPTURE

Consider this prophecy about Christ's forerunner in Isaiah 40:3-5:

verse 3	The voice of him that crieth in the wilderness, Prepare ye the way of the Lord, make straight in the desert a highway for our God.
verse 4	Every valley shall be exalted, and every mountain and hill shall be made low: and the crooked shall be made straight, and the rough places plain:
verse 5	And the glory of the Lord shall be revealed, and all flesh shall see it together: for the mouth of the Lord hath spoken it.

Verse 3 was fulfilled by John the Baptist. Verses 4-5, though, will not be fulfilled until Jesus comes again. This is a 2000-year span! Not only does the text contain no hint of a gap, but it reads as if everything is joined together in *one event.*

Another amazing prophecy is Zechariah 9:9-10:

verse 9	Rejoice greatly, O daughter of Zion; shout, O daughter of Jerusalem: behold, thy King cometh unto thee: he is just, and having salvation; lowly, and riding upon an ass, and upon a colt the foal of an ass.
verse 10	And I will cut off the chariot from Ephraim, and the horse from Jerusalem, and the battle bow shall be cut off; and he shall speak peace unto the heathen: and his dominion shall be from sea even to sea, and from the river even to the ends of the earth.

Only verse 9 was fulfilled at Jesus' first coming. If you tried to tell an Old Testament believer that the King will not have "dominion from sea even to sea" until His second coming, he would accuse you of chopping up the text and inventing two comings when there is only one. I can hear him now: "If there were *two* comings 2000 years apart, the Bible would say *two* comings instead of one!"

Second Thessalonians: Glory

Isaiah 9:2-7 goes back and forth between the first and second comings. I can imagine a staunch theologian in those days using this passage as proof conclusive that there is only one coming because of the way the two aspects are mingled together.

first coming	The people that walked in darkness have seen a great light: they that dwell in the land of the shadow of death, upon them hath the light shined (compare Matthew 4:14-16).
second coming	Thou hast multiplied the nation, and not increased the joy: they joy before thee according to the joy in harvest, and as men rejoice when they divide the spoil. For thou hast broken the yoke of his burden, and the staff of his shoulder, the rod of his oppressor, as in the day of Midian. For every battle of the warrior is with confused noise, and garments rolled in blood; but this shall be with burning and fuel of fire.
first coming	For unto us a child is born, unto us a son is given:
second coming	and the government shall be upon his shoulder: and his name shall be called Wonderful, Counsellor, The mighty God, The everlasting Father, The Prince of Peace. Of the increase of his government and peace there shall be no end, upon the throne of David, and upon his kingdom, to order it, and to establish it with judgment and with justice from henceforth even for ever.

Another passage that reverses the order is Isaiah 65:17 and 20. Mere order of mention, therefore, proves nothing about the order of occurrence or the time of occurrence.

Isaiah 61:1-3 gives no indication whatsoever that Christ's coming would be in two stages:

The Spirit of the Lord God is upon me; because the Lord hath anointed me to preach good tidings unto the meek; he hath sent me to bind up the brokenhearted, to proclaim liberty to the captives, and the opening of the prison to them that are bound; to proclaim the acceptable year of the Lord

THE PRE-TRIBULATION RAPTURE

> and the day of vengeance of our God; to comfort all that mourn; to appoint unto them that mourn in Zion, to give unto them beauty for ashes, the oil of joy for mourning, the garment of praise for the spirit of heaviness; that they might be called trees of righteousness, the planting of the Lord, that he might be glorified.

I can hear the theologians now: "This has to be one coming because only an 'and' connects the two." Jesus knew better, though, and when He was reading the text He knew where the break was. He broke off in the middle of a verse and made a separation where there was a conjunction (see Luke 4:16-21).

Malachi 3:1-5 begins with a prophecy of John the Baptist and continues with the Lord coming "suddenly" in judgment. Surely, if the other passages don't, this passage "proves" only one coming.

John the Baptist	Behold, I will send my messenger, and he shall prepare the way before me:
second coming	and the Lord, whom ye seek, shall suddenly come to his temple, even the messenger of the covenant, whom ye delight in: behold, he shall come, saith the Lord of hosts. But who may abide the day of his coming? and who shall stand when he appeareth? for he is like a refiner's fire, and like fullers' soap: and he shall sit as a refiner and purifier of silver: and he shall purify the sons of Levi, and purge them as gold and silver, that they may offer unto the Lord an offering in righteousness. Then shall the offering of Judah and Jerusalem be pleasant unto the Lord, as in the days of old, and as in former years. And I will come near to you to judgment; and I will be a swift witness against the sorcerers, and against the adulterers, and against false swearers, and against those that oppress the hireling in his wages, the widow, and the fatherless, and that turn aside the stranger from his right, and fear not me, saith the Lord of hosts.

As it turned out, it was not "suddenly" then, but 2000 years later He will come "suddenly" in judgment. No hint whatso-

Second Thessalonians: Glory

ever of a gap before His sudden coming.

Now for the grand finale:

> Now we beseech you, brethren, by the coming of Our Lord Jesus Christ [after the tribulation], and by our gathering together unto him [rapture] (2 Thessalonians 2:1).

"Surely this proves that Christ's coming after the tribulation brings the rapture because they are mentioned together." If this is supposed to be post-trib "proof" then this is mighty shaky proof indeed.

Why Are They Mingled? When God mingles two comings in one passage is He playing word games with us? No, I believe in God's mind this *really is* all one event. That is why it is written this way. Important are the events in God's program; less important is the number of years in between. Like mountain peaks separated by valleys, God steps from mountain to mountain while we have to tread through the valleys in order to get to the next mountain. We know that we must tread the valleys of time, but sometimes God takes us under His wing and lets us see things from His vantage point.

That is one reason, but there is another reason that both aspects of Christ's coming blend into one in the Old Testament. If the nation of Israel had believed the first time, *there really would have been only one coming:* "And if ye will receive it, this is Elias, which was for to come" (Matthew 11:14). The glory of Christ would have followed immediately upon His suffering. The kingdom would have been set up right then: "From that time Jesus began to preach, and to say, Repent: for the kingdom of heaven is at hand" (Matthew 4:17). That is why the *time interval* is not revealed in the Old Testament.

In the New Testament it is the opposite. For those who do *not* believe there will only be one coming. They will *miss* the rapture and meet only the coming in judgment. And contrary to Old Testament saints New Testament believers can clearly distinguish a time interval because we will participate in *both* comings.

	Condition	Result
Old Testament	if believe	one coming
	if disbelieve	two comings
New Testament	if believe	two comings
	if disbelieve	one coming

Why can *we* clearly distinguish two future comings when the Old Testament believers could not? This question used to puzzle me until I discovered Matthew 11:14 and the above chart.

This did not excuse Old Testament believers from distinguishing the two aspects of Christ's coming (Luke 24:25-27). *Suffering* and *glory* were clearly predicted (1 Peter 1:11). But it was not clear that there would be a *time interval* between the two aspects. New Testament believers likewise should recognize two aspects to Christ's future coming, *salvation* and *glory* (2 Thessalonians 2:13-14). Even post-tribulationists can see these two aspects without seeing a time interval in between.

Those who are well grounded in God's normal pattern of revelation find this double-reference a pleasure instead of a problem. Does it still bother anyone that both aspects of Christ's coming are run together as one event in the Thessalonian epistles? Is it disturbing that Paul's picture of two distant mountain peaks appear as one? If so, they will have to request God to rewrite the Old Testament. To hide a 2000-year gap like that is inexcusable. Yet for some reason we gladly accept the 2000-year interval but reject a 7-year interval. We have swal-

Second Thessalonians: Glory

lowed the camel and are straining at a gnat.

What About the New Testament? It is fine for the Old Testament to be written so loosely, some may say, but isn't the New Testament more rigid and precise? Well, Gundry finds a gap of 1000 years right in the middle of Matthew 25:31.[2] All premillennialists agree on a similar gap in John 5:28-29 where two resurrections are lumped into one hour.

But what about the second coming terminology? Some claim that certain New Testament words are technical terms and are rigid in meaning. The words, "coming," "appearing," "revealing," and "end," are said to uniformly refer to the end of the tribulation. Let us examine these terms and see if these words are actually so rigid that they do not allow for flexible usage.

The word "coming" is used not only of the second coming of Christ, but also of the *first* coming of Christ in 2 Peter 1:16. If the word can be used for *both* of those comings, it is not a rigid term, and there is nothing in the word itself to prevent it from being used for both aspects of the second coming.

Likewise the word "appearing" is used of Christ's *first* coming in 2 Timothy 1:10. The mere use of the word "appearing," then, does not prove an after-the-tribulation event.

The word "revealing" is made specific only by each context as it mentions a certain thing which is revealed. The preciseness rests in the context, not in the word itself. The revealing of His glory necessarily occurs after the tribulation (1 Peter 4:13). On the other hand, His revelation through the person of Paul occurred during that period of time (Galatians 1:16). He reveals himself in one sense to believers at the rapture, and He reveals himself in another sense to the whole world when He returns to earth. To convince me of the meaning of "revealing," you would have to argue from the *context* in *each occurrence*. The word itself in an ambiguous context carries no weight.

The word "end" in some places obviously means the end of the tribulation. But must it *always* mean that? Hebrews 9:26

uses the word "end" for the *first* coming of Christ. Therefore, it is not a rigid technical term. Generations of Christians now dead have kept Christ's works unto the "end" without being *on earth* until the "end."

I cannot be boxed in by mere terminology, because these terms are not technical and rigid as some suppose. As in the Old Testament, there is nothing in the New Testament to eliminate a double coming. Some passages clearly refer to either the pre-trib coming or the post-trib coming. Other passages are not so clear, and these may possibly be double-reference. We will know for sure when we get to heaven whether these ambiguous passages are double reference or not. In a later chapter we will demonstrate a clear and unmistakable double-reference.

WHERE DO WE BEGIN?

Now we see the folly of those who depend on the Thessalonian epistles for their doctrine of the post-trib rapture. If the most that God allowed Paul to see was the two aspects of the second coming, without letting him know if they were identical in time or not, then we cannot make the epistles teach more than they were intended to teach. Before we jump to any conclusions, let's wait until all the evidence is in.

"But the Thessalonian epistles make such a nice starting place, a logical beginning point, because they talk about the second coming." Well, other passages talk about the second coming too. They also are inspired and of equal value for doctrine. Let's wait until all the evidence is in, shall we?

Our Hope Is Not Nearsighted. In light of what we have been talking about, another class of problem passages in the New Testament now becomes understandable. Some passages exhort or encourage us in view of the *post-tribulational* coming (such as 1 Corinthians 1:7-8; Philippians 1:6; 1 Peter 4:13). These passages are not a problem if we recognize that the Bible *normally* looks at the far event as closely linked with the near event. This dual vision is perfectly consistent with pre-tribulationism. I will let you be the judge of this if you will let me be the lawyer and appeal to the precedent of the Old Testament which mixes the near and far views.

My Big Moment. We must remember too, even apart from dual vision, the church does have a real hope anchored in the post-tribulational coming. We discussed this previously under 2 Thessalonians 1:6-7. Certain things happen at that "big moment" that do not happen at the rapture. At that moment comes glory and vindication. Our rejoicing is enhanced. God confirms us unto the ultimate day because our hope is ultimate. Even though I happen to believe the rapture comes before the tribulation, in a real sense I do look for the blessed hope after the tribulation. My big moment is not just going up in the air, but my big moment will be when I come riding down from the sky on my white horse. And I don't have to be on earth for those last seven years in order to look forward to it.

The church will not go through the tribulation, but we are interested in tribulation events. It is not a shallow interest in mere "signs" to satisfy our curiosity. It goes deeper than that. It goes beyond the mind to the heart. God wants us to become involved in the battle of the ages between good and evil, whether we are on earth or whether we are in heaven, and so He causes us to be concerned about tribulation events because they lead to final vengeance on the wicked and the revealing of God's glory.

I hope this explanation will broaden the view and help post-tribulationists to better understand our position. Our interest in Christ's return after the tribulation is in no way lessened by intervening events. If post-tribulationists can look forward to His coming even though tribulation events intervene, then surely pre-tribulationists can look forward to His post-tribulational coming even though the rapture intervenes. They look for intervening signs while we look for an intervening rapture. But neither obscures our main hope, the coming of Christ

THE PRE-TRIBULATION RAPTURE

in glory.

I hope this will also broaden the vision of pre-tribulationists who have narrowed their focus to the rapture. God's plan is wider than that. Only one chapter in the Bible describes the rapture. But two entire books, namely 2 Thessalonians and Revelation, are devoted to God's vindication as the wicked march into destruction. We have looked at one of these books, and now in the next chapter let's look at the second book.

1. Gundry, *The Church and the Tribulation,* p. 127.
2. Ibid, p. 168.

"And they had on their heads crowns of gold" (Revelation 4:4).

7
Revelation

Revelation, the last book of the Bible, is exactly what its name implies, a revelation. It is not a dark mystery book sealed to our understanding. It is open. "Seal not the sayings of the prophecy of this book: for the time is at hand" (Revelation 22:10). As the time becomes more and more at hand, people are understanding the book more and more. Some of the symbols, of course, await the events to occur to clear them up. But most of the symbols we understand already, and the main message of the book is open. (The book of Daniel also is becoming more and more unsealed as the time of the end approaches in fulfillment of Daniel 12:9.)

This book climaxes the entire Bible in many ways. In the progress of revelation this forms the capstone. This being so, we would expect the time of the rapture to be more clear in Revelation than it was in Thessalonians. And so it is. First Thessalonians reveals a description of the rapture, but not the time. Now Revelation reveals the time. This is all according to God's pattern of revealing truths one step at a time.

THE DUAL PURPOSE OF REVELATION
God gave this book "to show unto his servants things which

must shortly come to pass" (1:1). This raises the question: What does the church care about tribulation events if we will not even be around then?

The answer is the same here as it was in 2 Thessalonians because Revelation is a companion volume to 2 Thessalonians. Both books were occasioned by persecution (2 Thessalonians 1:4; Revelation 1:9), and both show the recompense for persecution by dealing with events during the great tribulation climaxing with the return of Christ in glory.

The church has a live interest in these events even though we will not be on the earth. As we discussed in our chapter on 2 Thessalonians, we desire God to reveal His glory to the world and take vengeance on the wicked. The first generation Thessalonian believers are in heaven now and so are the church members to whom John wrote Revelation. Were these books irrelevant to them? Of course not! They met a real need in their lives. They offered hope and encouragement when they needed it most. And now that they are in heaven I'm sure their prayer still is, "Thy kingdom come. Thy will be done, as in heaven, so in earth" (Luke 11:2). My point is this: our desire for God's judgment is not diminished just because we are in heaven—it is enhanced.

In fact, Revelation is written from the heavenly point of view. Ask an alumnus in the grandstands if he cares who wins the homecoming game. Sure, he is no longer a student. Sure, he is not playing in the game. Does this mean he doesn't care? More than spectators from the grandstands, those in heaven actively participate in the battle between good and evil. Some join the fight (angels) and others are cheerleaders (men). We care who wins.

Ask the souls under the altar if they care. Just because they are in heaven does not prevent them from crying with a loud voice, "How long, O Lord, holy and true, dost thou not judge and avenge our blood on them that dwell on the earth?" I'm sure they would never say that presence in heaven diminishes interest in tribulation events.

Revelation

Revelation has a purpose not only for the church, but also for tribulation saints. For some of the symbols in the book the meaning will unfold only as the events transpire. I am sure tribulation saints will keep one eye on Revelation and one eye on the world. Just as a baseball fan follows a program to tell the players, so tribulation saints will use Revelation to give them understanding of surrounding events.

If Revelation is written for tribulation saints also, does that not prove that tribulation saints and church saints are one and the same? Not necessarily, because it is perfectly legitimate for a later group to read Scripture originally written for an earlier group. We profit from reading the Old Testament even though it was originally written for Israel. "All Scripture is given by inspiration of God, and is profitable" (2 Timothy 3:16). I am not the type of dispensationalist who chops off portions of God's Word saying that it does not apply to us. (For example, the "Feast of Trumpets" has application to the church as well as to Israel as we saw in chapter five.) Both church saints and tribulation saints, two distinct groups, profit from Revelation.

Have you ever noticed the *double introduction* to Revelation? Verses 1-3 are addressed to the "servants" of God. This term is broad enough to apply to tribulation saints and for them these events will "shortly come to pass." Tribulation saints will be able to "keep those things which are written therein" because they will be alive to refuse the mark of the beast.

Then verse 4 starts all over again with another introduction just as though the previous introduction didn't exist. The second introduction is addressed specifically to the "churches" (verses 4-6).

The Revelation of Jesus Christ, which God gave unto him, to show *unto his servants* things which must shortly come to pass; and he sent and signified it by his angel unto his servant John: who bare record of the word of God, and of the testimony of Jesus Christ, and of all things that he saw. Blessed	INTRODUCTION TO TRIBULATION SAINTS

THE PRE-TRIBULATION RAPTURE

> is he that readeth, and they that hear the words of this prophecy, and keep those things which are written therein: for the time is at hand.
>
> John *to the seven churches* which are in Asia: Grace be unto you, and peace, from him which is, and which was, and which is to come; and from the seven Spirits which are before his throne; and from Jesus Christ, who is the faithful witness, and the first begotten of the dead, and the prince of the kings of the earth. Unto him that loved us, and washed us from our sins in his own blood, and hath made us kings and priests unto God and his Father; to him be glory and dominion for ever and ever. Amen.

— INTRODUCTION TO THE CHURCH

THE CHURCH AND THE TRIBULATION

Revelation 3:10 gives a wonderful promise to the church that she will not go through the tribulation: "Because thou hast kept the word of my patience, I also will keep thee from the hour of temptation, which shall come upon all the world, to try them that dwell upon the earth." Pre-tribulationists take this to mean that we will be raptured before the tribulation.

"Keep Thee from the Hour of Temptation." Post-tribulationists view this promise differently. To them the word "keep" means *protection during* the tribulation. And to them the word "from" (*ek,* also translated "out of") implies existence *in* the tribulation before we can come *out* of it. The identical preposition is used in Revelation 7:14: "These are they which came *out of* great tribulation." To clinch their point they use John 17:15 which uses both words together: "I pray not that thou shouldest take them out of the world, but that thou shouldest *keep* them *from* the evil." They use this verse to show that we are "kept from" *while still in the world.*

Their logic seems airtight at first glance, yet through all of these arguments one thing has escaped notice. It is like a young boy swinging a hammer who has hit all around the nail without

Revelation

once hitting the nail on the head.

What have they missed? It is the force of the *unique combination* of the words "keep" and "from (out)." Suppose we approach a high voltage area and we see a sign in big red letters with two words on it, "KEEP OUT." That means if we go into this high voltage area we will be *kept* safely so that we won't get electrocuted. OUT. That means if we go in, we are guaranteed to *come out* safely. The sign says we can go in safely. Let's go. Forget the high chain link fence and the barbed wire. Let's go in.

You see, you can't divorce the words and reason that way. You have to take the words as they come, *together*. Together they mean something that separately they do not. The *unique combination* is the key. If God promised I will be *kept out* of the hour of temptation, it means exactly that.

Now for a Biblical illustration of the same point, let's go to John 17:15, and I will illustrate my point from the post-trib's own verse:

> I pray not that thou shouldest take them out of the world, but that thou shouldest *keep them from the evil [one]*.

In this verse, what is the *object* of "keep from"? Is it the "world"? No. It is "the evil one." We are kept from the evil one! If we were kept from the world we would not have been born. This verse proves nothing about our presence or absence in the world during the tribulation, because our word "keep" is not used in connection with the world.

Let us analyze this further. What does it mean to be kept from the evil one? Does this mean we are kept *in* the evil one? Or does it imply existence *in* the evil one and God wants to take us out? God forbid! The believer is so kept that "that wicked one toucheth him not" (1 John 5:18). To be kept from something means that it will not even touch you! This verse illustrates our meaning beautifully. Just as we are not in the evil one, so we will not be in the tribulation.

THE PRE-TRIBULATION RAPTURE

"keep from the evil [one]" (John 17:15)	"that wicked one toucheth him not" (1 John 5:18)
"keep from the hour of temptation" (Revelation 3:10)	that hour toucheth us not

"Ah, but we are in the *sphere* of the evil one," some may say. "God wants to keep us while in the sphere of the evil one." Let me remind you, though, the object of "keep from" is *not* "the sphere" but "the evil one." All I am asking is that we take the verse straight without inserting additional words.

It is objected that Peter was under the power of the evil one because Jesus prayed for him. A close reading of Jesus' words, though, shows that Satan did *not* have him. Jesus says only that "Satan hath *desired* to have you . . . *but* I have prayed for thee that thy faith fail not" (Luke 22:31-32). This was spoken the same night as the prayer of John 17, and it is further evidence that the disciples were *not in Satan* at that time. First John 5:18 is a foolproof commentary as to the extent of any believer's being in the evil one.

It is further said that the word "keep" necessarily implies the *presence* of danger which in turn implies presence in the tribulation. These implications do not necessarily follow. Since the church is carried up to the brink of the tribulation and since she would plunge into it except for the Lord's intervention, we can truthfully say that our prior separation is in light of a present danger looming before us. Even if "keep" did imply a continual keeping *throughout* the tribulation, it is still possible to keep something *in heaven* (1 Peter 1:4)! The post-trib implications don't stand up.

Again I say, the unique combination of "keep" and "from" is critical. Let us just separate the two words and see what happens. A different preposition with "keep" is used in Acts 12:5: "Peter therefore was kept *in* prison." Obviously, he was not prevented from entering the place. But if the passage read that Peter was "kept from prison," then you would know that he never entered prison in the first place.

A different word before "from" (or "out of") also changes the meaning. Those who "*came* out of great tribulation" (Revelation 7:14) obviously were not prevented from entering it. Likewise to "*take* them out of the world" (John 17:15) implies previous existence in the world. A similar preposition is used in Jeremiah 30:7 which speaks of Israel being in "the time of Jacob's trouble, but he shall be *saved* out of it." All these passages imply previous existence within by the words "came" out, "take" out, or "save" out. The word "out" by itself implies nothing. It alone does not tell you if the meaning is "out beforehand" or "out afterwards." But putting it with *another word* tells the whole story. I can tell you I "stayed out" of a bar or I "came out" of a bar, and you would get the picture very swiftly. The unique *combination* of words is the key.

Different word combinations give different meanings. To communicate *deliverance afterwards* you would say "save from." To emphasize *protection during* you would say "keep in." But to promise *prior prevention* you would say, "keep from." (This is part of the contrast in John 17:15. Instead of belated separation from the world, Jesus asks *prior* separation—even stronger—from the devil.)

WORD COMBINATION	MEANING	TIME INDICATED
keep from	prevention	beforehand
keep in	preservation	during
save from	deliverance	afterwards

THE PRE-TRIBULATION RAPTURE

"Kept from the hour" signifies separation from the *events* of the hour. By God's prior prevention we will be kept from entering into the events of the tribulation so that they "touch us not." Here lies one difference between John 17:15 and Revelation 3:10. Whereas it is possible to be totally separated from the evil one while still in the world, it is *not* possible to be totally separated from the events of the tribulation while still in the world as we will demonstrate below.

John 17:15	Revelation 3:10
Separation from the evil one does not require separation from the world.	Separation from tribulation requires separation from the world.

The Purpose of the Hour. Further support for the rapture of the church prior to the tribulation comes from the *purpose* of the hour. The purpose according to Revelation 3:10 is "to try" those who dwell upon the earth. That is why it is called an "hour of testing." ("Temptation" here means "testing" instead of "temptation to sin.") That period has a purpose for tribulation saints because they have yet to be tested (Daniel 12:10), but the church has *already* been tried. "Because thou hast kept the word of my patience . . . ." The church has successfully passed the test and kept the word of His patience. As a reward God will keep her from further and unnecessary trial. Our trial is past! There is *no purpose* for the church in the tribulation! If there is a purpose, what is it?

One approach says that we will be exempt from God's *judgments* during the tribulation, but we will not be exempt from *persecution.* In other words, Revelation 3:10 promises protection from *only one aspect* of the tribulation. There are five reasons I have difficulty accepting this theory.

First, it would be difficult to separate persecution from the hour of testing in the light of other Scripture. Matthew

Revelation

24:15-21 indicates that persecution upon believers is a part of the great tribulation. The word "temptation" is elsewhere used for persecution of believers (see Acts 20:19 and 1 Peter 1:6). Second, Daniel 12:10 shows that saints during the tribulation *will* experience trial. Tribulation saints are *not* kept. (See Revelation 6:11; 13:7; 14:13. Except for Jewish saints, Daniel 12:1; Revelation 7:1-8, there is no promise of protection in the tribulation. Isaiah 26:20 refers not to the tribulation, but to when the Lord returns from heaven after the tribulation; notice 26:21—27:1.)

Third, Revelation 1:9 provides a contextual setting for Revelation 3:10, revealing one aspect of the tribulation which is in view. Revelation 1:9 (using the word "tribulation") clearly speaks of the patience of believers in *persecution.*

Fourth, those who have "kept the word of (His) patience" in Revelation 3:10 are those faithful in *persecution* (not the judgments of God). The reciprocal promise to keep them would miss the mark if it too did not include persecution.

Fifth, to promise partial exemption (exemption from the judgments of God, but not from persecution) is to weaken the promise of Revelation 3:10. God is promising a *reward.* What kind of reward would it be to say, "Since you have been faithful you will not have to suffer certain things during the tribulation, even though that hour will bring *greater* suffering for you in terms of fleeing for your life, and the chances are that you will be killed. But at least you have this reward: you will be exempt from the other judgments." That type of reward does not sound too compelling or convincing. Christian prisoners behind the Iron Curtain who have been tortured for years would not be impressed by such a promise. I could promise *un*believers a reward of equal size: "For not believing I promise you will be exempt from persecution." What is the difference in the size of rewards as far as the time span of the tribulation is concerned?

For these reasons I believe exemption from *all* the events of the tribulation are in view in Revelation 3:10. Other Scriptures indicate that persecution is included in the hour of temptation, Daniel 12:10 includes tribulation saints in the testing, contextual evidence includes persecution in the hour of testing, and the promised reward to be meaningful must be full. Therefore, if the "hour of temptation" signifies the events within that hour, then persecution must be included as one of those events, and to be kept from persecution we must be taken out of the world.

"All the World." "All the world" is the scope of the tribulation according to Revelation 3:10. This tells me that the verse is talking about the great tribulation of the future rather than some period of persecution in past history. It is true that persecution would try Christians, but it would not try all "them that dwell upon the earth." (By the way, Revelation 3:3 shows that these things have application to the last generation as well as the first generation.)

I have two questions about "all the world" for post-tribs. Do you believe the word "all" includes both believers and unbelievers? If you do, then persecution of believers must be included in the "hour of temptation," and we would have to be raptured in order to be kept, not killed.

Second question. Do you believe "all" refers only to unbelievers? If you do, how can "all the world" consist of unbelievers *if believers enter* the tribulation? Only under pre-tribulationism does "all the world" consist of unbelievers at the outset of the tribulation because all the believers will have been "caught up."

The promise of Revelation 3:10 is clear. When God puts a promise in the Bible, He intends for us to take it at its full face value. He does not intend for us to try to find a way around it. If some string were attached He would say so. The simplest interpretation, the one a child can understand, is usually the best.

Contrast 2:10 and 3:10. The church in Smyrna was warned, "Ye shall have tribulation ten days" (2:10). Note the contrasts between 2:10 and 3:10. One says "you," the other says "them." One is obviously a local and earlier tribulation; the other is worded with wider application.

With the unique combination of "keep" and "from" implying prior separation, the church is left with no fair forewarning if she is to go through the tribulation. On the other hand, Israel is expressly told in no unmistakable terms that they will be in that time (Jeremiah 30:4-7; Daniel 12:1,10). The church in Smyrna received a forewarning of a smaller-scale tribulation. If the church at large is going through the great tribulation, is it fair that she should receive no such clear forewarning?

Other Prepositions? Gundry asks the question, "Why was not another preposition used (*apo,* "away from," instead of *ek,* "out from") which did not imply previous presence within?"[1] Actually the two words became so close in meaning by New Testament times that the difference between them was not critical. They are even used interchangeably in parallel passages. The preposition *ek* was strong enough and clear enough for Jesus to express prior separation from the devil in John 17:15. Linked together with "keep" it does imply prevention. Only with different verbs does it imply previous presence within.

Maybe some Greek scholar has more light than I have, but perhaps the only reason *ek* was chosen over *apo* is that *ek* happens to be a more common word in the New Testament, and *especially* in John's writings. Gundry suggests five other prepositions which are even less common. Since the more common preposition expressed the idea strongly enough there was no demand to go to a less common or to a rare preposition.

On the other hand, the preposition "through" (*dia*) is just as common as *ek,* and "in" (*en*) is far more common than either. If post-tribulationism were correct, there would be a demand to say "kept safely *in*" or "preserved *through*" in order to avoid the idea of prior separation which "from" has when used with "keep."

THE PRE-TRIBULATION RAPTURE

Gundry's own explanation for the usage of "from" (*ek*) is that the emphasis is on emergence. (As the promise was fulfilled for the first generation Philadelphian church, they did not emerge from the tribulation because they did not live to enter it. The only way the promise could hold true for them is if prior prevention were in view.) However, if the emphasis were on emergence, then why the word "keep" (*tereo*) instead of "deliver" (*hruomai*)? "Deliver" would better fit the concept of emergence, it is commonly used with "from," and so we would expect it to be used. "Keep," however, is rare with "from" and it better suits prevention instead of emergence. The two words "keep" and "from" are working against each other, like mules pulling in opposite directions if one emphasizes preservation and the other emergence. The words don't cooperate with each other unless you understand this, not as deliverance afterwards, not as preservation during, but as prior prevention.

"As a Thief" (3:3; 16:15). Revelation 3:3 contains a warning addressed to the church in Sardis: "If therefore thou shalt not watch, I will come on thee as a thief, and thou shalt not know what hour I will come upon thee." This raises a question. If Christ's coming "as a thief" is *after* the tribulation (as it uniformly is in other contexts), then how can this be addressed to the church?

The answer lies in the probability that those given the warning are *unbelievers* within the local church. As unbelievers they will miss the rapture and go through the tribulation and meet Christ's coming "as a thief."

Why do I suspect that these are unbelievers rather than believers? These people in Sardis are described as spiritually "dead" (3:1) and it is implied that their names are not in the book of life (3:5). As to the possibility of unbelievers in other local churches see Revelation 2:14-15,20; 3:17-20. These references include Balaamites, Nicolaitanes, Jezebel, and those unclothed with white raiment with Christ outside the door of their

Revelation

heart. It should never be that unbelievers are allowed to become church members, but unfortunately it happens.

When we approach the end of the tribulation in Revelation 16:15, we find the statement again: "Behold, I come as a thief." Here it does not say, as in Revelation 3:3, "Thou shalt not know what hour I will come upon thee." Why the omission? The reason is that 16:15 is addressed, not to unbelievers only, but to *both* believers and unbelievers. Unbelievers will not know the hour the thief comes, but tribulation saints will know the hour (compare Luke 12:39).

THE TIME OF THE RAPTURE

As you remember, First Thessalonians gave a description of the rapture without revealing the time. It left us hanging in the air. Revelation builds on that, not repeating the full description, but it does reveal the time. Revelation 4:1 locates the time at the beginning of the tribulation:

> After this I looked, and, behold, a door was opened in heaven: and the first voice which I heard was as it were of a trumpet talking with me; which said, Come up hither, and I will show thee things which must be hereafter.

Symbolism Used. The "trumpet" in connection with the words "come up hither" identify this as symbolizing the rapture. (There is no trumpet at Revelation 11:12.) Also the heavens open only twice in Revelation, once here at Christ's pre-trib coming and once in 19:11 (same event as 6:14) at His post-trib coming. The heavens open only for His coming.

Let it be clear that I never use this verse to "prove" a pre-trib rapture. I take my proof from elsewhere in the Bible that the rapture *cannot* occur at the *end* of the tribulation. Some of this evidence we saw in chapters two, three, and four, and even stronger evidence is coming in the chapters following. Having seen the evidence against a post-trib rapture, the only remaining question is: *When* does it occur? If it does not occur at the end, does it occur in the middle of the tribulation, or at the

THE PRE-TRIBULATION RAPTURE

beginning, or sometime before the beginning? Since Revelation is the capstone in the progress of revelation it is only natural that it should answer this one last question. Revelation 4:1 is not the foundation to my belief; it is the capstone sitting on top of all the other evidence.

Do you wish that this verse spelled out the rapture in straightforward language instead of using symbolic language? This is only what we would expect in Revelation because God told us in Revelation 1:1 that He is communicating this book by "signs" (". . . He sent and *signified* it by his angel unto his servant John"). So it is perfectly normal for the rapture to be portrayed in symbolic language. Post-tribs likewise see a symbolic representation of the rapture in Revelation 14:14-16. So we are not asking you to accept anything unusual. Of course, the symbolism in no way denies that John also was *literally* caught up to heaven in Revelation 4.

As with any symbol there is always the danger of making the symbol stretch too far. Anyone who does stretch a symbol will find that it does not fit in all details, because a symbol is designed to communicate the central facts only. In this case the "trumpet" in connection with "come up here" are sufficient to identify this as the rapture without any stretching of the symbolism or of the imagination. Trumpets occur elsewhere without signifying the rapture, but here the trumpet *in combination with* "come up here" is the tip-off.

The Twenty-four Elders. The scene is definitely set in heaven in the following verses.

> And round about the throne were four and twenty seats [thrones]: and upon the seats I saw four and twenty elders sitting, clothed in white raiment; and they had on their heads crowns of gold (Revelation 4:4).

The controversy about the twenty-four elders involves the question: Do they represent the church, and if so, do they represent a raptured church? I will follow a different (and easier) line of argument here than is usually taken. I will not try to prove that they are the church, I will only try to prove that they are *men*. This is easy enough to prove from their characteristics.

Elsewhere in the Bible *only men* are "elders."
Only men sit on thrones (except God and Satan).
Only men wear white raiment (*himation* in Greek).
Only men wear crowns. This is fitting because the Greek word means a "victorious crown" rather than a "kingly crown." The Greek distinguishes between the two types of crowns. A heavenly being may wear a kingly crown, but no heavenly being has gone through the battle of life on earth in order to earn the victor's crown. (Revelation 9:7 is unique because a figurative creature is involved. Even here, though, these locusts are not heavenly beings, and it is expressly stated that their faces are as "men." Revelation 14:14 also fits the pattern because Christ as "the son of man" is a *man* as well as God.)

All four characteristics constitute sufficient evidence that the twenty-four elders are *men*. It might be possible to discount one or two of them if that were all there were. But four characteristics all at once is too much to get around. To try to explain these away, or to try to get around them one by one, is like trying to hold down four jack-in-the-boxes with one hand. The same hand that holds down one lets the other three jump up. A comprehensive and unified explanation is impossible unless we understand that these are men. (Not the church necessarily, just *men*.)

It may be objected, "We cannot be certain who the twenty-four elders are." (They cannot be angels, Revelation 7:11. If not men or angels, what other possibilities are there?) But remember, Revelation is an *unsealed* book (22:10). Maybe some minor things in Revelation we do not understand yet, but the twenty-four elders are *major*. They are the first thing mentioned in the heavenly scene after God Himself. They figure prominently no less than four times in chapters four and five.

THE PRE-TRIBULATION RAPTURE

Later in the book they reappear several times at strategic events. Can we not understand a *major* item in an *unsealed* book? Obviously, God intends for us to know who they are.

God has made their identification clear, not only from their characteristics, but also from the previous context. In Revelation 2 and 3 He promises, "I will give thee a crown of life . . . white raiment . . . to sit with me in my throne." In light of these promises in the previous context, to see the elders sitting on thrones, wearing white raiment and crowns, it is impossible to miss their identity. What can Revelation 4 be if it is not the fulfillment of these promises? The promises (in chapters 2 and 3) match the fulfillment (in chapter four) as perfectly as a glove fits on a hand. Or would God fool us by giving us a host of false and misleading clues in a book that is unsealed? If so, the title of the book should be changed from "Revelation" to "Obscuration."

After establishing that the twenty-four elders are men, the second step in our line of argument is to notice that they have crowns on their heads.

Third, the time for men to receive crowns is *at the coming of Christ,* not before (2 Timothy 4:8; 1 Peter 5:4). (Exceptions occur later in Revelation in the more symbolic visions of John. However, for real men this is the rule. Of course, in 14:14 Christ wears a crown because He is resurrected and glorified as we will be at the rapture. The rapture and crowning occur *simultaneously.* This accounts for John's seeing the elders with crowns the moment he was caught up to heaven.)

Fourth and finally, if men's crowns are received at the coming of Christ, and if these twenty-four men have crowns, then *there must have been a coming of Christ prior to this.* If all three previous points are correct, then we are committed to a pre-trib rapture. (If this scene of the twenty-four elders comes at the beginning of the seven years, then this rules out a mid-tribulation rapture.)

Now we went through this entire argument without once assuming that the twenty-four elders represent the church.

Revelation

After finishing the argument, however, I can safely conclude that they represent New Testament saints only, because the resurrection of Old Testament saints occurs after the tribulation (Daniel 12:2).

Let us pause here to catch a glimpse of the amazing privilege God has given us. The thrones of these elders surround God's throne. This indicates that we will be *associated with God as co-rulers with Him* in the judgments of the tribulation! We will be on top instead of down under. What an encouragement to remain patiently under our problems just awhile longer. We also learn from the elders' attitude of praise that *prayer* is a high privilege. We do not have to wait to enter into this privilege, but we can live *now* like the kings and priests God has called us to be by offering intercession and praise.

THE CHRONOLOGY OF REVELATION

We owe a debt to Gundry for enlightening many of us on the chronology of Revelation.[2] Seven seals, seven trumpets, and seven vials outline the events of the book. Normally we would think that they follow one another in succession. But Revelation was not written in our modern times; it was written according to the Semitic style of apocalyptic literature. The seals, trumpets, and vials run concurrently instead of successively. The seals cover the *entire* tribulation, the trumpets back up and elaborate on approximately the last half of the tribulation, and the vials back up again and elaborate on the cluster of events at the end.

When you watch a television program with the "flashback" method, you find no fault with the chronology. No one says, "Hey, this TV program is out of order. Those producers had better get their chronology straight." No one objects because the "flashback" method is a perfectly accepted literary device of our day. Likewise, the chronology of Revelation follows the normal pattern of the day in which it was written.

If we did not know about the Semitic pattern of apocalyptic literature, we would still have a way of knowing that the seals stretch to the end of the tribulation. Under the sixth seal the sun and moon are darkened and the stars fall (6:12-13). According to Matthew 24:29 these events occur *after* the tribulation. (Isaiah 2:10-21 pinpoints this time as the day of the Lord.) This will be significant as we discuss the winepress in chapter ten.

Likewise the seventh trumpet occurs at the end, as a simple reading of its contents will tell you (11:15-19; compare 10:7). It is the time of God's reigning, wrath, judgment, and reward. This is significant because it tells us when the two witnesses minister. The death and resurrection of the two witnesses occur shortly before the seventh trumpet (11:14). If their 1260-day ministry ends shortly before the end, this means their ministry begins a few days before the middle of the tribulation when antichrist is revealed. Their career almost parallels that of antichrist providing an alternative and a challenge to him. The chronology is significant also because it undermines those who use the seventh trumpet as a basis for the mid-tribulation rapture theory.

The resulting picture is that the seals, trumpets, and vials all stretch to the end of the tribulation. They run concurrently instead of consecutively. The *sixth* seal is the end because the *seventh* seal gives rise to the seven trumpets. The seventh trumpet, in contrast, does not give rise to the seven vials. In other words, the sixth seal, the seventh trumpet, and the seventh vial all synchronize, occurring at the end.

```
Seals                        1  2  3  4  5  6
Trumpets (7th seal ──▶)                  1 2 3 4 5 6 7
Vials                                         1234567
```

"LEND ME YOUR EARS" (13:9)

Chapters two and three repeat over and over again, "He that hath an ear, let him hear what the Spirit saith unto the churches." This phrase occurs not once, nor twice, nor even three times, but seven times it is repeated "unto the churches."

Post-tribulationists discount the fact that the church is not mentioned on earth in Revelation 4—19. (I believe the church is mentioned in heaven in the form of the twenty-four elders who inherit the thrones, raiment, and crowns promised to the church.) Perhaps they are right. Maybe it is too much to expect the church to be mentioned. But Revelation 13:9 is a different story: "If any man have an ear, let him hear." Here we would *expect* the church to be mentioned because of the consistent pattern previously. Why the omission of "unto the churches"? Is the church no longer on the earth?

At the very least, Revelation 13:9 dulls the sharp edge of the contention that Revelation is written *only* to the church. As we saw earlier, the church is interested in all the contents of Revelation, but those alive during the tribulation also will have a vital interest in it.

NEITHER JEW NOR GREEK (7:1-8)

> "There is neither Jew nor Greek . . . for ye are all one in Christ Jesus" (Galatians 3:28).

How different is the account of the 144,000 Israelites in Revelation seven! God is dealing with Israelites in a special way! To set them aside unto a special group tribe by tribe, and to even set a seal on their foreheads is something He never did in the church age. Obviously the tribulation period is *distinct* from the church age.

Today whenever a person believes, he automatically becomes a member of the church, Christ's universal body. This is true for Jew *or* Gentile, for in the church there is no difference between Jew and Gentile; it is all one. There is no such thing as non-Jewish believers belonging to the church while Jewish believers do not belong. Even post-tribs admit a distinction between two groups of believers, Jews and non-Jews, in Revelation seven. That distinction is fine for the tribulation, but there is no such distinction in this age. The church must be raptured and taken out of this world altogether before such a distinction can take place.

Can we explain it away by saying the 144,000 are figurative? No, because John lists 12,000 from each tribe. And he *names* each tribe. John went to a lot of trouble and detail in order to explain who these 144,000 are. They are literal.

If the church age extends into the tribulation period, then how do we explain God's special dealing with Israelites?

"FIRSTFRUITS" (14:4)

"Firstfruits" are the first part of the harvest from the field. Scripture applies the term also to a spiritual harvest of men. For example, Epaenetus was "the firstfruits of Achaia unto Christ" (Romans 16:5). In other words, he was one of Paul's first converts in that region.

The tribulation period also has firstfruits. Revelation 14:4 says the 144,000 "were redeemed from among men, being the *firstfruits* unto God and to the Lamb." In what sense are the 144,000 the firstfruits of redeemed men? How could that be? By now millions the world over have been harvested into the church. The time for firstfruits has passed!

They could only be firstfruits if God were starting over again with a *new class* of converts during the tribulation. This tells me the church has been completed and raptured before the tribulation.

In order to get around this some post-tribs may object, "The 144,000 are firstfruits of the *millennium* rather than firstfruits of the tribulation." This objection cannot stand because the evidence shows that they are converted *during* the tribulation instead of after. What evidence? The seal. They have the seal of the living God on their foreheads (7:2-3) in contrast to the mark of the phony god which unbelievers wear. If they wear the seal of God, they must belong to God. This is no ordinary seal. It is no less than the "Father's name written in their foreheads" (14:1). Unbelievers? With God's seal? Incredible!

Therefore, the 144,000 "were redeemed from among men [during the tribulation], the firstfruits unto God and to the Lamb" (14:4). Being "firstfruits," the 144,000 are some of the *first* converts in the tribulation. Although most Jews will be converted at the end, just before Christ returns as we saw in chapter three, a few will be converted earlier (see Daniel 12:1,10; Matthew 24:9). The 144,000 are "firstfruits." If they were converted at the *end* they would be "lastfruits."

(If the 144,000 constituted the Jewish remnant converted at Christ's return, as some post-tribs say, then multiplying that figure by three should result in the present world population of Jews. Zechariah 13:8-9.)

THE HARVEST (14:14-20)

Revelation 14:14 pictures the coming of Christ after the tribulation as a harvest:

> And I looked, and behold a white cloud, and upon the cloud one sat like unto the Son of man, having on his head a golden crown, and in his hand a sharp sickle.

What is the sharp sickle for? One view is that He swings the sickle to catch up believers (post-tribulationism). The other is that He swings the sickle in judgment (pre-tribulationism). Which is right? Is Christ reaping believers or unbelievers?

Let us run to the commentary for help. The best commentary on this passage was written by the prophet Joel, because Joel forms the backdrop for this passage in Revelation. Let us put his explanation alongside of Revelation 14:14-20:

THE PRE-TRIBULATION RAPTURE

Revelation 14:14-20

14. And I looked, and behold a white cloud, and upon the cloud one *sat* like unto the Son of man, having on his head a golden crown, and in his hand a sharp sickle.

15. And another angel came out of the temple, crying with a loud voice to him that sat on the cloud, Thrust in thy sickle, and reap: for the time is come for thee to reap; for *the harvest of the earth is ripe.*

16. And he that sat on the cloud thrust in his sickle on the earth; and the earth was reaped. [Compare Matthew 13:38, "The field is the world."]

17. And another angel came out of the temple which is in heaven, he also having a sharp sickle.

18. And another angel came out from the altar, which had power over fire; and cried with a loud cry to him that had the sharp sickle, saying, Thrust in thy sharp sickle, and gather the clusters of the vine of the earth; for her grapes are fully ripe.

19. And the angel thrust in his sickle into the earth, and gathered the vine of the earth, and cast it into the great winepress of the wrath of God.

20. And the winepress was trodden without the city, and blood came out of the winepress, even unto the horse bridles, by the space of a thousand and six hundred furlongs.

Joel 3:12-13

12. Let the heathen be wakened, and come up to the valley of Jehoshaphat [compare "valley of decision" in verse 14]: for there will I *sit* to judge all the heathen round about.

13. Put ye in the sickle, for *the harvest is ripe:*

Come, tread [the winepress]; for the press is full, the fats [vats] overflow; for their wickedness is great.

Revelation

Thank you, Joel, for explaining it for us. We see now that the sickle is for judgment. Pure judgment from start to finish. The sickle is not aimed at believers, but unbelievers.

Let's look at some of the details. Judgment lies in the very name of the valley. "Jehoshaphat" in Hebrew means "Jehovah judges," and so the valley of Jehoshaphat is the valley of "the Lord's judgment." The valley also goes by the name, "the valley of decision." "Decision" has double meaning in Hebrew. It can mean "decision" or "cutting." How fitting it is, because the decision of the Lord is the cutting of the Lord as He swings His sharp sickle to reap the wicked. The sickle signifies cutting, decision, judgment.

The judging takes place in two phases, the reaping and the treading. First, the Son of man reaps (Revelation 14:15-16). This is the cutting-off point for every person in the whole world. Not just believers are reaped, but the entire "earth" is reaped (compare Matthew 13:38, "The field is the world," not the church). As the Son of man reaps He makes His decision concerning every individual, saying, "This man believes in me, that one rejects me." This is the cutting-off point. Repentance now is too late. Those who are wicked now will be wicked forever. Those who are righteous now will be righteous forever. The final results are in. The earth is reaped.

After the Son of man passes judicial sentence, the angels carry out the execution of that sentence as phase two of the judgment, the treading (Revelation 14:17-19). After the Son of man has reaped, the angels gather the grapes and cast them into the winepress. Then comes the invitation to the Son of man to tread, according to our commentator, Joel. (The KJV in Joel 3:13 reads "get you down," but "tread" is generally accepted to be the correct reading.) When the press is filled to overflowing the Son of man treads the winepress (Revelation 14:20).

So the reaping of Revelation 14 does not picture the rapture at all. After the tribulation comes, not rapture, but judgment. From start to finish it is judgment. Judgment in two phases, reaping and treading, or to put it another way, cutting and casting.

It is well-known that Revelation constantly alludes back to Old Testament passages. When John wrote the book, he assumed knowledge of the Old Testament on the part of his readers. All I am asking is that we interpret Revelation 14:14-20 in light of Joel 3:12-13 as John intended for us to do. To divorce the two passages is to interpret in the dark.

The harvest of Revelation 14 not only accords with Joel, but it also harmonizes with the *proper order* of gatherings. In the next chapter we will learn from Matthew 13 that the *wicked* are gathered *first*. The post-tribulational interpretation of Revelation 14:14-20 is precluded by the mere fact that they have the wrong order. They see a gathering of the righteous (verses 14-16) *before* the wicked (verses 17-20). Since the order is wrong this *cannot* picture the gathering of the righteous. Rapture doesn't fit here at all.

Where does this leave us? Since the rapture is *not* pictured in Revelation 14, this means there is no description of the rapture whatsoever in the entire book of Revelation unless there be a symbolic representation of the rapture in 4:1, and that would place the rapture before the tribulation.

THE ARMIES IN HEAVEN (19:14)

The account of Christ's returning on a white horse in Revelation 19 mentions white-robed armies following with Him. These saints coming with Him are those *already* "in heaven." No mention of any saints "caught up" to join Him. Why the omission of saints caught up, or raptured, to join the armies already in heaven?

Post-tribs would say the omission is not significant and does not prove anything. I agree that omissions in some places are not significant, but here? Here is the *climax* of the whole book! At this climactic point in the drama I think that John would want to highlight and make the most out of the victorious King of Kings and His accompanying armies. What makes more sense? To strengthen a climax or to weaken a climax? What author of a novel would build up to the climax only to dissipate it? What playwright would purposely weaken the high point in his drama? Likewise, it doesn't make sense for John to leave out saints "raptured" here if there really were a rapture here.

Unless he omitted the rapture accidentally. But that couldn't happen because the Holy Spirit was guiding every word John wrote. It has to be a purposeful omission.

According to post-tribulationism the armies in heaven are *souls* not yet resurrected. How easy it is to picture resurrected church saints riding down from the sky in one smooth descent. However, post-tribs insert the resurrection into the middle of the descent. Now imagine yourself as one of those white horses. You leave heaven with a soul on your back. But when you reach cloud level you halt while the horseless soul swoops down to the ground to get its body. A moment later the body hops on your back and you resume your descent. Not impossible, of course, but interesting. Not to mention the horses that must leave heaven empty so that *living* saints caught up from the earth will have something to ride on.

THE FIRST RESURRECTION (20:4-6)

After the tribulation we find an account of the "first resurrection" (20:5). Why is it called "*first* resurrection" if there is another resurrection seven years earlier at the rapture?

Well, let's think about it. We know that Christ arose, along with other believers in Jerusalem (Matthew 27:52-53). This happened 2000 years ago. Also the two witnesses arise *before* the end of the tribulation (Revelation 11:12-14). If the first resurrection does not nullify these earlier resurrections, then to be logically consistent, neither does it eliminate an earlier resurrection with the rapture.

If earlier resurrections happen, then why is this called the "first" resurrection? If the terminology is not meant to exclude earlier resurrections, then there must be another reason for the word "first." The answer, as usual, lies in the context. In the context following we find the "second death" (20:14). The

THE PRE-TRIBULATION RAPTURE

reason for the term "first resurrection" is to contrast the "second death." A sharper contrast cannot be found. "First" contrasts "second" and "resurrection" contrasts "death." There is no "second resurrection," strictly speaking, the second is not a resurrection, but a death. How terrible a fate for the unbeliever. His body becomes alive again only to suffer a living death in the lake of fire for ever and ever.

How wonderful, in contrast, is the destiny of the believer who partakes of the first resurrection. Believers are in the first resurrection; unbelievers are in the second death. This is the contrast and this is the purpose of the terminology in this context. A word takes on meaning only as we use it in a context. If the word "first" had arms and hands so that it could push, it would not be pushing against earlier resurrections; it would be pushing against the "second death." All I am asking is that we let the context give us the meaning of the word instead of inserting our own definition for "first resurrection."

If the first resurrection allows for earlier resurrections, this also helps to explain a similar problem in 1 Corinthians 15:54:

> So when this corruptible shall have put on incorruption, and this mortal shall have put on immortality, then shall be brought to pass the saying that is written, Death is swallowed up in victory.

This passage quotes from Isaiah 25:8 which according to the context there places the time of victory over death at the *end* of the tribulation. Here is the problem. If 1 Corinthians 15 is talking about victory over death at the *rapture,* then how can the rapture occur at the *beginning* of the tribulation if Isaiah 25:8 places victory over death at the *end* of the tribulation? Why the discrepancy of time between the two verses?

I can best answer this by giving you another example. By comparing Joel 2:28 with Acts 2:17 we see a similar problem regarding the time of the pouring out of the Spirit. The church has already entered into the promise of Joel 2:28 early, only about 2000 years early. My point is this: *nothing in the Bible prevents an earlier and partial fulfillment of Old Testament prophecies.* If the church can enter into one promise 2000 years early, then surely she can enter into another promise seven years early. All I am asking for is consistency of interpretation.

Shall we forget early fulfillment and be strict about the time? All right, let us be very strict about the time and see what happens. The promise from Isaiah 25:8, "He will swallow up death in victory" in its final fulfillment, comes *75 days too late* to be a resurrection at a post-trib rapture! I'll show you what I mean.

The resurrection of Revelation 20 includes the resurrection of Old Testament saints. We all agree on this. Now Daniel was an Old Testament saint, wasn't he? Again we agree.

Now let me ask you one question: When is Daniel's resurrection? When? You'll find the answer in the last verse of his book:

> But go thou thy way till the end be: for thou shalt rest, and stand in thy lot at the end of the days (Daniel 12:13).

When is Daniel's resurrection? At the end of the days. When is that? As we pointed out in chapter two, Daniel's last chapter gives three dates:

1260 days	When is Daniel's resurrection?
1290 days	
1335 days	At the end of the days.

When is Daniel's resurrection? The end of the days is the *1335th day.* Since Christ returns on day 1260, as we saw in chapter two, then Daniel's resurrection comes *75 days too late* to be a rapture resurrection! Therefore, the resurrection of Revelation 20 *cannot* take place at the rapture.

We will learn more in the next chapter about this 75-day gap between the tribulation and the millennium. Rather than taking place at the end of the tribulation, the resurrection of Revelation 20 occurs later, at the beginning of the millennium. Notice the context. Revelation 20 comes after Christ returns and destroys the Armageddon armies. You see, this tiny overlooked detail from the context places the resurrection after Christ sets foot on earth, not while He is still in the air as it would happen at the rapture. The order of Revelation 19 and 20 accords with 1 Corinthians 15:26, "The *last* enemy that shall be destroyed is death." He must put the Armageddon armies under His feet before He destroys death at the resurrection. This resurrection occurs even after Satan is bound. The visions of chapters 19-20 are chronological; they are not part of the overlapping visions of chapters 6—18. Even if we did change the order of the visions, the first resurrection still occurs in the *same vision* as the millennium (20:4-10) which is 75 days too late for the post-trib scheme.

Shall we be strict about the time? Not only is Daniel's resurrection 75 days too late, not only does the resurrection of Revelation 20 occur at the outset of the millennium, but also the promise of Isaiah 25:8, "He will swallow up death in victory," occurs in a pre-millennial context. This evaporates the argument that the resurrection of Revelation 20 is identical to the resurrection of 1 Thessalonians 4 and that the time of the rapture can be proved by the "first resurrection."

SUMMARY

In summary of Revelation, let me leave you with the following questions which I hope will stimulate all of us to dig into our Bibles a little deeper:

Is not the church interested in the contents of Revelation as heavenly participants—exactly the role of the first generation church—even though we will not be earthly observers?

In Revelation 3:10, why the unique combination of "keep" and "from"?

How could the twenty-four elders have crowns if Christ had not come previously?

Why does Revelation 13:9, contrary to expectation, contrary to the consistent pattern, address individuals instead of churches?

Why does God deal in a special way with 144,000 Israelites,

something that He does not do during this church age?

Why are the 144,000 called "firstfruits" instead of "lastfruits" unless a brand new class of converts arises during the tribulation?

How can the harvest of Revelation 14:14-16 be the rapture when Joel explains it to be the harvest of the wicked?

Why are the white-robed armies all *in heaven* before Christ leaves heaven to return to earth?

If the resurrection of Revelation 20 is the rapture resurrection, then why does it occur well *after* Christ sets foot on the earth?

1. Gundry, *The Church and the Tribulation,* pp. 57-58.
2. Ibid, pp. 74-77.

"Gather ye together first the tares"
(Matthew 13:30).

8
Which Comes First?

Post-tribs see virtue in harmonizing the two aspects of the second coming into one event. Let me remind you, however, that there is no virtue of itself in harmonizing events. The virtue lies in harmonizing passages of Scripture.

In this chapter I want to show you a harmony of Scripture which is written in parallel columns in the chart. This harmony reveals an amazingly consistent pattern which uncovers a surprising fact. The moment Christ returns to earth after the tribulation, He does not gather any believers in any way. No gathering of believers occurs until well *after* Christ sets His foot upon the earth!

Let me now point out the significant features of the harmony which you see in the parallel columns.

HARMONY OF SCRIPTURE

The crucial passage in the harmony is the parable of the tares in Matthew 13, because this clearly puts the gathering of the wicked *first*, before the gathering of the righteous. "Gather ye together *first* the tares." What does this prove to you? Does it prove pre-trib or post-trib? This has been used against pre-

Which Comes First?

tribulationism, but we will turn it around and demonstrate that it disproves post-tribulationism.

The order of gatherings is crucial, because the order is *opposite* to the post-trib scheme. Post-tribs say the righteous are raptured "from among" the wicked at the end of the tribulation. But Jesus says that at that time the angels shall "sever the wicked from among the just." The order is exactly the opposite. They both can't be right.

So, let's take time to scrutinize the post-tribs' objections closely.

Who Are the Tares? One objection is that the tares represent only a *portion* of the wicked. The tares are professing Christians in the church, not true believers, who are gathered *before* Christ returns. This supposedly allows a gathering of the tares first, the rapture of believers next, and the dealing with the rest of the wicked later so that the order will come out correct.

Often we do not even have to interpret the Bible, because the interpretation is given right there. All we have to do is read it. Simply read it. In this case, Jesus Himself explains "the field is the world." The field is not the church. The field is the *world*. According to Jesus the tares represent people in the world, not the church only.

He further explains that the tares are "the children of the wicked one." Again, no limitation to professing Christians. "The children of the wicked one" encompasses all unbelievers the world over. If the wheat is *all* the believers, it is consistent for the tares to be *all* the unbelievers in the whole world.

That is Jesus' interpretation of the parable. Simply read it. What right do we have to *re*-interpret His interpretation?

The objection comes back: Do not the tares sown especially among the wheat signify unbelievers especially in Christian circles? Well, the location of the tares does not prove anything, because the *wheat is in the world,* and so the tares likewise are *in the world.* If a limited sphere were intended, Jesus could have said that the field is the church and that the wheat and the

THE PRE-TRIBULATION RAPTURE

THE TIME OF HARVEST

	Matthew 13:30, 40-42, 49	Revelation 14:14-20	Mark 13:26-27 (compare Matthew 24:30-31)	Revelation 13:5; 20:6; Daniel 12:7,11,12-13
Before the Harvest	Let both grow together			And power was given unto him to continue *forty and two months* [1260 days]. It shall be for a *time, times, and an half* [1260 days]; and when he shall have accomplished to scatter the power of the holy people, all these things shall be finished.
The Decision	until the *harvest*:	And I looked, and behold a white *cloud*, and upon the *cloud* one sat like unto the Son of man, having on his head a golden crown, and in his hand a sharp sickle. And another angel came out of the temple, crying with a loud voice to him that sat on the cloud, Thrust in thy sickle, and *reap*: for the time is come for thee to *reap*; for the *harvest* of the earth is ripe. And he that sat on the *cloud* thrust in his sickle on the earth; and the earth was *reaped*.	And then shall they see the Son of man coming in the *clouds* with great power and glory.	
	and in the time of harvest I will say to the reapers, *Gather* ye together first the tares, and bind them in bundles to burn them: As therefore the tares are	And another angel came out of the temple which is in heaven, he also having a sharp sickle. And another angel came out from the altar, which had power		

192

Which Comes First?

Gathering of the Wicked	gathered and burned in the fire; so shall it be in the end of this world. The Son of man shall send forth his angels, and they shall gather out of his kingdom all things that offend, and them which do iniquity (and sever the wicked from among the just); And shall cast them into a furnace of *fire*: there shall be wailing and gnashing of teeth.	over *fire*; and cried with a loud cry to him that had the sharp sickle, saying, Thrust in thy sharp sickle, and *gather* the clusters of the vine of the earth; for her grapes are fully ripe: And the angel thrust in his sickle into the earth, and gathered the vine of the earth, and cast it into the great winepress of the wrath of God	And from the time that the daily sacrifice shall be taken away, and the abomination that maketh desolate set up, there shall be *a thousand two hundred and ninety days*.
Gathering of the Righteous	but *gather* the wheat	And then shall he send his angels, and shall *gather* together his elect from the four winds, from the uttermost part of the earth	*Blessed* is he that waiteth, and cometh to the *thousand three hundred and five and thirty days*. *Blessed* and holy is he that hath part in the first resurrection: on such the second death hath no power, but they shall be priests of God and of Christ, and shall reign with him a thousand years. Thou [Daniel and Old Testament saints] shalt rest, and stand in thy lot at the *end of the days*.
The Harvest Ended	into my barn.	to the uttermost part of heaven.	

tares were sown in the church. Why didn't He say this? No, the field is still the world, for both wheat and tares. The wheat is in the world and the tares cannot be limited any more than the wheat is.

The objection might be pressed that not all the wicked are included because of the companion parable of the fishnet. The net gathers all kinds of fish *out of* the sea, not *all* the fish in the sea. This objection would stand *if* it could be shown that the sea is the world and the net is the church. However, using Christ's interpretation as our only guide, we see that *the net in one parable corresponds to the field of the other parable,* because each denotes the sphere of separation between the good and the bad. Jesus makes no mention of separation in the sea since it is merely an addition to the story which points to the main object, the net. By correspondence, then, if the field is the world, then the net is the world, and the sphere of separation is still the world, not the church.

Now forget all my arguments for a minute, and let's suppose that the field were the church and that the tares were unbelievers in the professing church. Suppose that we let them grow together with no attempt to separate them as the parable says to do. Now how will we explain to the Lord our refusal to expel false members in the church? How will we face the charge of insubordination to commands like these: "Deliver such an one unto Satan . . . Purge out therefore the old leaven . . . Put away from among yourselves that wicked person" (1 Corinthians 5:6,7,13), and, "But I have a few things against thee, because thou hast there them that hold the doctrine of Balaam . . . So hast thou also them that hold the doctrine of the Nicolaitanes, which thing I hate. Repent . . . I have a few things against thee, because thou sufferest that woman Jezebel . . ." (Revelation 2:14,15,20)?

These are commands to expel, not commands to tolerate. The difference of commands proves the difference of spheres. Do we expel them or do we let them grow together? It all depends. In the church we expel them; in the world we let them

Which Comes First?

grow. Therefore, the sphere of separation in Matthew 13 is the world, not the church.

Is the Order Important? If it be agreed that the scope of separation is the entire world, it may yet be objected that the *order* of separation is not to be pressed. But why would Jesus make a special point to say the tares are gathered *first* when He could just as easily have said the opposite or not have made a point of it at all? If it were not true it would be misleading for Him to put it the way He did. Also, this is no isolated mention of the wicked's being gathered first. In the companion parable of the fishnet, the angels "sever the wicked from among [literally, *out of the midst of*] the just" (Matthew 13:49). The order is repeated. It must be real.

The time of burning the tares is irrelevant. The order of gatherings is what counts.

It's Only a Parable. I can think of one more objection that post-tribs may try to make. "It's only a parable. You can't prove doctrine from parables, because you can make a parable say anything you want to."

In response, let me say, "I agree with you." I do not so much depend on the parable of the tares, or the parable of the net, but I depend on *Jesus' interpretation of these parables*. It is Jesus' interpretation which says that the wicked are severed from among the just instead of the other way around. It is Jesus' interpretation that explains the field to be the world. I don't make the parable say anything I want to by making the field the church or by limiting "the children of the wicked one" to *some* of the children of the wicked one, or by inserting any foreign material whatsoever. All I am asking is that we let Jesus' interpretation be our interpretation.

Another point, if the sphere of separation were the church, and if the Lord supposedly roots out false members *before* He returns, then tell me, *when* is the harvest?

Even if the tares were unbelievers in the church, there is no record of any future rooting out of all false believers *before* Christ returns. It simply will not be fulfilled. It is true that Babylon is destroyed before Christ returns (Revelation 17—18), but how does the destruction of one city exterminate false Christians worldwide?

THE TIME OF THE HARVEST

It is time we quit trying to figure out our own interpretations and let Scripture give its own interpretation. This drives us to the second feature of our harmony, a passage which pinpoints the *time* of the harvest.

Revelation 14:14-20 places the time of harvest *after* the tribulation *at the return of Christ.* The time is specific—this is the moment for reaping (verse 15).

Other evidence backs up what Revelation 14:15 says about the time of harvest. If the harvest is the end of the world (Matthew 13:39), then Matthew 24:3 shows the end of the world to be the end of the tribulation. If the reapers are the angels (Matthew 13:39), then nowhere else do we find angels reaping but at the end of the tribulation (Revelation 14:17-19 and Matthew 24:31). If after the harvest the righteous shall shine in the kingdom of their Father (Matthew 13:43), then Matthew 26:29 places the kingdom of the Father in the millennium. Finally, Joel 3:13 places the harvest at the end of the tribulation.

Of course, in one sense there is a harvest of men's souls going on right now as we win them to the Lord (John 4:35). But in another sense, Scripture reveals only one time of harvest in the end of the age. Our job is to harvest as many as we can now before the angels step in and do their harvesting.

Concerning the Rapture. "In the time of harvest" is the answer to the post-trib argument against pre-tribs. Some suppose that the rapture could not be *before* the tribulation because that would place the gathering of the righteous *first.* We are accused of being out of order. But Jesus said—this is His interpretation, not mine—the order of separation applies

Which Comes First?

to "the time of harvest" (Matthew 13:30), and Revelation 14:15 places the time of harvest at the end of the tribulation. *The order of gatherings at the end of the tribulation is what counts.* A rapture seven years earlier, seven years before the time of harvest, does not enter into the order of gatherings at all.

Suppose I told you to buy eggs on Monday. Then on Friday told you to buy meat and eggs in that order—meat first, eggs second. Would you conclude that you were not supposed to buy eggs on Monday because the order would be wrong? Of course not! The order on Friday has nothing to do whatsoever with the purchase on Monday. Likewise, the order of harvest at the end of the tribulation has nothing to do with the rapture at the beginning of the tribulation.

A pre-tribulation rapture does not interfere in any way with the order of gatherings *in the time of harvest*. The rapture does not keep saints and sinners from growing together until the end of the age. The rapture does not interfere with the main point of the parable, that the wicked are not to be rooted out until the end. The rapture does not interfere with a gathering of the righteous *after* the wicked. At no point does a pre-trib rapture make this parable untrue.

For the post-tribulationist, however, problems multiply. Not only does he have to reckon with the *order,* but also if he theorizes a harvest of the wicked *before* the time of harvest, then he is premature on the *time.* Revelation 14:15 nails down the time.

Revelation 14 not only nails down the time; it also confirms the *order* of Matthew 13. That is why I put these passages in parallel columns so that you can see the harmony. If, as post-tribs suppose, verses 14-16 described the rapture, and verses 17-20 described the gathering of the wicked, then Revelation 14 would be *out of order*! However, if we take verses 14-16 as judgment, and verses 17-20 as the gathering resulting from that judgment, then we have no problem with the order, and it harmonizes perfectly with Matthew 13. (For other reasons why

THE PRE-TRIBULATION RAPTURE

Revelation 14:14-16 cannot be the rapture, see our discussion in the previous chapter.)

Concerning the Gathering. If believers are gathered after the tribulation, and if this gathering is not the rapture, then who is gathered and why are they gathered? To find the answer we go to the third feature of our harmony, Mark 13:27 and Matthew 24:31. First of all, notice how these passages confirm the *order* which we have been talking about. Even though these passages omit the harvest of the wicked, we can still perceive an order of events. First Christ comes (the whole world sees Him); *then* He gathers the elect. Have you ever noticed that before? If post-tribulationism were correct we would think that the believers are gathered first, *then* the world sees Him coming in the clouds with the saints. Some post-tribs even guess that there might be a period of several hours between the gathering and the coming. But it's pretty hard to squeeze even one hour in there, because the world sees Him coming *before* He gathers the saints. How ironic! The very verses which have been used to prove a post-trib rapture have the wrong order!

If this is not the rapture gathering, then what gathering is it? Who is gathered, when are they gathered, and how are they gathered? The answer lies in two Old Testament passages, because Matthew 24 and Mark 13 allude to these passages. Whenever the New Testament alludes to the Old Testament, it helps to read the New in light of the Old. This is sound interpretation. Here are the two Old Testament passages:

> And [He shall] gather together the dispersed of Judah from the four corners of the earth (Isaiah 11:12b). (The gathering of verse 12 comes after the slaying of the wicked in verse 4.)

> And ye shall be gathered one by one, O ye children of Israel. And it shall come to pass in that day, that the great trumpet shall be blown, and they shall come which were ready to perish in the land of Assyria, and the outcasts in the land of Egypt, and shall worship the Lord in the holy mount at Jerusalem (Isaiah 27:12b-13).

Which Comes First?

What, then, is the gathering? It is a gathering of *Israel* to *Jerusalem*, not a gathering of the church in the air. (Israel is called the "elect" in Isaiah 45:4 and 65:9.) Furthermore, it is a gathering "one by one," not a gathering en masse. They will come by ship, plane, car, or whatever means of transportation is available, as other nations assist the Israelites in their gathering to the land (Isaiah 49:22 and 66:20).

This chart shows the utter difference between the two gatherings.

WHO?	GATHERING OF ISRAEL	RAPTURE OF THE CHURCH
WHERE?	to Jerusalem	in the clouds
HOW?	one by one	en masse
WHEN?	after the return of Christ	at the return of Christ

Now let's go to the next question. How soon after Christ's return will the gathering of Israel take place? Daniel indicates a 75-day gap between the return of Christ and the beginning of the millennium. Daniel's twelfth chapter mentions three dates, "time, times, and an half" (1260 days), 1290 days, and 1335 days. What happens on these three dates? We saw from chapter two that Christ returns on the 1260th day. But what happens on the other two dates?

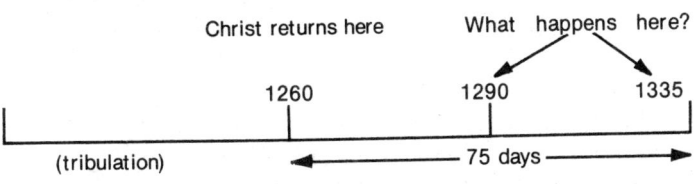

On the last of these dates is Daniel's resurrection, because Daniel 12:13 says, "For thou shalt rest, and stand in thy lot at

THE PRE-TRIBULATION RAPTURE

the *end* of the days." Since the resurrection begins the millennium according to Revelation 20:4, then this makes a 75-day gap between the tribulation and the millennium.

What happens in between? Scripture does not spell it out, but let me share with you my guesses which I think are based on Scripture. You be the judge. The first 30 days allows time for the rooting out of the tares. How will Christ do this? In chapter 10 we will see how Christ treads the winepress, beginning at the Mount of Olives, going to Edom, and returning again in victory. These 30 days of destroying the wicked may be concluded on day 1290 by the chaining of Satan (Revelation 20:1-3).

Then—according to the proper order of Matthew 13, tares first, wheat second—begins the gathering of the elect from the four corners of the earth. They are gathered "one by one" for 45 days. Then on day 1335 the gathering is completed to the uttermost part of heaven as the believing souls join new bodies in the resurrection. Thus this 75-day "time of harvest" allows 30 days for the destruction of the wicked and 45 days for the gathering of the righteous, and it is all according to the proper order of Matthew 13.

This outline of events is one possible way to account for the events which must transpire between the tribulation and the millennium. Maybe I am all wrong, but at least this scheme allows for the proper *order* of gatherings as well as the *time* needed for each (treading the winepress to Edom and gathering "one by one"). It also accounts for the 1260, 1290, and 1335 days of Daniel. If this outline is anywhere near correct, then the post-tribulational gathering occurs weeks after Christ sets His foot upon the earth, not while He is still in the air.

Back to our two Old Testament passages, if you took the time to read the entire chapters of Isaiah 11 and 27 you would see that each context associates the gathering with the *beginning of the millennium.* For example, the gathering occurs *after* the "serpent" is dealt with (Isaiah 27:1—compare the time of the chaining of Satan in Revelation 20:1-3). So even the Old Testament puts the gathering *after* Christ sets His foot

Which Comes First?

upon the earth.

Scripture will harmonize itself if we will let it. I'm not depending on just one or two parables but the united testimony of Matthew 13, Matthew 24:31, Mark 13:27, as well as Isaiah 11:12 and 27:12-13; all combine into a *consistent* testimony concerning the order and time of the gatherings. Overwhelming harmony. And furthermore, *no* passage—I say *no* passage—specifically puts a gathering of the elect of any kind *at* Christ's post-trib return. Surprising absence. Even that favorite verse in the hands of post-tribulationists, Matthew 24:31, turns out to be the opposite of what they thought it was.

We conclude that the very assumption of post-tribs can be used against their own position:

> ... direct unquestioned statements of Scripture that Jesus Christ will return after the tribulation and that the first resurrection will occur after the tribulation, coupled with the absence of statements placing similar events before the tribulation, make it natural to place the rapture of the church after the tribulation. . . .[1]

Reasoning similarly, I could say, "Direct unquestioned statements of Scripture that the gathering of believers is *after* the post-tribulational return, coupled with the *absence* of statements placing such a gathering *at* His post-tribulational return, make it natural to place the rapture of the church at a *time different* than after the tribulation."

The weakness of post-tribulationism now comes to light. They assume a post-trib rapture *contrary* to the order and time of gatherings. We now see that the assumptions are on the other side. Pre-tribulationists now have the impregnable position, because there is nothing forbidding a rapture before the tribulation, whereas the order of gatherings forbids any rapture after the tribulation.

Nothing Forbidden. We have said that nothing in Scripture forbids a pre-trib rapture. Some may think that Acts 3:21 for-

THE PRE-TRIBULATION RAPTURE

bids it because it says of Christ, "Whom the heaven must receive until the times of restitution, of all thing." If Christ must remain in heaven until the restitution, that is, until He sets up His kingdom upon the earth, then this prevents Him from leaving heaven for a pre-trib rapture, so the argument goes.

The whole argument stands or falls on the definition of the word "heaven." "Heaven" is used in different ways in the Bible. "Heaven" can be where God lives, or "heaven" can be where the birds fly, or "heaven" can include both. Flip back a couple chapters from Acts 3:21 and look at Acts 1:9-11:

> And when he had spoken these things, while they beheld, he was taken up; and a cloud received him out of their sight. And while they looked stedfastly toward *heaven* as he went up, behold two men stood by them in white apparel; which also said, Ye men of Galilee, why stand ye gazing up into *heaven*? this same Jesus, which is taken up from you into *heaven*, shall so come in like manner as ye have seen him go into *heaven*.

Into which heaven were the men gazing? Could they see up into the heaven where God lives? No, all they could see was the heaven where the clouds were. Into which heaven did Christ ascend? Into the heaven of clouds *and* into the heaven beyond.

If Acts 1 uses "heaven" in this way, why not Acts 3? Thus the argument disappears. At the rapture when Christ meets us in the air He remains in the cloudy heaven and the requirements of the verse are fulfilled. To disprove a pre-trib rapture one would have to prove that "heaven" excludes the cloudy heaven.

Another passage used similarly against pre-tribulationism is Hebrews 10:12-13. But "henceforth" in the original language refers to *time,* not to *location.*

Therefore, no verse, not Acts 3:21, not Hebrews 10:12-13, nor any other verse forbids a pre-trib rapture. But the order of gatherings forbids a post-trib rapture.

It is asserted that the burden of proof rests on the pre-tribulationists. We already *know* that Christ will return *after* the tribulation; so it is up to pre-tribulationists to prove that He will come at *another* time. I agree. It is only proper and fair that we assume this burden of proof; so that is what I have done in this chapter. I have faced the issue squarely and have given *Scriptural evidence* that the *order* and *time* of gatherings is wrong for a post-trib rapture. In light of this evidence, the burden of proof has now *shifted* to the post-tribulationists.

1. Gundry, *The Church and the Tribulation,* p. 10.

"The one shall be taken, and the other shall be left" (Luke 17:34).

9
Luke Seventeen

Luke 17 provides further powerful proof of the order of gatherings, as if the harmony of several passages so far were not enough. "I tell you, in that night there shall be two men in one bed; the one shall be taken, and the other shall be left" (Luke 17:34). Who is the one taken? Who is the one left? At the rapture, of course, believers are taken. But at the end of the tribulation, it happens again, only the other way around. *Un*believers are taken. It is like a rapture in reverse.

Surprising? Let us see what Luke 17 says.

When I first read Luke 17, I ran into some interpretive problems, and I couldn't figure out what it was saying. Why does God allow problems in the Bible? Problems we find in the Bible are not there to tease us, but to cause us to dig deeper to find solutions and thereby to discover things we would otherwise never dream of. Problems make us study the Bible. If it were easy we wouldn't study it as much. Once we solve the problems in Luke 17, we will have another strong evidence for pretribulationism.

"DAY" AND "DAYS"

The first problem I had when I read Luke 17 is the confusing

Luke Seventeen

use of "day" and "days" (verses 22-37). What time period is meant? Is it the tribulation period, the end of the tribulation, or the millennial kingdom? Does "day" mean one thing and "days" mean another? The usage is not consistent, and this bothered me until I finally came to accept the fact that "day" and "days" are used in a loose sense, not in a technical sense. Luke uses the words in different ways, depending on the context, just as we do sometimes. Once I stopped getting bogged down in tight meanings, I discovered that each context makes each word clear. Luke was not a careless writer because, as we shall see, he compiled Jesus' words in a beautiful and orderly manner which makes the meaning clear in the end.

As an example of the loose terminology, "the days of the Son of man" in verse 22 refers to the kingdom period (see verses 20-24). On the other hand, verse 26 uses "the days of the Son of man" for the tribulation period because of the comparison to the days of Noah *before* the flood. But in verse 24 "day" pinpoints the *end* of the tribulation. If we hold to strict terminology we become hopelessly confused. If we allow the *context* to interpret the terms for us, everything remains clear.

A particularly tough case is verses 30-31. Is the time *after* the tribulation or *during* the tribulation?

> 26. And as it was in the days of Noe, so shall it be also in the days of the Son of man.
> 27. They did eat, they drank, they married wives, they were given in marriage, until the day that Noe entered into the ark, and the flood came, and destroyed them all.
> 28. Likewise also as it was in the days of Lot; they did eat, they drank, they bought, they sold, they planted, they builded;
> 29. But the same day that Lot went out of Sodom it rained fire and brimstone from heaven, and destroyed them all.
> 30. Even thus shall it be in the day when the Son of man is revealed.
> 31. In that day, he which shall be upon the housetop, and his stuff in the house, let him not come down to take it away: and he that is in the field, let him likewise not return back.

Verse 30 is *after* the tribulation because that is when "all the wicked" are destroyed (see verses 27 and 29). On the other hand, verse 31 stretches the term "day" to include the tribulation period because it takes us back to the abomination of desolation (see Matthew 24:15-21). So we have to let the context rule and let the terminology be flexible. Context is rule number one in interpretation.

NOAH AND LOT

With the flexible use of "day" and "days" in the back of our minds, we learn from Luke 17 the answer to two questions concerning Noah and Lot. First, who do Noah and Lot typify? Church saints or tribulation saints? They typify tribulation saints. Here is why.

Jesus is explaining the events which immediately precede the visible aspect of the kingdom. The days of Noah and Lot immediately precede the *total destruction* of the wicked (which happens at the *end* of the tribulation), not *partial destruction* (which happens *during* the tribulation). In other words, Noah's flood symbolizes Armageddon, not the tribulation itself. (In another application of Noah's flood, 2 Peter 3 makes the destruction by water a foretaste of destruction by fire after the millennium—both water and fire cleanse the old world preparing the way for the new.) Lot's wife who was slow to flee Sodom typifies those who are slow to flee at the abomination of desolation, and this is *during* the tribulation. Verse 37 mentions the eagles being gathered together over dead bodies, and this happens at the end of the tribulation (see Matthew 24:28). All these considerations from the context reveal that Noah and Lot represent saints *during the tribulation period.*

Second question, what does the *escape to safety* of Noah and Lot represent? "Noah entered into the ark" and "Lot went out of Sodom." What parallel do these escapes have in the latter days? Is it the rapture? Primarily Luke applies it to those who escape at the abomination of desolation at the midpoint of the tribulation (compare verse 31 to Matthew 24:15-18). Lot's wife represents those who hesitate at this time while Lot typifies

Luke Seventeen

those who quickly flee without turning back (see Genesis 19:26).

Why does Luke make a special point of escaping at this time? Why this time rather than some other time? As we discussed in chapter two, the abomination of desolation is the point when antichrist assumes world prominence and this is when he begins his persecution of the saints. At the abomination people are forced to decide. Will they follow Christ or antichrist? They are forced to decide because at this point, or shortly thereafter, they are forced "to receive a mark in their right hand, or in their foreheads" (Revelation 13:16). Since "no man might buy or sell, save he that had the mark" (Revelation 13:17), men will be tempted to save their lives by accepting the mark. Those who refuse the mark may lose their lives. It will be a tough decision for many and that is why Luke records in verse 33:

> Whosoever shall seek to save his life shall lose it; and whosoever shall lose his life shall preserve it.

The truth of these words comes to light in Revelation 14:9b-10:

> If any man worship the beast and his image, and receive his mark in his forehead, or in his hand, the same shall drink of the wine of the wrath of God, which is poured out without mixture into the cup of his indignation; and he shall be tormented with fire and brimstone in the presence of the holy angels, and in the presence of the Lamb.

In other words, Jesus is saying in Luke 17:31-33, "Do not give in to antichrist and the temporary security his mark offers. Don't remain behind and become part of the system, but flee; seek eternal salvation rather than temporal salvation. Lot's wife is an example for anyone who wants to remain a part of the system." Of course, the disciples did not understand all these implications when Jesus spoke, but He spoke *through* the disciples *to* the saints who would be alive at that time.

THE PRE-TRIBULATION RAPTURE

Although Luke applies the escapes of Noah and Lot primarily to those who flee at the midpoint of the tribulation, it is evident that all those saved during the entire seven-year period also "enter into the ark of safety" since they also escape the destruction. The flexible use of "day" allows for this extended time period. Just as the abomination of desolation occurs the "same day"—so to speak—as the day the Son of man is revealed (verses 30-31), so also believers "enter the ark of safety" the "same day" the final destruction comes (verses 27,29,31). The usage of "day" in these verses indicates that the seven-year period is all one day of entering the ark as far as God is concerned. The seven years of entering might be illustrated in that Noah took seven days to gather everything into the ark (Genesis 7:1-10).

One more observation. If the entire seven-year period amounts to "one day" of entering the ark of safety, and if *all* the saved of that period are like Noah who enters the ark, then those who "enter the ark" at the *very beginning,* namely those raptured, might also be included in the ark of safety. We cannot be positive of this, but since "day" is used of the entire period it may include the beginning also. I include this, not as proof, but as a matter of interest.

"ONE SHALL BE TAKEN"

Now we come to the crucial question. The previous questions about the escapes of Noah and Lot have prepared us for this one.

> I tell you, in that night there shall be two men in one bed; the one shall be taken, and the other shall be left. Two women shall be grinding together; the one shall be taken, and the other left. Two men shall be in the field; the one shall be taken, and the other left (Luke 17:34-36).

The question here should not be "*When?*" but "*Who?*" We already know *when.* Since Noah and Lot represent tribulation saints, and since this entire section is in a tribulation context as we have pointed out earlier, then the time has to be *after* the

Luke Seventeen

tribulation. Of course, I happen to believe that "the one shall be taken, and the other left" before the tribulation also, but that is not what this passage is talking about. This passage is *after* the tribulation. Remember verse 37 compared with Matthew 24:28 nails down the time pretty tightly.

Now let's get to the crucial question. Who? Who is the one taken? And who is the one left? Post-tribs say believers are taken in rapture. But pre-tribs say unbelievers are taken in judgment since the rapture occurred seven years earlier. Who is taken? Believers or unbelievers?

The disciples asked where they are taken, and Jesus' answer is revealing. He said, "Wheresoever the body is, thither will the eagles be gathered together" (verse 37). "Eagles" is better translated "vultures" (birds of prey), and "body" is explained in Matthew 24:28 as "corpse." Vultures. Corpse. What does that tell you about who is taken? "Vultures" and "corpse" are not exactly a fitting description for the destination of believers. Those taken are *unbelievers.*

Further evidence. I want to show from the context, from the flow of thought in this entire section, that there is only one possible answer to who is taken. When we finish you will not only see the answer to our question, but you will see that Luke is a very organized writer, living up to his name as a reputable historian.

I've found that in trying to figure out the flow of thought in a passage, an outline helps me best. The outline is a valuable tool in the interpreter's kit. Notice from the following outline that Luke recorded Jesus' words in a very organized manner.

OUTLINE OF LUKE 17:20-37

I. Answer to the Pharisees—you expect the kingdom wrongly (20-21)
II. Answer to the disciples—here is how to expect the kingdom rightly (22-37)
   A. Do not expect to be able to watch it come gradual-

THE PRE-TRIBULATION RAPTURE

        ly (22-23)
- B. Do expect it to come suddenly (24-37)
    1. Its suddenness and its delay (24-25)
    2. The sudden coming illustrated (26-37)
        a. The examples of Noah and Lot—escape and destruction (26-30)
        b. The explanation of the examples (31-37)
            1) The escape from destruction (31-33)
            2) The taking in destruction (34-37)

Beginning with the examples of Noah and Lot we notice two main threads of thought, *escape* and *destruction*. Read closely: "Noah entered into the ark [escape], and the flood came and destroyed them all [destruction]." "The same day that Lot went out of Sodom [escape] it rained fire and brimstone from heaven, and destroyed them all [destruction]." That's not all. Both threads of thought have their parallel in the last days, for "according to these things [literal Greek] shall it be in the day when the Son of man is revealed" (verse 30).

The latter-day parallel includes *both* escape and destruction, just as the examples of Noah and Lot did. *Escape* is explained in verses 31-33 ("let him likewise not return back . . . whosoever shall lose his life shall preserve it") while *destruction* is explained in verses 34-37 ("one shall be taken"). It is all very organized. Jesus mentions the escape of Noah first; afterwards the destruction of the flood. He mentions the escape of Lot first; afterwards the destruction of Sodom. Likewise, in the latter-day parallel, He explains the escape first (31-33); afterwards the destruction (34-37). It matches perfectly. See how the passage fits together into a smooth flow of thought?

Luke Seventeen

	ESCAPE	DESTRUCTION
EXAMPLES	Noah entered into the ark	the flood came and destroyed them all
	Lot went out of Sodom	it rained fire and brimstone from heaven and destroyed them all
EXPLANATION OF EXAMPLES	In that day, he which shall be upon the housetop, and his stuff in the house, let him not come down to take it away: and he that is in the field, let him likewise not return back. Remember Lot's wife. Whosoever shall seek to save his life shall lose it; and whosoever shall lose his life shall preserve it (verses 31-33).	I tell you, in that night there shall be two men in one bed; the one shall be taken, and the other shall be left. Two women shall be grinding together; the one shall be taken, and the other left. Two men shall be in the field; the one shall be taken, and the other left. Where the corpse lies, the vultures will gather (verses 34-37).

Even thus shall it be in the day when the Son of man is revealed

The outline makes it clear that verses 34-37 explain *destruction* rather than escape. For if they explained escape, then the entire section (verses 31-37) would dwell on escape and where would be the reference to destruction? The explanation would not fit the example; it would make the entire section disjointed. The escapes of Noah and Lot would have latter-day parallel, but the destruction would have no parallel.

Rather than omitting the destruction of the latter days, it is given the stronger emphasis in verses 34-37. Of the two themes, destruction is more prominent than escape. In the example of Noah, destruction is a main part of the sentence, while Noah's escape is confined to a subordinate clause. Identically with Lot.

And likewise with the latter-day parallel. Even the escape paragraph (31-33) has destruction in close view in the background as though to make the reader expect an account of the destruction shortly. Our expectations are met as verses 34-37 answer how the one who saves his life shall lose it. As destruction is prominent from the beginning, so the passage winds up with destruction as the climax.

Now that we understand the point of verses 34-37, that it explains the climactic destruction of the latter days, it becomes clear that "the one shall be taken" in judgment, not rapture. Who is taken? Unbelievers. Who is left? Believers.

It is like a rapture in reverse. And since believers are *not* "taken" after the tribulation, this is formidable evidence that there is *no rapture after the tribulation*!

One post-trib to whom I have written surprisingly agrees that the wicked are "taken" and the righteous are "left." It is surprising because if the righteous are "left" they are not left for long according to the post-trib scheme. Only seconds later they too are "caught up" at the rapture. He may solve one problem this way, but he runs squarely into another problem: "Who will populate the millennium?" If all the wicked are "taken," then by his own admission no one is left with natural bodies to populate the millennium. He has run from a lion and into a bear.

It might be objected that Luke is emphasizing the destruction of the "one left" instead of the "one taken." This cannot stand, however, because the disciples ask, "Where?" In other words, "Where are they *taken*?" It makes no sense to ask, "Where are they left?" The disciples' question assumes the prominence of "taken"; so unbelievers are *taken* in destruction rather than left for destruction.

Since believers are *not* the ones taken after the tribulation, evidence for a post-trib rapture has vanished. Rapture in reverse? Yes. Rapture? No.

To sustain a rapture after the tribulation, post-tribulationists would have to make an adjustment or two in Luke 17. They would have to interrupt Luke's smooth flow of thought by making "one taken and one left" represent escape rather than destruction. Thus the escape of Noah and Lot would be paralleled *twice* (verse 31 *and* verses 34-37) and the destruction by the flood and the destruction of Sodom would be deprived of a latter-day parallel. Or they may prefer to adjust the disciples' question to mean, "Where are they left?" Finally, they would have to adjust the Lord's answer and change the meaning of "vultures" and "corpse."

Even if they succeed in making all these adjustments, they still have to reckon with the WINEPRESS. . . .

"And the angel thrust in his sickle into the earth, and gathered the vine of the earth, and cast it into the great winepress of the wrath of God. And the winepress was trodden without the city, and blood came out of the winepress, even unto the horse bridles, by the space of a thousand and six hundred furlongs [200 miles]" (Revelation 14:19-20).

10
The Winepress

The most terrifying ordeal for any human being, outside of hell itself—what is it? The winepress.

I want to tell you about the winepress because it will demonstrate the harmony of the Bible by answering several puzzling questions and because it will teach us some important principles about God and our lives. Here are some of the questions we hope to answer in this chapter:

If after the tribulation "the one shall be taken, and the other left" (Luke 17:35), *where* is the one taken to?

If blood comes out of the winepress as high as the horse bridles for as long as 200 miles (Revelation 14:20), where does all that blood come from?

If blood flows out of the winepress beginning at Jerusalem for 200 miles, to where does the 200 miles extend?

With that much blood flowing out of the winepress, where does it empty out?

I would like to show you how the Bible answers all these questions with one harmonious story. These questions are only a sample. As we go along you will see that several other ques-

The Winepress

tions also find their solution as the Bible talks about the winepress.

WHERE ARE THEY TAKEN?

In the last chapter we examined Luke 17 which says that at the end of the tribulation this will happen:

> Two men shall be in the field; the one shall be taken, and the other left. And they answered and said unto him, Where, Lord? (Luke 17:36-37a).

The disciples questioned, "Where?" The last chapter left this question hanging in the air and we hope now to answer the question, "Where are they taken?"

Of course, God could take them and supernaturally kill them. He could just zap them and that would be the end of them. But God has a habit of using *natural* means to destroy wicked people. To destroy the old world He used a flood. To destroy Sodom and Gomorrah He used fire and brimstone. I believe the end-time destruction is no exception. He will use natural means. So we ask the question, "Where are the wicked taken?"

Let's look at Jesus' answer to the disciples' question:

> And they answered and said unto him, Where, Lord? And he said unto them, Wheresoever the body is, thither will the eagles be gathered together (Luke 17:37).

Does Jesus' answer tell you anything? He did not come right out and tell the disciples the whole story right away. But He did give a hint. He said that their bodies will be taken to the same place to where the eagles will gather. Where does this clue lead you? It leads me to Revelation 19:15b-18:

> . . . He treadeth the winepress of the fierceness and wrath of Almighty God. . . . And I saw an angel standing in the sun; and he cried with a loud voice, saying to all the fowls that fly in the midst of heaven, Come and gather yourselves together unto the supper of the great God; that ye may

THE PRE-TRIBULATION RAPTURE

> eat the flesh of kings, and the flesh of captains, and the flesh of mighty men, and the flesh of horses, and of them that sit on them, *and the flesh of all men,* both free and bond, both small and great.

Where is this place? It is in the vicinity of Jerusalem because this is where the armies descend according to Zechariah 12:2,9. Yes, the armies are there with their kings and captains, and the birds will feast on their flesh, but more than that, the birds will feast on the flesh of *all men.* This is the place they are taken to. This is the winepress. (Also see Isaiah 34:15 and context.)

We arrived at this answer by comparing two passages. But is there a single passage which tells the whole story at once? Yes, there is. Revelation 14:19-20 says:

> And the angel thrust in his sickle into the earth, and gathered the vine of the earth, and cast it into the great winepress of the wrath of God. And the winepress was trodden without the city [Jerusalem], and blood came out of the winepress, even unto the horse bridles, by the space of a thousand and six hundred furlongs.

This single passage combines the taking, the casting, and the location. At Christ's return, all unbelievers from all over the globe are instantly taken and cast into the winepress just outside Jerusalem.

At this point some might wonder, "Isn't Revelation 14:19-20 figurative?" Two generations ago Bullinger wrote:

> Whereas today, *"Figurative language"* is ignorantly spoken of as though it made less of the meaning, and deprived the words of their power and force. A passage of God's Word is quoted; and it is met with the cry, "Oh, that is figurative"—implying that it's meaning is weakened, or that it has quite a different meaning, or that it has no meaning at all. But the very opposite is the case. For an unusual form (*figura*) is never used except to *add* force to the truth conveyed, emphasis to the statement of it, and depth to the meaning of it.[1]

Yes, it is figurative. But any figure of speech has a literal meaning behind it. The figure of the sickle stands for reaping men. The figure of the vine stands for unbelieving men. The figure of the winepress stands for Christ treading on men. And the location is not figurative; that is plainly given. Read it again:

> And the angel thrust in his sickle into the earth, and gathered the vine of the earth ["the one shall be taken, and the other left"], and cast it ["Where, Lord?"] into the great winepress of the wrath of God. And the winepress was trodden without the city.

SO MUCH BLOOD?

This conveniently answers the question, "Where does all that blood come from?"

> And the winepress was trodden without the city, and blood came out of the winepress, even unto the horse bridles, by the space of a thousand and six hundred furlongs [almost two hundred miles].

Even if you were to pack the Armageddon armies together like sardines, you still could not drain enough blood from them to reach the horse bridles for a distance of 200 miles. Their bodies alone would hardly fill that distance. It would take more than the armies. It would take every unbelieving body in the whole world to be cast into one place, like grapes piled into a winepress, in order to have a source for that much blood.

In this way we are free to interpret Scripture *literally*. There remains no need to say this blood is figurative or an exaggeration. It is real.

WHICH DIRECTION?

If the winepress begins outside Jerusalem, which direction does it extend? North to Armageddon? No, the distance from Jerusalem to Armageddon falls far short of 200 miles. Apparently, Armageddon is a place for the assembling of armies, not for the battle itself. After the armies assemble, they converge on Jerusalem according to Zechariah 12:2,9.

Does the winepress extend to the west? No, the Mediterranean Sea is in the way.

How about east? Zechariah 14:4 says:

THE PRE-TRIBULATION RAPTURE

> And his feet shall stand in that day upon the mount of Olives, which is before Jerusalem *on the east,* and the mount of Olives shall cleave in the midst thereof toward the east and toward the west, and there shall be a very great valley; and half of the mountain shall remove toward the north, and half of it toward the south.

When the mountain splits in two what do we have? We have a newly-formed valley running eastward outside Jerusalem. Does this mean that blood runs out of the winepress for 200 miles going straight east? We are coming to that in a moment. But first a question about the valley itself.

WHAT HAPPENS IN THE VALLEY?

What is the purpose of this valley formed by the splitting of the mount of Olives? Some feel that it will provide a shelter for the saints as they flee into it. Let us consider the possibility, though, that those fleeing into this valley are *unbelievers.* Instead of a shelter, the valley may be a *trap.* The next verse says:

> And ye shall flee to the valley of the mountains; for the valley of the mountains shall reach unto Azal: yea, ye shall flee, like as ye fled from before the earthquake in the days of Uzziah king of Judah: and the Lord my God shall come, and all the saints with thee (Zechariah 14:5).

Picture unbelievers fleeing with terror into the valley, with God and the saints in hot pursuit. What do they do after they are trapped in the valley? Revelation 6:12-17 gives the awful picture:

> And I beheld when he had opened the sixth seal, and, lo, there was a great earthquake; and the sun became black as sackcloth of hair, and the moon became as blood; and the stars of heaven fell unto the earth, even as a fig tree casteth her untimely figs, when she is shaken of a mighty wind.

Matthew 24:29 places these signs *after* the tribulation.

The Winepress

And the heaven departed as a scroll when it is rolled together; and every mountain and island were moved out of their places.

And the kings of the earth, and the great men, and the rich men, and the chief captains, and the mighty men, *and every bondman, and every free man,* hid themselves in the dens and in the rocks of the mountains;

And said to the mountains and rocks, Fall on us, and hide us from the face of him that sitteth on the throne, and from the wrath of the Lamb: for the great day of his wrath is come; and who shall be able to stand?

This may be the point of Christ's return.

Every man, not just the armies, are here because they were "taken" and cast into this place.

This has to be *after* Christ's return, because *before* Christ's return people are peacefully working or sleeping (Luke 17:34-36).

For the reasons given above at the side, I believe this passage describes people cowering in the valley of the winepress.

WHICH VALLEY?

The valley of the mountains (formed by the east-west splitting of the mount of Olives as Christ sets foot on it) would form a suitable winepress where the Son of man could vent His fury upon those who blasphemed His name. There is another valley, however, which we should consider:

> I will also gather all nations, and will bring them down into the *valley of Jehoshaphat,* and will plead with them there. . . .
>
> Let the heathen be wakened, and come up to the *valley of Jehoshaphat:* for there will I sit to judge all the heathen round about. Put ye in the sickle, for the harvest is ripe: come [tread], for the press is full, the [vats] overflow; for their wickedness is great. Multitudes, multitudes in the *valley of decision:* for the day of the Lord is near in the *valley of decision* (Joel 3:2a, 12-14).

"Jehoshaphat" in Hebrew means "Jehovah judges." The valley of Jehoshaphat is where the Lord judges. That is why it

THE PRE-TRIBULATION RAPTURE

is also called the valley of decision (the Lord's decision to punish the wicked).

Where is this valley of Jehoshaphat? No one knows for sure, but it seems to be close to Jerusalem. Church tradition says it is the valley of Kidron east of Jerusalem. Maybe it is the valley which will be formed by the splitting of the mount of Olives, and maybe not. At any rate, these two valleys, the valley of the mountains and the valley of Jehoshaphat, should be considered as likely sites for the winepress. (Perhaps both constitute the winepress as men flee from one valley to the other or as the blood runs from one to the other. The ancient presses for grapes had two troughs, one for the trampling, and one for the juice to run into. The armies gather ahead of time to the valley of Jehoshaphat. If it forms part of the winepress, then the angels gather the rest of the wicked also into it. Apparently the bloody winepress will be cleansed later by the river from the sanctuary in Jerusalem. See Zechariah 14:8 and Ezekiel 47:1-5.)

HOW FAR

We have seen that Christ first touches earth on the mount of Olives and begins trampling outside Jerusalem on the east. How far does He go? According to Isaiah the Lord thrusts into Bozrah, the capital of Edom. This is across the Jordan river to the east. Read the graphic description in Isaiah 34:3-8:

> Their slain also shall be cast out, and their stink shall come up out of their carcases, and the mountains shall be melted with their blood. And all the host of heaven shall be dissolved, and the heavens shall be rolled together as a scroll: and all their host shall fall down, as the leaf falleth off from the vine, and as a falling fig from the fig tree [compare these events to Revelation 6:13-14 which we quoted earlier]. For my sword shall be bathed in heaven: behold, it shall come down upon Idumea, and upon the people of my curse, to judgment. The sword of the Lord is filled with blood [compare this sword to the one at Christ's return in Revelation 19:15,21]; it is made fat with fatness, and with the blood of lambs and goats, with the fat of the kidneys of rams: for the Lord hath a sacrifice in Bozrah, and a great slaughter in the land of Idumea. And the unicorns shall come down with

The Winepress

them, and the bullocks with the bulls; and their land shall be soaked with blood, and their dust made fat with fatness. For it is the day of the Lord's vengeance, and the year of recompences for the controversy of Zion.

Once you know about the winepress, you see that the Bible is full of it. The classic Old Testament passage on the winepress is Isaiah 63:1-6:

Who is this that cometh from Edom, with dyed garments from Bozrah? this that is glorious in his apparel, travelling in the greatness of his strength? I that speak in righteousness, mighty to save. Wherefore art thou red in thine apparel, and thy garments like him that treadeth in the winefat? I have trodden the winepress alone; and of the people there was none with me: for I will tread them in mine anger, and trample them in my fury; and their blood shall be sprinkled upon my garments, and I will stain all my raiment. For the day of vengeance is in mine heart, and the year of my redeemed is come. And I looked, and there was none to help; and I wondered that there was none to uphold: therefore mine own arm brought salvation unto me; and my fury, it upheld me. And I will tread down the people in mine anger, and make them drunk in my fury, and I will bring down their strength to the earth.

This passage pictures the Lord returning in victory from Bozrah in Edom. It also vividly pictures His personal vengeance and active fury, a side of God that we need to know about.

WHERE DOES IT EMPTY?

If you are checking your map closely you are noticing that Bozrah is not *directly* to the east of Jerusalem. To get to Bozrah you have to *cross the Jordan river* and then *curve southward.* Also you will notice that Bozrah is *not* 200 miles from Jerusalem. It is less. Remember, Revelation 14:20 says, "Blood came out of the winepress . . . by the space of a thousand and six hundred furlongs [200 miles]."

Even if Bozrah is less than 200 miles from Jerusalem, the geography has given us a clue to pursue. If you were to continue drawing the line southward from Bozrah, where would you end up? The Red Sea! How far is that from Jerusalem?

Two hundred miles! This provides a most satisfying answer to the question, "Where does all the blood drain out?" The Red Sea has a continuous current, the top waters flowing in and the undercurrent flowing out. A most logical place.

But is there any Scripture to support it? Jeremiah 49:7-22 tells the story of Edom's destruction. The destruction begins when the Lord "shall come up like a lion from the swelling of Jordan" (verse 19). After He crosses Jordan He curves southward to Bozrah (verse 22). Finally, "the noise thereof was heard in the Red Sea" (verse 21)!

The winepress theory is not finished with answering questions. Here is another one. Why was the Red Sea named the Red Sea? No one seems to know. They can only speculate as to the reasons. But I believe that God, who knows the outcome of all things, looked ahead to the ultimate purpose the sea would fulfill, and He caused it to be named the Red Sea because the blood of His vengeance would turn it red.

PROPHECY IN COLOR

Can a color be a prophecy? Not only is the Red Sea prophetic, but also the name "Edom," the country of the winepress, is prophetic. "Edom" means "red." If you go back to the story of Jacob and Esau you will see prophecy in embryo:

> And when her days to be delivered were fulfilled, behold, there were twins in her womb. And the first came out red, all over like an hairy garment; and they called his name Esau. And after that came his brother out, and his hand took hold on Esau's heel; and his name was called Jacob . . . and the boys grew . . . And Esau said to Jacob, Feed me, I pray thee, with that same red pottage; for I am faint: therefore was his name called Edom (excerpts from Genesis 25:24-30).

Esau's name was changed to Edom and Jacob's name was changed to Israel. The two brothers became two nations, and ever since the beginning Edom has been an enemy of Israel. But as "Edom" means "red," it pictures the land being soaked with blood in the latter days.

The Winepress

HOW WILL IT HAPPEN?

The winepress theory has answered many questions that would otherwise remain unanswered, and it has demonstrated the harmony of the Bible. The strength of this theory is that it allows many Scriptures to be interpreted in their plain and normal sense. It is a weak position that has to resort to figurative or imaginative interpretations.

We will solve more puzzles later, but right now let's back up and ask, *How* does this all happen? *How* will the wicked be taken and cast into the winepress? *How* will Christ tread the winepress?

This is not an area for dogmatism; all I can do is share with you what the Scripture says on these subjects. First, let's take the question, "How are the wicked taken and cast into the winepress?" On one occasion before, two men were standing together. One was taken and the other was left. How was he taken? The two men were Elijah and Elisha. Elijah was taken by a whirlwind (2 Kings 2:11).

Of course, Elijah was not an unbeliever and we are talking about unbelievers being taken. But the example of Elijah proves the possibility. It shows that a *literal whirlwind* could take somebody away. It happened once; it *could* happen again. Read what the following Scriptures have to say about this:

> Therefore prophesy thou against them all these words, and say unto them, The Lord shall roar from on high, and utter his voice from his holy habitation; he shall mightily roar upon his habitation; he shall give a shout, as they that *tread the grapes,* against *all* the inhabitants of the earth. A noise shall come even to the ends of the earth; for the Lord hath a controversy with the nations, he will plead with *all* flesh; he will give them that are wicked to the sword, saith the Lord. Thus saith the Lord of hosts, Behold, evil shall go forth from nation to nation, and a great *whirlwind* shall be raised up from the coasts of the earth. And the slain of the Lord shall be at that day from one end of the earth even unto the other end of the earth ["earth" can be translated "land"]: they shall not be lamented, neither gathered, nor buried; they shall be dung upon the ground (Jeremiah 25:30-33).
>
> Behold, the *whirlwind* of the Lord goeth forth with fury, a continuing

> whirlwind: it shall fall with pain upon the head of the wicked. The fierce anger of the Lord shall not return, until he have done it, and until he have performed the intents of his heart: in the *latter days* ye shall consider it (Jeremiah 30:23-24; see also Jeremiah 23:19-20; Isaiah 40:22-24; Psalm 58:9-10; Proverbs 1:27-28).

As you read these Scriptures you can decide for yourself what will happen. Personally, I suspect that a whirlwind of some sort will take the wicked away to the winepress.

HOW WILL CHRIST TREAD THE WINEPRESS?

When Christ treads the winepress will He literally stomp on men's bodies as a treader of grapes tramples the grapes? I wouldn't rule this out, because we already read about His personal vengeance in Isaiah 63:1-6, and we read there how the blood will be splattered all over His garment so that it looks like it was dyed red.

I do not know exactly how Christ will trample, but the Bible does give us a preview of methods of destruction He will use. He will use a sword, probably not a sword of metal because this sword comes out of His mouth instead of being held in His hand:

> And out of his mouth goeth a sharp sword, that with it he should smite the nations: and he shall rule them with a rod of iron: and he treadeth the winepress of the fierceness and wrath of Almighty God (Revelation 19:15).

> For my sword shall be bathed in heaven: behold, it shall come down upon Idumea [Edom], and upon the people of my curse, to judgment. The sword of the Lord is filled with blood, it is made fat with fatness, and with the blood of lambs and goats, with the fat of the kidneys of rams: for the Lord hath a sacrifice in Bozrah, and a great slaughter in the land of Idumea (Isaiah 34:5-6).

Since the sword comes out of His mouth it probably represents the dynamic power of His spoken Word (compare Ephesians 6:17) to harness the forces of nature. He will say, "Fire," and there will be fire:

> Our God shall come, and shall not keep silence: a *fire* shall devour before him, and it shall be very tempestuous round about him (Psalm 50:3).

> A *fire* goeth before him, and burneth up his enemies round about. His lightnings enlightened the world: the earth saw, and trembled. The hills melted like wax at the presence of the Lord, at the presence of the Lord of the whole earth (Psalm 97:3-5).

> For, behold, the Lord will come with *fire,* and with his chariots like a whirlwind, to render his anger with fury, and his rebuke with flames of *fire.* For by *fire* and by his sword will the Lord plead with all flesh: and the slain of the Lord shall be many (Isaiah 66:15-17).

As the Lord tramples he will shout, "Hail," and suddenly 125-pound stones will rain from the sky:

> And there fell upon men a great hail out of heaven, every stone about the weight of a talent: and men blasphemed God because of the plague of the hail; for the plague thereof was exceeding great (Revelation 16:21).

THE SEVENTH VIAL

At this point some sharp Bible student may ask, "How did hail get into the winepress? I thought the hail happened *during* the tribulation, not after."

It is true that the hail is part of the seven vials which the angels pour out in the book of Revelation. But the hail is in the *seventh* vial (Revelation 16:17-21), and part of the seventh vial is *after* the tribulation, *after* the return of Christ.

Why do I say this? All right, let me give you a riddle. Revelation 15:1 says, "And I saw another sign in heaven, great and marvellous, seven angels having the seven last plagues; for in them is filled up the wrath of God." Now, if all seven vials were completed *during* the tribulation, and if the seven vials "fill up" the wrath of God, then how can there be any more wrath in the winepress which follows? You see, if the wrath of God is "filled up" in the seven vials, then part of the seventh vial has to include the winepress. This is how hail gets into the winepress.

Placing the return of Christ *during* the seventh vial, instead of after it, harmonizes with the rest of Revelation. We have already seen that Christ returns *during* the sixth seal (Revelation 6:12-17; compare Matthew 24:29). Likewise, Christ returns *during* the seventh trumpet, because during the seventh trumpet "it is done" (Revelation 16:17). Whether it is seals, trumpets, or vials, it is the last one in each series during which Christ returns.

MANY SCRIPTURES HARMONIZE

Once you know about the winepress many Scriptures open up with new light. For example, look what it does to an ordinary passage like Proverbs 2:21-22:

> For the upright shall dwell in the land, and the perfect shall remain in it. But the wicked shall be cut off from the earth, and the transgressors shall be rooted out of it.

Another example is Psalm 110:

> The Lord said unto my Lord, Sit thou at my right hand, until I make thine enemies thy footstool. . . . He shall fill the places with the dead bodies.

As Christ treads the winepress His enemies literally become His footstool (compare 1 Corinthians 15:24-26). I believe this Psalm is fulfilled at the winepress because Christ remains in heaven only "until," not "after," His enemies become His footstool.

THE SHEEP-GOATS JUDGMENT

The winepress theory is a possible answer to another question that Gundry has pointed out. He says pre-tribs face a dilemma because we apparently leave no "goats" for the sheep-goats judgment. We believe all the wicked shall be taken away after the tribulation (Luke 17:34-36). If this is true, then where do the "goats" come from in the following account:

> When the Son of man shall come in his glory, and all the holy angels with

The Winepress

> him, then shall he sit upon the throne of his glory: and before him shall be gathered all nations: and he shall separate them one from another, as a shepherd divideth his sheep from the goats: And he shall set the sheep on his right hand, but the goats on the left (Matthew 25:31-33).

How can any wicked remain to face this judgment if they have all been taken away previously? A possible answer is simply this: the taking and casting into the winepress is the result of the judgment. Judgment first, winepress second. This solves the problem logically, but is there Scripture to back it up?

Fortunately Scripture does not leave us in the dark. Joel 3:2, 12-14 does us the favor of linking the judgment and the winepress together:

> I will also gather all nations, and will bring them down into the valley of Jehoshaphat, and will plead with them there for my people and for my heritage Israel, whom they have scattered among the nations, and parted my land. . . . Let the heathen be wakened, and come up to the valley of Jehoshaphat: for there will I sit to judge all the heathen round about. Put ye in the sickle, for the harvest is ripe: come, [tread]; for the press is full, the [vats] overflow; for their wickedness is great. Multitudes, multitudes, in the valley of decision: for the day of the Lord is near in the valley of decision.

According to Joel the nations are gathered into the valley of Jehoshaphat for two reasons, to be judged and to be trampled. Notice that Joel describes the Lord as *sitting* while He judges: "I will *sit* to judge all the heathen [nations] round about."

The nations are gathered here not only to be judged, but also to be trampled. Verse 13 says, "Come, tread, for the press is full."

The total picture is this: first the Lord passes sentence (verse 12), then He executes the sentence (verse 13). Judgment and winepress, Joel ties the two together.

This places the time of the sheep-goats judgment *at* the Battle of Armageddon as it is called, not sometime after it as a separate event. First, the armies gather at Armageddon; then they descend upon Jerusalem where the winepress is located, then the angels gather the rest of the wicked ("all men" in Revelation 19:18) and cast them into the winepress.

Is Joel 3 the only Scripture which ties the two together? No, Psalm 110:6 says, "He shall judge among the heathen [judgment], he shall fill the places with the dead bodies [winepress]."

Also, Revelation 14:14 says the Son of man "sat" on a white cloud just before treading the winepress. He sits on the cloud, which is really His throne of glory, to judge between the sheep and the goats, and immediately He swoops down from the cloud to trample the goats which He has judged.

SHEEP-GOATS JUDGMENT	WINEPRESS
passing sentence (Joel 3:12)	executing sentence (Joel 3:13)
reaping (Rev. 14:14-16)	casting (Rev. 14:17-20)
as Christ returns	*after* Christ returns

I give this as a possible answer because Gundry's own view of the sheep-goats judgment has a possibility of being correct. He places this judgment, not at the end of the tribulation, but at the end of the millennium, 1000 years later. To support his view he gives many Scriptures and sound arguments which I will not repeat here.[2]

So there are arguments on *both* sides. Joel seems to place the judgment *before* the millennium, while other arguments place the judgment *after* the millennium. Either time may be true, or *both* times may be in view. It is well known that much of Old Testament prophecy contains *both* the near and far view. It is possible here also.

At any rate it does not hurt my pre-trib position to place the sheep-goats judgment at the end of the millennium as Gundry does. I do not depend on this judgment whatsoever to prevent the wicked from entering the millennium. A host of other Scriptures, much more clear, preclude the wicked from entering the millennium. I gave a long list of these Scriptures in

The Winepress

chapter three.

GOD HATES SIN

When you read about the winepress, how does it make you feel? Isn't it a terrible and frightening thing to think about? The winepress helps us to realize how much God hates sin. Sin is an awful thing. We don't even know how awful it is, but the winepress helps us to see it. How can we even think of dabbling in sin when we know that sin is the reason for the winepress?

POWER FOR PATIENCE

The winepress teaches us another lesson. It teaches us that we can afford to be patient. When we think of all the wrongs that we suffer in this world, we don't have to worry about them because God will take care of them. We don't have to take vengeance because God will take vengeance in due time. We can afford to have all the patience in the world.

I have no excuse to have a tinge of bitterness in my heart. If a non-Christian wrongs me, God will take care of that at the winepress. If a Christian wrongs me, God has already judged that at the cross. Take the long look. Those injustices you suffer that you think are so big, they are just small things, such little things. Return good for evil now, while you have opportunity. If your enemy does not come to the cross he will get all he deserves at the winepress.

MOTIVATION FOR WITNESSING

Motivations for witnessing are many, and to me the winepress is one of them. I don't desire for anyone to be cast into the winepress, and I know that God cares infinitely more than I do. He went as far as He could to keep men from that fate without forcing their wills. He sent His only begotten Son, Jesus Christ, to die on the cross in our place. He has waited patiently these many years, putting off His vengeance as long as He can. During the tribulation He will give men a foretaste and a forewarning of the winepress and the lake of fire, trying to save as many of them as possible.

Yes, He cares more than I ever will. I just want to fit into God's purpose and God's plan. If He is delaying His coming so that more people might be saved, then our goal also should be the salvation of people. His purpose should be our purpose. Let's harmonize with His will.

WILL IT BE HIS BLOOD OR YOUR BLOOD?

When you take the Lord's Supper and drink of the cup, what are you drinking? It is the fruit of the vine which represents the blood of Jesus. How was this drink made? It was made by crushing grapes so that the juice would run out—in other words, a winepress. Jesus suffered a winepress, so to speak, and His blood ran out. Suffering the winepress Himself, He has earned the right to tread the winepress. "Thou art worthy . . . for thou wast slain, and hast redeemed us to God by thy blood . . ." (Revelation 5:9).

Whenever I take the Lord's Supper now, I am reminded that He suffered the winepress so that I don't have to suffer the winepress. I deserve to be there, but He took my place.

Are you not sure that you are saved? You don't have to hope or wonder if you might make it through the pearly gates someday. You can be *certain* of salvation more than you can be certain of anything else in this world. Turn away from your sins and turn to Jesus as your *only* hope. Give up your stubbornness and yield your life completely to Him. Trust, believe, have full confidence, that Jesus spilled *His* blood so that He won't have to spill yours. Surrender your life to the One who died in your place.

---

1. E. W. Bullinger, *Figures of Speech Used in the Bible* (Grand Rapids, MI: Baker Book House, reprinted 1968), p. vi.
2. Gundry, *The Church and the Tribulation,* pp. 163-171.

"So shall also the coming of the Son of man be" (Matthew 24:37).

11
The Olivet Solution

One day Jesus sat down on the mount of Olives and the disciples came up to Him and asked about His second coming. Jesus revealed to them signs that would precede His coming, including the Great Tribulation, and He told them of His coming with power and great glory after the tribulation. Jesus concluded this portion of the discourse in an unexpected way. He said of His coming, "But of that day and hour knoweth no man, no, not the angels of heaven, but my Father only" (Matthew 24:36). "Watch therefore, for ye know neither the day nor the hour wherein the Son of man cometh" (Matthew 25:13).

Doesn't it seem strange that the *strongest statements of imminency* in the entire Bible occur in this post-tribulational context? Very puzzling after what we learned in chapter two that believers can count 1260 days from the abomination of desolation to the return of Christ. Is this a contradiction? Is the Olivet Discourse an insoluble riddle? Or can we find a solution?

THE OLIVET PROBLEM

These statements of imminency have been a "hot potato"

THE PRE-TRIBULATION RAPTURE

for pre-tribulationists to handle. They have faced the embarrassing choice of being accused of interrupting the flow of the context by saying that they refer to the *beginning* of the tribulation or of ignoring them altogether by depending on other and weaker verses for their doctrine of imminency. The latter choice is like running from the ocean in order to dive into a bucket, and the first choice is like trying to turn a mule around who doesn't want to be turned around.

For post-tribulationists the Olivet Discourse has been a fortress, for they are pleased to see that surprise can fit into a post-tribulational setting. Yet there is a crack in that fortress because they are hard put to explain the outright contradiction of the unknown day when Daniel and Revelation give the exact day.

Both sides, then, face a problem.

HORNS OF A DILEMMA

day is known — day is unknown

I myself faced this dilemma for quite awhile without any solution in sight. If I grabbed one horn, the bull would jab me with his other horn. On the one hand, I had to believe that the day of the post-tribulational return could be calculated because Daniel and Revelation said so. At the same time the post-tribulational context in Matthew 24 pressed down upon me with increasing force. I felt I was facing a brick wall. Why does God give us problems like this? He gives us problems to cause us to seek Him, to meditate, to dig a little deeper. Several times while researching this subject I have faced a brick wall. It was those occasions which led to the greatest discoveries.

So as I faced the problem of the Olivet Discourse, I sought

The Olivet Solution

an answer from God. After the answer came it seemed so simple that I wondered what had been so hard about it. I laughed at myself for not knowing it long before.

The Precedent. A similar dilemma faced the Jews of Old Testament times. They looked at passages in which two irreconcilable prophecies were woven together. Would the Messiah come suffering or would He come ruling? Who would ever dream that He would come *twice,* once to suffer and once to rule! Imagine the debates that could have gone on, each side trying to interpret it their way at the expense of the data on the other side. Then Jesus came and opened the Scriptures and made it clear.

Much of prophecy has double reference. This is a recognized and common rule of interpretation for the Old Testament. If for the Old, why not for the New? When we come to Matthew 24—25 maybe we can save ourselves a lot of argument if we will let this prophecy be like much other prophecy. Perhaps we can tackle the bull if we grab *both* horns. The perfect solution to the problem would be to let "the coming of the Son of man" refer *at the same time* to the post-trib *and* the pre-trib coming.

Double reference in Old Testament prophecy is readily accepted. Is double reference accepted in New Testament prophecy also? Yes, a passage that is generally agreed to have double reference is Luke 21:12-24 (part of the Olivet Discourse, by the way). In that passage the destruction of Jerusalem in A.D. 70 prefigures the destruction of Jerusalem during the tribulation. Therefore, we cannot limit double reference prophecy to the Old Testament. It happens in the New also.

When it first hit me that the solution to Matthew 24 might be double reference, I said to myself, "I must run back to Matthew 24 and read it again. I've got to check it out to see if it's really true or not."

The Clue. I grabbed my Bible and reread the illustration of the days of Noah very carefully (verses 37-42).

THE PRE-TRIBULATION RAPTURE

> But as the days of Noah were, so shall also the coming of the Son of man be. For as in the days that were before the flood they were eating and drinking, marrying and giving in marriage, until the day that Noah entered into the ark. And knew not until the flood came, and took them all away; so shall also the coming of the Son of man be. Then shall two be in the field; the one shall be taken, and the other left. Two women shall be grinding at the mill; the one shall be taken, and the other left.
>
> Watch therefore: for ye know not what hour your Lord doth come (Matthew 24:37-42).

In this illustration Jesus compares the surprise of His coming to the surprise of the flood. "And [they] knew not until the flood came, and took them all away . . .watch, therefore; for ye know not what hour your Lord doth come." When I read that I noticed a strong incongruity there. Do you see it? How strange that believers should be compared, not to Noah, but to the *wicked*. *"They* knew not . . . *Ye* know not." I had read that many times before without being struck by this riddle. But now I was baffled.

Then I saw that it was more than a riddle; it was a clue. It was a clue to a whole new way of looking at Matthew 24.

But I am getting ahead of my story. First I want to back up and talk about the "fig tree" and "this generation" which occur earlier in Matthew 24.

TEMPORARY DIGRESSION
The Fig Tree. Look at these verses:

> Now learn a parable of the fig tree; when his branch is yet tender, and putteth forth leaves, ye know that summer is nigh: so likewise ye, when ye shall see all these things, know that it is near, even at the doors (Matthew 24:32-33).

What does the fig tree represent? Does it represent the nation Israel? What does the putting forth leaves represent? Does it

The Olivet Solution

speak of Israel's becoming a nation in 1948? Does the budding of the fig tree mean that we can approximate the time of the rapture? How can we know the correct interpretation?

Jesus gives the interpretation, and this should erase all doubt as to the meaning. Jesus says the putting forth of leaves represents the coming to pass of "all these things." What are "all these things"? The very things He has just spoken of, namely events to occur during the tribulation period. Read Matthew 24 and see if Jesus speaks of Israel's becoming a nation. I can't find it. Jesus does speak of the "beginning of sorrows" and the "great tribulation." These two time periods, I tend to believe, form the two halves of the seven-year tribulation. Whether or not you agree with this, one thing remains clear: Jesus never spoke of Israel becoming a nation. So there is no contextual basis for reading the nationhood of Israel in the fig leaves. Safety of interpretation comes only by sticking to Jesus' own interpretation.

One may object that if the nationhood of Israel is not in the context, then it finds its basis from other Scripture, for the fig tree commonly represents Israel in Scripture. Well, all it takes to answer that is a little counting. Remember, a concordance is a Bible student's best friend. If you were to consult your best friend and count the references, you would discover that the fig tree stands for Israel only *one-tenth* of the times it is used in the Bible. Furthermore, even the few verses where the fig tree does stand for the nation, not one of them supports the idea that the leaves represent Israel's *becoming a nation.*

Consider also, the parallel passage in Luke 21:29. From it we learn that Jesus is not singling out the fig tree over any other tree, because He is actually referring to "all the trees." This should disperse any idea of one particular symbol for Israel being on Jesus' mind. According to Luke 21:31 the fig tree signals the kingdom of God (millennium), not the pre-trib rapture.

What do the leaves of the fig tree represent? They represent the coming to pass of "all these things" that Jesus has spoken of earlier in Matthew 24. Notice the word "all." It reads not,

THE PRE-TRIBULATION RAPTURE

"When you see these things *begin* to come to pass." No, not the beginning, not *some* of these things, but when you see *all* these things, *then* the fig tree has budded, *then* you know the end is near. Have you seen the abomination of desolation? If not, then you haven't seen the fig tree bud.

If the rapture were a hundred years away, that future generation would still see "all these things" that Jesus listed in Matthew 24. From the little word "all" to the broad context in Matthew 24, the budding of the fig tree refers to the tribulation events Jesus has named, not to some event in 1948.

Can we approximate the time of the rapture by watching the fig tree? No, the fig tree will bud after we are gone. I don't want to be around to watch "all these things" which Jesus spoke of. I hope I am raptured before that.

This Generation. Then consider these verses:

> Verily I say unto you, This generation shall not pass, till all these things be fulfilled. Heaven and earth shall pass away, but my words shall not pass away (Matthew 24:34-35).

What does "this generation" mean? Does it mean the generation living which sees these signs? Or does it mean the race of Israel? The former interpretation defines a generation as 30, 40, or 70 years. The latter interpretation allows the generation (or race) of Israel to span the centuries. Which is correct? Both meanings are theoretically possible for the Greek word "generation." But which meaning makes sense in this context?

Does a generation of 30 or 40 years make sense? If Jesus meant a generation of 30 or 40 years dated from the time of the signs (which are tribulation signs, remember), then Jesus would be saying, "Thirty or forty years shall not pass before seven years of tribulation passes." This does not make sense.

It does make sense, though, to say that the race of Israel will not pass from the earth until all the things promised her have been fulfilled. She will not be wiped out by her enemies; she will survive until God finally gathers her from the four corners of the earth into her own land in peace and prosperity.

Not only does the latter interpretation make more sense to *us*, but it would have made more sense to the disciples who were listening. Rather than being concerned about a far-off generation which watches end-time events, they were concerned about the national promises to Israel. They became concerned when Jesus told them the temple would be demolished so that not one stone would be left upon another. If the temple would pass away, what would happen to God's promises to Israel? This made them ask about His coming (which they knew would involve a restoration of the temple and of the nation). The disciples' questions arose out of concern for their race, and so they would understand when Jesus responded, "This race shall not pass, till all these things be fulfilled."

This interpretation not only makes more sense in the context, but it better suits the grammar. "This" generation points to something close at hand, namely, the existing nation. If a far-off generation were intended, more likely the word would have been "that" generation. The demonstrative pronoun is the tip-off.

For more confirmation we can go to the following verse (verse 35) which illustrates and illuminates the meaning. "Heaven and earth shall pass away, but my words shall not pass away." Such a grand statement is more fitting to guarantee the security of a race. The race is more secure than "heaven and earth." "My words shall not pass away" corresponds to the sure promises to that race.

ISRAEL'S GUARANTEE

VERSE 34	This generation (race) shall not pass,	till all these things be fulfilled.
VERSE 35	Heaven and earth shall pass away,	but my words shall not pass away.

THE PRE-TRIBULATION RAPTURE

The Greek language has another word which means "nation." This made me wonder why Jesus didn't say "nation" instead of "generation" if that is what He meant. Perhaps "nation" wouldn't fit because the nation as a political unit *did* pass away—they had no nation of Israel for centuries—but the race, the stock of people, continued on.

Why do we say all this about the "fig tree" and "this generation"? Because we want to show that the rapture *cannot be dated*. Some zealous and well-meaning Christians try to predict the rapture using the budding of the fig tree and calculating a generation of years. Various calculations use various starting points and various lengths of generations, showing that the entire speculation is not on solid ground.

Interpreting from the context, the fig tree buds *after* the rapture and "this generation" refers to the race of Israel rather than to a period of 30, 40, or 70 years. This means *we cannot calculate the time of the rapture.* It will come as a surprise.

(Perhaps in a secondary sense "this generation" refers to the forty years from the time of Christ to the destruction of the temple in 70 A.D. If so, this would answer the disciples' question about when the temple would be destroyed. But because of the connection of verses—or disconnection—I cannot tell if this is the case.)

What About "Signs of the Times"? If the fig tree has not yet budded, then of what significance is 1948 when Israel became a nation? That event sets the stage for the drama of the tribulation. Since we know that during the tribulation Israel will be a nation in their land, it can be argued that Israel must become a nation *before* the tribulation. On the other hand, it could be argued that the covenant between antichrist and Israel at the *beginning* of the tribulation (Daniel 9:27) could itself signal the forming of the nation. As long as the latter option was possible, there was nothing to say that Israel *had* to become a nation before the tribulation. However, God chose to let it happen ahead of time.

Some claim that the recapture of Jerusalem in 1967 was a fulfillment of Luke 21:24. However, Jerusalem will be overrun by Gentiles again during the tribulation (Revelation 11:2). This means that Luke 21:24 is not yet fulfilled, and it means that we cannot look to Luke 21:24 for a "pre-tribulational sign."

What about the other "signs of the times" like earthquakes and famines? Are they not increasing today? A certain pastor told me how he figured this out. Some books he read said that no sign whatsoever comes before the rapture. Other books said that we have "signs of the times" to tell us the rapture is approaching. Which was right? Signs or no signs? Well, this pastor said he sat back in his chair, wiggled his toes, and thought, "Technically speaking, the 'signs' belong to the tribulation period, but some signs 'slop over' into the church age. What some call 'signs of the times' are really a slopping over of tribulation signs." I think he's right. God is giving us a foretaste of what is to come. No signs are *necessary* before the rapture, but God in His mercy allows His bride to see some signs making her more eager for the meeting in the air.

At any rate, these signs give *no time indication in terms of years*; they merely tell us that the time is approaching. Personally, I think He will come soon. But I don't want you to be discouraged if He comes later than we expect.

It might come sooner than we expect. We cannot guess the time of the rapture. It comes in surprise. Remember this, because it is one key which unlocks the mystery of the Olivet problem.

THE RIDDLE OF NOAH

Now we are ready to return to our riddle about Noah. Study this passage closely and then we will consider some questions.

> But as the days of Noah were, so shall also the coming of the Son of man be. For as in the days that were before the flood, they were eating and drinking, marrying and giving in marriage, until the day that Noah entered into the ark, and knew not [*they knew not,* in Greek] until the flood came,

THE PRE-TRIBULATION RAPTURE

and took them all away; so shall also the coming of the Son of man be. . . . Watch therefore: for *ye know not* what hour your Lord doth come (Matthew 24:37-39,42).

Let me ask you a couple easy questions first, before I ask you a stumper.

Question one, the flood victims. Who do the flood victims represent? Jesus relates this illustration in order to make a comparison to the end-times; so the flood victims must represent someone in the end times. Who? Remember the context. Jesus has been talking about the tribulation, and He told about His return after the tribulation. In this context, who do the flood victims represent?

The flood victims correspond to unbelievers who are destroyed at Christ's return. Just as the flood destroyed unbelievers of old, so Christ's return will destroy unbelievers of the end-times. Just as the flood took those unbelievers by surprise, so Christ's return will take these unbelievers by surprise. This is obvious from the context, even to post-tribs, and it also harmonizes with Luke 17 where, as you recall, the flood represented Christ's return *after* the tribulation rather than the tribulation itself.

Question two, Noah. If the flood victims represent unbelievers during the tribulation, then who does Noah represent? Believers during the tribulation. This accords with Luke 17 where Noah represents tribulation saints.

Flood victims represent tribulation unbelievers
Noah represents tribulation saints

Question three, the stumper. Why does Jesus compare the disciples to the flood victims instead of to Noah? It doesn't fit. Are the disciples unbelievers? Will they be destroyed? Then why are they compared to the flood victims? Why not compare them to Noah? If Noah represents tribulation saints, then surely the disciples ought to be compared to Noah if the disciples represent tribulation saints. How *do* the disciples fit into the picture? Which category do they fall into?

INTO WHICH CATEGORY WILL YOU PUT THE DISCIPLES?

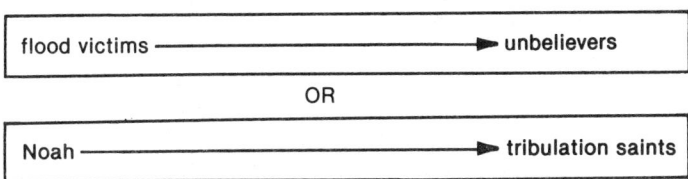

Quite a stumper, isn't it? *Neither category* seems to fit. The disciples don't fall into the category of unbelievers. Yet Jesus refrains from putting them into the category of Noah.

The solution is quite simple. The disciples form a *third category* namely, *church saints* who will be raptured before the tribulation. Instantly the riddle dissolves. Now, instead of forcing the interpretation where it doesn't fit, the interpretation fits as naturally as a baby in a cradle.

Watch.

Surprised, But Safe. The disciples are like the flood victims in one respect—they are surprised. The disciples are like Noah in another respect—they are safe. The disciples are *un*like the flood victims, because the flood victims are unbelievers. The disciples are *un*like Noah, because Noah *knew the day* the catastrophe would come (Genesis 7:4).

Therefore, the disciples have similarities and dissimilarities to both groups, but they fit perfectly a third group, namely church saints who are surprised but safe. This diagram shows how the characteristics of all three groups easily fall into place without forcing one word of Scripture:

THE PRE-TRIBULATION RAPTURE

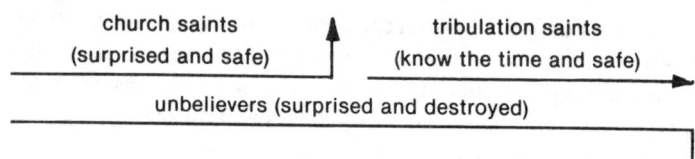

The arrows depict the destination of each group. Looking at the diagram you can see how easily the disciples fit into the category of church saints, and they cannot be stuffed into either of the other two categories even with a very large shoehorn.

Why did Jesus compare the disciples to the flood victims instead of to Noah? Because Jesus wanted to illustrate *surprise,* and Noah was *not* surprised. Noah *knew* the day, just as tribulation saints will know the day. We will *not* know, and so, believe it or not, in one respect we *are* like unbelievers—we both will be *surprised.* Yes, unbelievers will be surprised because they will be deceived by antichrist and they will not be counting the days.

Because Jesus is coming in surprise for the church, He told us to "watch" (verse 42). "Watch" is in the present tense and the intended sense is, "Be continually watching now." This command has force under pre-tribulationism, but a post-trib could more easily be tempted to say to himself, "I will not watch now; I will wait until the tribulation begins, to start watching." Watching *now* is confirmed by the *reason* for watching, "for ye know not what hour . . . ." This implies that it *could* be any day now rather than implying that it *could not yet* be any of these days.

Why did Jesus not compare the disciples to Noah? We would expect Him to make the comparison to Noah, because Noah was saved and protected from wrath, but Jesus could not make the comparison to him because Noah knew seven days ahead of time, and Jesus was illustrating surprise. If the prophecy were *single in viewpoint,* then the disciples would have been compared to Noah, for church saints and tribulation saints would

The Olivet Solution

be one and the same and so the comparison would be between the two. But since there are *two* different saved groups (one knowing and one not knowing) and since there are *two* different groups not knowing (one saved and one not saved), Jesus is giving the prophecy from a *double viewpoint*. The double viewpoint illuminates the comparisons and apparent contradictions, while the single viewpoint is stuck with disjointed comparisons and insoluble contradictions. How many times have we all read this passage before, not noticing the inconsistency that arises from the single viewpoint?

Am I trying to make all the details fit too perfectly? Maybe the illustration of Noah wasn't meant to fit like a hand in a glove. After all, this is a historical illustration and there aren't that many historical illustrations that Jesus could choose from. Even though He was the Master Teacher, maybe He couldn't think of a perfectly appropriate illustration and this was the best He could come up with.

With a historical illustration maybe He would have a limited repertoire to choose from, but what about the next illustration? It is *not* a historical illustration—it is one that Jesus designed from scratch so that it would suit His purpose to a tee. Why does it follow the same pattern as the Noah illustration? In fact Jesus gives not just one illustration, nor two illustrations, but three illustrations, and *they all follow the same pattern*.

THE RIDDLE OF THE GOODMAN

> But know this, that if the goodman of the house had known in what watch the thief would come, he would have watched, and would not have suffered his house to be broken up. Therefore be ye also ready: for in such an hour as ye think not the Son of man cometh (Matthew 24:43-44).

Ready for another quiz? A couple of easy questions first. Jesus said *if* the goodman had known he would have watched. This implies that if the goodman did *not* know he would *not* have watched. We have, therefore, two hypothetical goodmen.

THE PRE-TRIBULATION RAPTURE

GOODMAN #1	knows and watches
GOODMAN #2	knows not and watches not

First question, who does goodman number one represent? What end-time group knows and watches? Tribulation saints.

Second question, who does goodman number two represent? What end-time group knows not and watches not? Unbelievers.

Now for the stumper. Which goodman are you? Stop reading for a minute and ponder it.

Are you goodman number one? Surely you are watching for the Lord's return, but do you know the hour? No, you can't be goodman number one.

Are you goodman number two? Surely you know not the hour, but are you not watching? No, you can't be goodman number two.

What's the solution to the riddle? You are *neither*. You form a *third category,* namely church saints who know not the hour, yet watch.

GOODMAN #1	knows and watches	tribulation saints
GOODMAN #2	knows not and watches not	unbelievers
DISCIPLES	know not and watch	church saints

Or, to diagram it another way:

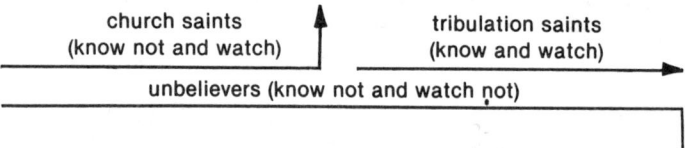

The three groups follow the *same pattern* as the Noah illustration. Coincidence? Or design?

To our delight the double-reference interpretation dissolves the riddles and solves the problem of the known day versus the unknown day. With two groups of redeemed people in mind, the apparent contradiction between the known day and the unknown day disappears, and the incongruities within Matthew 24 vanish. "Be ye (church saints) also (like tribulation saints) ready." If tribulation saints are ready because they know, then how much more should we constantly be ready because we do not know.

Sometimes people try to talk me out of the double-reference interpretation of Matthew 24. Somehow they think that this is a fanciful interpretation with no foundation in the text. Well, just look at the text and see what it says. According to verse 43, why does the goodman watch? Because he *knows.* According to verse 44, why do the disciples watch? Because they know *not.* The text gives *two opposite reasons* for watching! How can this be? Even if the unknown day had no conflict with Daniel and Revelation, we would still face this discrepancy within the illustration itself. It makes no sense unless there are two redeemed groups who watch for opposite reasons. All I am doing is noticing what is right there in the text, and all I am asking of my brothers and sisters in Christ is that they notice what is right there in the text.

THE RIDDLE OF THE VIRGINS

The parable of the virgins (Matthew 25:1-13), amazingly enough, follows the *identical pattern* of the Noah illustration and the goodman illustration. The double-reference interpretation fits snugly and comfortably, not only one way, or two ways, but in three ways.

> Then shall the kingdom of heaven be likened unto ten virgins, which took their lamps, and went forth to meet the bridegroom. And five of them were wise, and five were foolish. They that were foolish took their lamps, and took no oil with them: but the wise took oil in their vessels with their lamps. While the bridegroom tarried, they all slumbered and slept. And at

midnight there was a cry made, Behold, the bridegroom cometh; go ye out to meet him. Then all those virgins arose, and trimmed their lamps. And the foolish said unto the wise, Give us of your oil; for our lamps are gone out. But the wise answered, saying, Not so; lest there be not enough for us and you: but go ye rather to them that sell, and buy for yourselves. And while they went to buy, the bridegroom came; and they that were ready went in with him to the marriage: and the door was shut. Afterward came also the other virgins, saying, Lord, Lord, open to us. But he answered and said, Verily I say unto you, I know you not.

Watch therefore, for ye know neither the day nor the hour wherein the Son of man cometh.

Let me ask you a couple of easy questions first. The five wise virgins and the five foolish virgins are waiting to attend the wedding. Who do the five wise virgins represent? They represent tribulation saints. Remember, we are staying within the framework of the context which places these illustrations in a tribulational time setting.

Second question, who do the foolish virgins represent? The bridegroom says to them, "I know you not." So the foolish virgins must be unbelievers.

Now, into which category do the disciples fit? Not the foolish virgins. How about the wise virgins? Are the disciples like the wise virgins waiting to attend the wedding? Well, yes and no. The disciples will be at the wedding all right, but not as attendants. They are the *bride!* You and I are *not* virgins who attend the wedding, we are the *bride* at the wedding. If this parable were talking about the rapture of the bride, we might entitle it, "The Case of the Missing Bride."

Therefore, *neither* category fits the disciples perfectly, but the double-reference fits perfectly because it recognizes two groups of redeemed people.

| disciples (bride) | tribulation saints (wise virgins) |

unbelievers (foolish virgins)

The illustration of the virgins carries a different twist to it, because it dwells not so much on knowing or not knowing, but it emphasizes readiness or preparedness. Perhaps this is why it stands separate from Noah and the goodman instead of following immediately after them.

wise virgins	ready	attend wedding
foolish virgins	not ready	miss wedding
disciples	ready	bride at wedding

Some have said that the virgins represent the church because the church is called a "virgin" in 2 Corinthians 11:2. Others have said the virgins represent Israel because Israel is called a "virgin" in Jeremiah 18:13. But "virgin" in these verses is singular, not plural. Is the church ten virgins? Or are there ten Israels? No, rather than representing Israel or the church, the parable of the virgins depicts *people in general* living during the tribulation, saved and unsaved, Jew or Gentile. This interpretation avoids the oddity of the church being made up of multiple virgins, it allows the foolish virgins to be unsaved ("I know you not"), and it matches the illustrations of Noah and the goodman which depict the saved and the unsaved of the tribulation.

Viewing the bride and her attendants as two different groups harmonizes with common sense and with other Scripture. Just as we saw that a period following the rapture is to call out a righteous people to populate the millennium, so God has a period of time following the receiving of the bride in order to call out the bride's attendants. These are "the virgins her companions that *follow* her" (Psalms 45:14). The "friends of the bridegroom" are Old Testament saints (John 3:29). In this way the wedding is completely furnished—friends, bride, and attendants; none are missing, but all have their counterparts in real life as prophecy is fulfilled.

REMAINING QUESTIONS

We have surveyed the double-reference interpretation of the Olivet Discourse. More remains to be said, however, and several questions need to be answered. Let's handle the rest of the material in question and answer form.

Question: How Do I Separate the Double References? Does it all seem too fuzzy? Too blurred? Is the distinction between church saints and tribulation saints too hard to separate as you read through the passage? Then let me give you a practical hint that will help you to see it at a glance.

Take a pen and bracket Matthew 24:37-39 in your Bible. Beside the bracket write "tribulation illustration." Now bracket verse 42. (Verses 40-41 we will discuss later on.) Beside it write "church application." Also bracket verse 43 as "tribulation illustration" and bracket verse 44 as "church application." Finally bracket 25:1-12 as "tribulation illustration" and bracket verse 13 as "church application."

Now you can see that it is not mixed up. It follows a pattern. Actually it is easier for you to distinguish the double references than it was for Old Testament saints to distinguish their double references. The reason for this we discussed in our chapter on 2 Thessalonians.

When Jesus gave a "tribulation illustration" and a "church application" He was simply doing what preachers do every Sunday when they preach. You've heard the preacher as he tells a story from the Bible and then he concludes with, "Now this is what it means for you." He's taking the ancient story and *applying* it to modern life. You in the pew have no trouble separating the story from the application.

Jesus did identically. He first told the story about Noah. From that story he made *application* to the disciples. He first told the parable of the goodman. From that he drew an *application* to the disciples. He first told the parable of the virgins. From that, *application.*

All the way through the two parts are clearly distinguished. You can separate the double references of the Olivet Discourse just as easily as you can separate the application from the preacher's story.

Question: How Does it Fit the Context? I share the concern of many to remain strictly within the context and to do nothing whatsoever to injure the time-setting of the Olivet Discourse. Matthew 24:29 says "after the tribulation." That time-setting governs the illustrations which follow. The illustrations of Noah, the goodman, and the virgins all fall into the context of "after the tribulation."

This being so, how can I get a church reference out of a post-tribulational context? Am I not reading something into the text that is not there?

The answer is simple. I see *no church reference whatsoever* in the illustrations of Noah, the goodman, and the virgins. These three illustrations *remain strictly within the post-tribulational context.* The references to the church come in the applications *following* the illustrations, and nothing is more natural than a preacher drawing such applications to his hearers.

ILLUSTRATION OF NOAH	This primary reference *preserves* the tribulational context.
APPLICATION TO CHURCH	This secondary reference preserves the unknown day.

In this way we fully satisfy the demands of the context. Nothing is wrenched out of place, twisted, or distorted, but it all fits naturally.

Let me go even further. The double-reference interpretation has a *stronger view* of the context than post-tribulationism does. Surprising? I'll show you why. Jesus says, "The flood came and took them all away." We allow this statement its *full force.* Just as *all* the flood victims were taken away, so *all* the wicked of the end times will be taken away. We allow the illustration *full correspondence* with the end times just as Jesus intended it.

In contrast, post-tribulationists have a *lack of correspondence* to the end times. They cannot allow *all* the wicked to be destroyed as *all* the flood victims were destroyed. According to their scheme some wicked would have to survive to populate the millennium. In this way post-tribs muffle the comparison. The flood victims do not provide a true or a full comparison.

Rather than squelching the context, we are happy to allow the post-tribulational context its full force.

Question: Why Did Jesus Give Three Illustrations? He gave three so that we would be sure to get the point, to be ready for His return. They reinforce each other. I am glad He gave three so that I would be three times as sure of the double-reference interpretation. The strength of the double-reference interpretation is that it can handle all three illustrations in one swoop because they all follow the same pattern. The weakness of other interpretations is that they cannot come up with a unified explanation for the riddles each illustration presents. If they even try to answer the riddles at all, they might be able to juggle around an assortment of explanations hodgepodge style. But why try to juggle three balls with one hand, unless you're a juggling artist instead of an exegete?

The three illustrations reinforce each other, but also one builds upon the other in a progression of thought. The illustration of Noah and the flood teaches *surprise.* The illustration of the goodman teaches *readiness* in light of that surprise. And the parable of the virgins teaches *advance readiness.*

Question: Do Other Gospels Contain Double Reference? If Matthew's Gospel contains double reference, then what about other Gospels? Do they contain similar double references? Yes.

The Olivet Solution

What I learned from Matthew 24 helped me to understand Luke 12. For a long time I was puzzled by an incongruity in Luke 12:36, a riddle if you please. As you recall, this passage places Christ's return *after* the wedding processional, and it tells us to be like men who wait for His return after the wedding.

> And ye yourselves [be] like unto men that wait for their lord, when he will return from the wedding; that when he cometh and knocketh, they may open unto him immediately.

My puzzlement was this: I thought I was waiting for the wedding, the rapture. How could I be around to wait for His return *after* the wedding?

Double reference solves the riddle.

I am *not* one of those men who wait for His return after the wedding. I am merely *like* those men in that I, *like* them, am ready and waiting. Again the application does not fit the illustration unless we recognize that two distinct groups are in view. Church saints wait for the wedding, tribulation saints wait for His return after the wedding. This interpretation accepts the precise wording of the text as well as dissolving the riddle.

To help you remember this, bracket verses 35-39 in your Bible (this includes the illustration of the goodman also), and label this "tribulation illustration." Then bracket verse 40 as "church application."

THE PRE-TRIBULATION RAPTURE

	"the coming of the Son of man"		
	for tribulation saints	upon tribulation wicked	for church saints
Noah and the flood victims	knew and safe	knew not and destroyed	know not but safe
goodman of the house	knew and watched	knew not and watched not	know not but watch
wise and foolish virgins	ready	not ready	ready but bride
men waiting	ready after wedding		ready before wedding
	primary reference		secondary application

The remarkable feature is that the third group in each case is *distinct* from either of the first two groups. Either Jesus was poor in making His conclusions fit the illustration or else He had something different in mind than what we had noticed before.

Another case of double reference is Mark 13 because it addresses the church after talking about the tribulation.

> For the Son of man is as a man taking a far journey, who left his house, and gave authority to his servants, and to every man his work, and commanded the porter to watch. Watch ye therefore: for ye know not when the master of the house cometh, at even, or at midnight, or at the cockcrowing, or in the morning. Lest coming suddenly he find you sleeping. And what I say unto you I say unto all, Watch (Mark 13:34-37).

This illustration follows a different pattern; so for a post-trib this is no proof. But for those of us who are already pre-trib, we must see this as applying to the church because the time commences from *when the Son of man leaves*. This plants the illustration squarely in the church age.

Question: Can Christ Return at "Any Moment"? To disprove the idea that Christ can return at "any moment" post-tribulationists have argued that He could *not* have returned during the first few years of the church's existence. Time was needed for Peter to grow old and die (John 21:18-19), time was needed to fulfill the Great Commission (Matthew 28:18-20), and similar arguments.

How do I answer these arguments? I don't really need to answer them because I do not depend on the "any-moment" doctrine. The Bible does not say that Christ will return at "any moment." All it says is that He will return "at an hour when ye think not." Suppose it is true that He could not have come during the first generation of the church. What difference does it make *now?* Whenever He does come, He *still* will come "at an hour when ye think not." Maybe He could not have come at "any moment" during the first generation, but that does not prevent Him from surprising us in this generation.

Question: Can Noah Apply to Church Saints? We have explained that Noah represents tribulation saints. Can Noah also represent church saints who are raptured before the tribulation?

Maybe.

It is true that we are like Noah in *safety,* but Matthew 24 does not draw the comparison. As we have seen, Matthew 24 keeps Noah in a *strict tribulational context.* So he represents tribulation saints primarily, but if Noah represents church saints by *secondary application* we have to go to other Scripture, outside of Matthew 24, to find it.

In our chapter on Luke 17 we saw that "the day that Noah entered into the ark" refers not only to the end of the tribulation, but it also covers the entire period (Luke 17:26-31). It is all one day of entering the ark as far as God is concerned. *If* the seven years are one day from the rapture to the revealing, and *if* the "day that Noah entered into the ark" includes the rapture, then Noah himself can apply to the saints raptured. This is an inference based upon the use of "day" in Luke 17:31. (If this inference is correct, it is evidence that the tribulation begins the *same day* as the rapture.)

Genesis 7 tells the story of Noah. In Genesis 7:1 God says to Noah, "Come." This reminds us of the "come" of Revelation 4:1 which appears to be a veiled representation of the rapture, and the "come" of Revelation 11:12 which is a rapture-type event. Then God says His purpose is "to keep seed alive upon the face of all the earth" (Genesis 7:3). We have seen in chapter three that the pre-trib rapture followed by the calling out of saints during the tribulation is for the purpose of keeping a righteous seed alive upon the earth to populate the millennium.

Then God says, "For yet seven days, and I will cause it to rain . . . and Noah went . . . into the ark . . . and it came to pass after seven days, that the waters of the flood were upon the earth" (excerpts from Genesis 7:4-10). Likewise, church saints respond to the "come" seven years before the destruction. The Genesis account thus far sounds like Noah entered the ark *seven days before the flood,* and we would never think otherwise if the passage stopped here.

But a *second* account follows (Genesis 7:11-16) which shows that Noah actually entered the ark *on the very day* the flood began (implying that he was loading the ark for the seven days). Thus God inspired Moses to write a *double account* which fits a two-fold application of Noah. The first account envisions raptured saints and the second tribulation saints. Either the double Genesis account is a coincidence, or else God planned it that way.

Question: Do Some Know When the Thief Comes? As we mentioned in our chapter on First Thessalonians, Christ's com-

The Olivet Solution

ing as a thief is a post-trib figure rather than a pre-trib figure. Accordingly, the illustration of the goodman and the thief here in Matthew 24 occurs in a post-tribulational context. The question comes, "Does not the figure of the thief imply surprise? Doesn't this prove that tribulation saints will *not* know the day of Christ's return?"

The thief does come in surprise, but not all are surprised by the thief. Some *know* when the thief will come. "If the goodman of the house had *known* in what watch the thief would come, he would have watched" (Matthew 24:43). Do tribulation saints know only the "watch" (general time), but not the "hour" (specific time)? No, for Luke 12:39 says, "If the goodman of the house had known what *hour* the thief would come, he would have watched."

Therefore, those watching do know when the thief comes.

Question: Who Is the Servant? In the Olivet Discourse we have two parables about servants. How do they fit into our interpretation?

In Matthew 24:45-51 we have a faithful servant and an evil servant. The evil servant meets the post-trib coming. This is clear because he is cast into hell, and no one is cast into hell at the pre-trib coming. *"There* shall be weeping and gnashing of teeth." The word "there" is an adverb pointing to the *place* of punishment, namely hell. "There" looks like part of the verb as it is written in English, but in Greek it is clear that it means *"there—*in that *place* of punishment."

When I consciously sin, often I am guilty of the same attitude as that evil servant who said, "My lord delayeth his coming." I am tempted to reason this way: "The Lord has waited these many years; the chances are He will delay a little longer while I commit this sin."

This is the very attitude that Jesus teaches against. We should not use His delay as an excuse to sin. Of course, the evil servant was unsaved and went to hell, and if I am saved that is all the more reason I should have no part of that wicked attitude. Saved people should not act like unsaved people.

The evil servant meets the post-trib coming, but who is the faithful servant? Does he meet the pre-trib or the post-trib coming? This is not clear. The servant's duty and reward fits either church saints or tribulation saints. Jesus talks as though anyone can be that faithful servant. But if it is double reference I cannot prove it as I can the other three illustrations.

In the other parable of the servants and the talents (25:14-30) we have more to go on. The time span is *from when the Lord leaves* to when He returns to cast the wicked into hell, from the time the Lord's feet leave the mount of Olives until the time His feet touch the mount of Olives. This offers no proof to post-tribulationists, but to pre-tribulationists it shows that this parable covers the church age *and* the tribulation period. This makes the parable have double reference simply because it spans both time periods.

The first parable of the servant stresses *continual readiness* while the parable of the servants and the talents teaches *how* to be ready for the Lord's coming. Readiness means doing the job God gives us to do, thoroughly, faithfully, no matter how small a job it is. Being faithful each moment will not save us, but it is the way of readiness for those *already* saved (Ephesians 2:8-10).

Question: Who Is the One Taken and the One Left? After Jesus gives the illustration of Noah and the flood, He says,

> Then shall two be in the field; the one shall be taken and the other left. Two women shall be grinding at the mill; the one shall be taken, and the other left (Matthew 24:40-41).

Who is the one taken? Who is the one left? I've seen it argued both ways. We can say that Noah was taken into the ark and the rest were left to drown. Or we can say that the flood victims were taken away and Noah was left to live on the earth. The context can go either way. Which is right? Are the righteous or the wicked taken?

The Olivet Solution

The definition of "taken" can go either way also. In the Greek it is a compound word which means "take along" or "take with." This fits the taking of the saints along with Christ at the rapture. It also fits the taking of the wicked along with the "angel-reapers" to cast them into the winepress of the wrath of God. Elsewhere in the New Testament the word is used in both the good sense and the bad sense. So the definition of the word can go either way. Which is right?

One might argue that the word "took" in verse 39 (the flood "took" them all away) is a different Greek word than "taken" in verse 40 ("one shall be taken"). "Took" in verse 39 means "take up" or "take away." If you wanted to argue from this word you could say that the wicked are "taken away" after the tribulation or you could say that the saints are "taken up" at the rapture. In the latter case our likeness to the flood victims becomes two-fold, our not knowing and our being taken away. This fully satisfies the comparison Jesus makes between them and the disciples. All this would be by application only since the flood victims primarily represent the unbelievers who are destroyed after the tribulation.

Who is taken? The righteous or the wicked? You might argue that since these verses follow the illustration of Noah they fall into the same tribulational context. On the other hand they precede the application Jesus makes to His disciples, a church context. They are sandwiched between a tribulation illustration and a church application. Either single-reference interpretation accounts for *some* of the facts, but what interpretation accounts for *all* the facts?

Because these verses are sandwiched between the tribulation illustration and the church application, and because the meaning can go either way, I believe it is *double reference*. Who is taken? *Both* are taken. When are they taken? At *both* times. Church saints are taken at the rapture and unbelievers are taken after the tribulation.

Jesus left it ambiguous in order to include *both* times. If He intended one time only He certainly could have made it clear as

THE PRE-TRIBULATION RAPTURE

He did in Luke 17 (see chapter nine). But here He didn't. He stated it in such a way that it could apply to *both* times.

Since we mentioned Luke 17, let's learn something else by way of comparison. As you remember, in Luke 17 the emphasis was *destruction*. In Matthew 24 the emphasis is, not destruction, but *surprise*. Surprise fits *both* comings; destruction does not. Matthew 24 fits both comings, Luke 17 does not.

I always thought it strange that "one shall be taken and one left" in both passages where it occurred (Matthew 24 and Luke 17) should not refer to the rapture since it made such a perfect description of the rapture. I wondered why the Bible would omit describing the rapture in this way. But now I see that Matthew 24 includes the rapture, and I find it satisfying, not only to the brain, but also to the heart.

Question: If "No Man" Knows the Day, How Can Tribulation Saints Know the Day? We spent an entire chapter, chapter two, to prove that tribulation saints will know the day of Christ's return. If this is true, how do we explain Matthew 24:36?

> But of that day and hour knoweth no man, no, not the angels of heaven, but my Father only.

If only the Father in heaven knows the day and hour, then how can tribulation saints know it? If the angels don't know it, how can man know it?

An easy way to get around it would be to deny that this refers to the post-trib coming and to say that it refers only to the pre-trib rapture. But this would be to forget the context which places the verse squarely in a post-trib setting.

Post-tribs may use this verse as an easy out, as an excuse to ignore all the evidence in chapter two that tribulation saints will know the day. But that is not exegesis; that is merely throwing Scripture against Scripture, like trying to demolish a wall of bricks by hurling another brick at it.

The Olivet Solution

How can we find out what this verse is really saying? Let's begin with the tense of the word "know." It is present tense. No one knows *now*, in the *present*, but some may know *later*. This interpretation solves the problem, but is this a twisted interpretation forced upon the verse, or is this a natural interpretation arising out from the verse itself?

Let us let the angels answer that for us, shall we? Certainly the angels do not know the time *now* as the verse says. But the question arises, will the angels know *later* after the tribulation begins? Evidence indicates that they will. When Daniel asked the angel how long it was, he answered in a manner showing that he understood how long it was from the abomination of desolation (Daniel 12:6-13). The reason the angel did not make it plain to Daniel is not that he didn't know but because the book was sealed. He gave the impression that he himself would know when the time came.

If the angel in Daniel understood the chronology it is likely that the angels in Revelation also understood the chronology. It is an angel which transmitted the message to John (Revelation 1:1). Angels played key roles throughout the process of revealing the book to John. In transmitting the message the impression is given also that the angels understood the message. Not that they understand as much as God, but at least, being of great intelligence and with their understanding undimmed by sin, they would be able to know what is knowable, namely the revealed chronology from the abomination of desolation to the return of Christ.

Now Jesus' use of the angels is key to understanding the argument of the verse. The argument is that if angels, who are on a higher scale than man, whose intelligence is greater and undimmed by sin, if they do not know, then man who is on a lower scale and of lower intelligence, cannot possibly know. Jesus intends to impress upon us that knowledge of that day is so far out of reach that even the angels do not know. Angels are used as *proof,* then, proof that man cannot know the day of Christ's return.

THE PRE-TRIBULATION RAPTURE

Now, the crux of the matter is that if there comes a time when angels *will* know, then that proof vanishes. As the proof vanishes this leaves the door open for man to know the day also.

If Jesus intended to make an airtight case that man could *never* know the day of His return, then He would have used stronger proof than the angels. But His very choice of the angels as proof is a clue that when the ignorance of angels ceases, then the ignorance of man ceases also.

Is this argument from the angels not enough for you? That is all right. We do not lack for arguments. We have also the argument from the Son. This verse in Matthew does not mention the Son, but the parallel verse in Mark 13:32 includes the Son as being ignorant of that day. In His state of humiliation upon the earth the Son of God voluntarily gave up knowing some things. He no longer fully exercised His omniscience as God. But after the resurrection and ascension He returned to His former glory (John 17:5). *The Son's ignorance was temporary while upon this earth.* Maybe some will deny angels future knowledge of that day, even though Scripture indicates otherwise, but who would dare deny the glorified Son knowledge of that day?

Verse 36, then, speaks of *ignorance in the present*, thrice over, whether it be the present tense of "know" or the reference to angels or to the Son. Such a threefold clue is significant. The verse says nothing about ignorance in the future. Therefore, we are left with no verse in the whole Bible which proves that tribulation saints will not know the day of Christ's return. If there is such a verse, where is it?

Let's analyze this further. Some may reply that although this verse *by itself* does not prove permanent ignorance, with the *context* it does prove it. Does not the context show that Jesus is talking about ignorance of the post-trib return? Does not the context indicate that ignorance will *persist until* the return of Christ?

We can answer this in two ways. First, it is true that no one

The Olivet Solution

knows the time of the post-trib return *now*. No one can know that until after the tribulation begins or at the latest by the abomination of desolation which is the 1260-day landmark. We, as the disciples, view His coming from *this side* of the tribulation. From this time perspective, the verse is correct when it says that no one knows the day of the post-trib return.

But this is only part of the explanation because the context implies that ignorance of the day will persist until Christ's coming. The context which implies that ignorance will persist until Christ's coming is the same context which gives us *double reference*. When viewed in light of this double reference, the problems of the verse disappear like the fog vanishes before the morning sun.

It is true. Ignorance *does* persist for everyone until Christ returns. The unsaved will not know until He comes upon them in judgment and the saved will not know until He comes for them in rapture. For both groups existing presently, ignorance persists until one coming or the other. The double reference views both groups which exist in the present and which will continue until one coming or the other, but omits that group of the future, namely tribulation saints. In this way the verse conforms to the context, because it allows ignorance to persist until Christ returns, and it retains the reference to the post-trib return.

One might object that the expression "that day" does not admit a double reference because of the preceding context which speaks *exclusively* of the post-trib return. If the preceding context were the only consideration the force of that argument could be admitted, but there is not only a preceding context but there is also a context following. In fact, if one rope pulls it back, a stronger rope pulls it forward also, and that rope is the word "but" in the next verse. "But" introduces the explanation of "that day." As Jesus explains "that day," He gives the illustrations of Noah, the goodman, and the virgins, and He brings in the application to the church following each illustration. In other words, "that day" is explained in

THE PRE-TRIBULATION RAPTURE

terms of double reference.

So this verse has ropes pulling in both directions—it is the turning point in the argument of the Olivet Discourse. It is the point of transition from the exclusively post-trib coming to the dual aspect of His coming.

If Matthew 24:36 refers to *both* comings, why is it in the singular, "that day"? Christ's coming in the Old Testament was viewed as one, even though the suffering and ruling aspects of it have been separated by 2000 years. So it is perfectly natural for the two aspects of Christ's second coming to be viewed as one. Why swallow 2000 years and strain at a mere seven years, especially when the Bible views the seven years as one day (Luke 17:30-31)? Technically the New Testament does refer to the second coming as one coming even though there are two aspects to it. Sometimes we loosely call it two comings, and so post-tribulationists accuse us of believing in two comings when the Bible only speaks of one coming. But just as the Old Testament viewed the two aspects as one coming, so I believe the two aspects of Christ's second coming are properly viewed as one coming.

To help you remember all this, you can mark your Bible as suggested:

refers to both times	36 But of that day and hour knoweth no man, no, not the angels of heaven, but my Father only.
tribulation illustration	37 But as the days of Noe were, so shall also the coming of the Son of man be. 38 For as in the days that were before the flood they were eating and drinking, marrying and giving in marriage, until the day that Noe entered into the ark, 39 And knew not until the flood came, and took them all away; so shall also the coming of the Son of man be.
refers to both times	40 Then shall two be in the field; the one shall be taken, and the other left. 41 Two women shall be grinding at the mill; the one shall be taken, and the other left.

The Olivet Solution

church application	42 Watch therefore: for ye know not what hour your Lord doth come.
tribulation illustration	43 But know this, that if the goodman of the house had known in what watch the thief would come, he would have watched, and would not have suffered his house to be broken up.
church application	44 Therefore be ye also ready: for in such an hour as ye think not the Son of man cometh.

As we discussed in our chapter on Second Thessalonians, Isaiah 9:2-7 seesaws back and forth between the two comings. But you can understand Matthew 24 better than Old Testament saints could understand Isaiah 9. The reason for that is also in the chapter on Second Thessalonians.

Question: Why Did Jesus Not Come Right Out and Say So? Why did Jesus conceal the two aspects of His coming in double reference? If He was coming twice, why did He not come right out and say so? I could ask the same question about the Old Testament, but somehow that question doesn't seem to bother us.

Part of the answer is that God reveals truths progressively or in stages. He lays the basic foundation of surprise here in Matthew, describes the rapture in First Thessalonians, and nails down the time of the rapture in Revelation. Keeping this progress of revelation in mind will prevent us from being disappointed at the non-mention of the rapture in Matthew. Matthew in the New Testament is like Genesis of the Old Testament.

Genesis through Malachi gradually unfolds a progress of revelation concerning Christ's first coming. As the progression unfolds, there are *hints* that He will come *twice*, once to die and once to rule. But even then *we find no clear statement that He will come twice.* Likewise with the second coming, revelation indicates two aspects, and revelation on His second coming is even clearer chronologically than revelation on His first

THE PRE-TRIBULATION RAPTURE

coming. Maybe the Jews misunderstood the first coming, but there is no excuse for the church to fall into the same trap and misunderstand His second coming.

In addition to progressive revelation, another reason that Matthew conceals the pre-trib rapture in double reference is that this truth is not a "pearl to be cast before swine." In addition to being written for Christians, the book of Matthew served as an "evangelistic tract" intended to convince Jewish unbelievers. Now there is a potential danger in teaching an unbeliever either the pre-trib doctrine or the post-trib doctrine. The danger of the pre-trib doctrine is that someone may say, "I'll have a second chance. If I miss the first return, all I have to do is get ready for the second return." The danger of the post-trib doctrine is that someone may say, "I don't have to get ready yet; it is safe to wait at least until the tribulation starts, because I know Christ won't return before then." Both of these dangers undermine the main point Jesus is making, "Be ready *now!*"

A proper teaching of either doctrine should not result in such perversion, but the danger is on the part of the *listener* who may use either doctrine as an excuse to delay readiness. But the Master Teacher left no room for excuse. By viewing the two comings as one, He offered only one chance to get ready. If someone (in this age) does not watch, he will miss the rapture and enter into the tribulation as an unbeliever, and as such he will not be aware of Christ's second return when He breaks into his "house" as a thief.

If an unbeliever is reading this and thinking, "No, I've got it outsmarted—all I have to do is count 1260 days," then I reply: Antichrist *will get you to disbelieve* and forget about the 1260 days (2 Thessalonians 2:11-12; Daniel 12:10). The deception is so great even the believers are almost deceived (Mark 13:22); so there is no chance at all for unbelievers who refuse the truth in this age. Believe *now* before the deception comes.

Taking a tip from the Master Teacher, when I talk with unbelievers now, I am slow to tell them about the two phases of

The Olivet Solution

Christ's second coming. Usually I just tell them that Christ is coming and that they need to be ready.

RIDDLES OR SOLUTIONS?

To summarize the evidence for the double-reference interpretation of the Olivet Discourse, let me give you a list of questions. Maybe someone someday will offer better answers to these questions than I have. But as far as I know, the double-reference interpretation offers the only satisfactory solution to these riddles.

(1) How else can we reconcile the unknown day in Matthew and the known day in Daniel and Revelation?

(2) Why are we compared to the wicked flood victims?

(3) Why are we to watch for the *opposite reason* the goodman of the house watches?

(4) Why is the parable about "virgins" if we are the bride?

(5) Why are we to be like men who wait for their Lord *after* the wedding processional?

(6) If you have an explanation for each illustration, does each explanation follow the *same pattern* or are they merely an assortment of explanations? Is the Olivet Discourse harmony or hash?

(7) Why a two-fold account of Noah's entering the ark (Genesis 7:1-10 and 7:11-13) if it is not to picture two groups of redeemed people?

(8) Why does Jesus not explain who is the "one taken and the other left" if it does not refer to both times?

These questions remain riddles without the double-reference interpretation. But the double-reference interpretation exchanges these riddles for solutions. Which will you have, riddles or solutions?

These questions represent more than one or two coincidences; they reveal hard facts which demonstrate a *consistent pattern*. Seeing such harmony and consistency, I think God is trying to tell us something. Which will you have, riddles or solutions?

THE PRE-TRIBULATION RAPTURE

The remarkable pattern of Matthew 24 provides evidence that God inspired every detail of the Bible. Since Matthew did not understand at the time (to him the parable of the goodman would be illogical), he would more naturally remember it in a way that made sense to him. But the Holy Spirit caused him to remember and record it the way Jesus spoke it.

THE CHURCH AND ISRAEL

The double-reference interpretation not only solves the apparent contradiction between the known day and unknown day, it not only solves the riddles within the Olivet Discourse, but it also solves another problem disputed over for many years. Is the Olivet Discourse for Israel or for the church? Post-tribulationists have said it is for the church, since the church will go through the tribulation. Pre-tribulationists have said it is for Israel only, because the church will not go through the tribulation. Each side has brought forth convincing arguments from the context to support their view. Who is right?

The fact is, both are right. Valid arguments rest on both sides. We have been disagreeing over nothing. Either side you choose is "right," but the other side has valid arguments too. Only the double-reference interpretation does full justice to *all* the arguments and *all* the evidence.

Let me show you what I mean. When the disciples asked Jesus their questions (Matthew 24:3), they had in mind Israel only. They considered themselves Israelites and they were concerned with Christ's coming to set up the kingdom promised to Israel. So Jesus answered their questions honestly, according to how they asked them. That is why He gave the signs leading up to His post-trib return.

However, Jesus knew in the back of His mind that the disciples would form the nucleus of a new group, the church. He knew that the church would meet the pre-trib coming rather than the post-trib coming. He knew the pre-trib return would come as a surprise instead of coming at the end of a prescribed period. Knowing this, He could not mislead the disciples and leave them with the impression that they would be able to calculate the day of His return. He could not leave them without the proper application they needed, and so He concluded each illustration with a special application for them, saying, "In such an hour as ye think not the Son of man cometh."

Of course, He did not reveal everything all at once here, but He did give His disciples the minimum amount of information they needed, the fact that they could not calculate the day. That is all they needed to know for the time being. In this way Jesus was honest to their questions and honest to the facts. The disciples represent *both* Israel and the church because they *were in fact* part of Israel and the church.

TO STRENGTHEN YOUR VIEW

Although the double-reference interpretation solves many problems, it is no weak compromise. Actually it strengthens both views. Whatever your view is now, I would like to strengthen it.

Are you post-trib? Then I understand that you are vitally interested in the *post-trib context* in Matthew 24. You are even more concerned about the context than about the post-trib rapture, because one rests on the other. To strengthen the context, let us allow Matthew's chief tribulation sign, namely the abomination of desolation, its full force as far as its timing is concerned. Let us be free to understand all we read in Daniel about the abomination of desolation as Jesus told us to do, and let the 1260 days stand out strong in its normal meaning. Up until now you have been hindered in doing this because of the presence of "for ye know not the day nor the hour in which the Son of man cometh." But now, with the double-reference interpretation, you no longer have to weaken the significance of the chief tribulational sign. You can now allow the tribulational context its full force.

Are you a pre-trib? I want to strengthen your view. How do you handle the statement, "For in such an hour as ye think not the Son of man cometh"? Because this statement occurs in a post-trib context, many pre-tribulationists felt they had to forfeit their strongest statement of imminence in the entire Bible. Relying on weaker verses to prove their case for imminence has not been very convincing to post-tribulationists. Now, however, with the double-reference interpretation, this strongest statement of imminency is rescued for pre-tribulationists to use once again.

AN APPEAL

Double reference in prophecy is common; so it provides a perfectly acceptable solution. Neither side has to give up their strongest arguments. Pre-tribulationists retain their reference to Israel, while those who have been post-tribulationists retain their reference to the church. Everything is explained. The post-trib context is explained. The unknown day's apparent contradiction with the known day of Daniel and Revelation is explained. Now nothing remains to hold back both sides from this new ground of agreement. We all can unreservedly unite under one banner proclaiming the doctrine, "Be ye also ready for in such an hour as ye think not the Son of man cometh." And most importantly, this interpretation is not forced from the outside, but by answering the internal riddles it arises from the very text itself, and that, after all, is what sound exegesis is all about.

"All the law is fulfilled in one word..." (Galatians 5:14).

12
Now What?

Some men in our church were talking about the rapture and what our attitude should be toward those of a different viewpoint. One remarked, "Allen believes in pre-tribulationism, but he sees the possibility of both sides."

I responded, "No, not exactly. I don't believe post-tribulationism has any possibility of being correct. What you really mean is that I accept post-tribulationists as persons."

This conversation illustrates two points I want to bring out before I finish. First, on the basis of what the Bible says, we can believe without a doubt that the rapture will rescue believers prior to the coming great tribulation. Second, we as Christians must receive those who differ as equal brothers and sisters in Christ.

KNOW WHAT THE BIBLE TEACHES

There was a time when I wasn't sure if the rapture came before the tribulation or after. I had to find out. That need led to the search recorded here to find out what the Bible really said and how the Bible interpreted itself.

Now I am sure, and I believe everyone can be sure. We don't have to wonder any longer. Why? Because the Bible allows only one possibility. The arguments are simple enough and clear enough that anyone can believe on the basis of the Bible alone, no matter who says what.

Searching out the truth about the rapture has been sheer enjoyment. I learned much from reading the works of others and from talking with various people, scholars and laymen alike. This interaction caused me to dig and to search the Scriptures, setting aside some "pat answers" to discover things which I never would have thought of on my own. Rather than conclusions limited to my own thinking, I view this work as a triumph for cooperative interpretation.

Reasons for my writing are my desire to display the harmony of the Bible and my obligation to be a faithful steward of what God has given me. But one big purpose behind it all has been to bring us to a unity of faith on the rapture issue.

WORK FOR UNITY IN THE LORD

Even though I am sure about pre-tribulationism, I still accept post-tribulationists as people. We ought to fellowship with them. As in most any controversy each side has an aspect of the truth, and we can learn much from each other.

Let's look at the Biblical basis for receiving post-tribulationists. Ephesians 4 describes two kinds of unity, unity of the Spirit and unity of the faith:

> I therefore, the prisoner of the Lord, beseech you that ye walk worthy of the vocation wherewith ye are called, with all lowliness and meekness, with longsuffering, forbearing one another in love; endeavouring to keep the *unity of the Spirit* in the bond of peace.
>
> There is one body, and one Spirit, even as ye are called in one hope of your calling; one Lord, one faith, one baptism, one God and Father of all, who is above all, and through all, and in you all. But unto every one of us is given grace according to the measure of the gift of Christ. . . .
>
> And he gave some, apostles; and some, prophets; and some, evangelists; and some, pastors and teachers; for the perfecting . . . of the body of Christ: till we all come in the *unity of the faith,* and of the knowledge of the

Now What?

Son of God, unto a perfect man, unto the measure of the stature of the fulness of Christ:

That we henceforth be no more children, tossed to and fro, and carried about with every wind of doctrine, by the sleight of men, and cunning craftiness, whereby they lie in wait to deceive; but speaking the truth in love, may grow up into him in all things, which is the head, even Christ: from whom the whole body fitly joined together and compacted by that which every joint supplieth, according to the effectual working in the measure of every part, maketh increase of the body unto the edifying of itself in love (Ephesians 4:1-16).

Unity of the Spirit is a spiritual oneness while unity of the faith is a doctrinal oneness. Unity of the Spirit we have already while unity of the faith we are striving toward. Let's make sure we know how to distinguish between these two kinds of unity, because confusing the two leads to dissension between brethren.

Unity of the Spirit. The unity of the Spirit rests on what genuine believers have in common. Paul lists some items common to all genuine believers:
one body
one Spirit
one hope of your calling
one Lord
one faith
one baptism (compare 1 Corinthians 12:13)
one God and Father

By this list Paul draws the boundaries broad enough to include all genuine believers, but narrow enough to exclude all false believers. Paul is not talking about a unity like the worldly "ecumenical movement" which waters down basic beliefs. We hold strong to the basic beliefs and our unity rests solidly on that foundation.

Some people glibly say, "Oh, yes, we all believe in the same God." But this is not true. Many people believe in a god of their own mind instead of the God of the Bible. The Christ of the Bible, the Christ that Paul has been talking about in Ephesians, is above all other power in the universe:

> That the God of our Lord Jesus Christ, the Father of glory, may give unto you the spirit of wisdom and revelation in the knowledge of him . . . what is the exceeding greatness of his power to us-ward who believe, according to the working of his mighty power, which he wrought in Christ, when he raised him from the dead, and set him at his own right hand in the heavenly places, far above all principality, and power, and might, and dominion, and every name that is named, not only in this world, but also in that which is to come (Ephesians 1:17-21).

"Oh, yes, we all have faith." But the faith of the Bible, the faith that Paul has been talking about, is a faith that brings salvation apart from any works that we do. Good works are the *result* of salvation, not the cause of salvation (see Ephesians 2:8-10).

So Paul draws narrow boundaries, but he also draws them broadly. As long as a person is part of the same body, sharing one Spirit and one calling, how can I reject him? If we have one Lord, one faith, one baptism, what right do I have to refuse to fellowship with him? If we have one God and Father, can we not work together?

Unity of the Faith. We now move to the second kind of unity, the unity of the faith. This is not a unity that we already have, but it is a unity we are striving toward. We strive toward it because it goes beyond basic faith required for salvation and presses toward perfect knowledge of God. This is where apostles, prophets, evangelists, pastors and teachers come in. Their job is to instruct us regarding all the doctrines of the Bible, and their purpose is to bring us to a unity, or to an agreement, on all these doctrines. Quite a task, isn't it? This is why we are still striving toward the unity of the faith.

I am sure you have heard this idea: "It doesn't matter what we believe. It's not really important. We'll just enjoy our unity and cover up our differences."

Now What?

No, it doesn't work that way. If that were the case, what good are pastors? We don't need teachers. Throw away the writings of the apostles. No, God intends for us to receive solid teaching, and He intends for us to come to the unity of the faith.

Can we all come to the unity of the faith on the rapture issue? Yes, I think we can. Some may doubt this because, obviously, post-tribulationism is not taught by "cunning craftiness" warned of in Ephesians 4:14. But at the same time God intends for us to grow "unto a perfect man, unto the measure of the stature of the fulness of Christ" (Ephesians 4:13).

The chart below illustrates my Biblical basis for receiving post-tribs even though I happen to believe pre-trib.

UNITY OF THE SPIRIT (Ephesians 4:3)	UNITY OF THE FAITH (Ephesians 4:13)
already have it	progressing toward it
basis of fellowship	reason for teaching
receive post-tribulationists	believe pre-tribulationism

Why Now? Why Not Before? If we can come to a unity of the faith on the rapture issue now, then why has disagreement continued for so long? If pre-trib is clearly taught in the Bible, then why hasn't *everyone* seen this long ago? If we believe in the same rules of interpretation, why do we still disagree? These are good questions and I would like to offer two answers.

First, I think God is allowing the prophetic Scriptures to become more and more unsealed as the time of the end approaches. You can observe this for yourself when you go to your Christian bookstore. On the shelves you see more books and commentaries on Revelation and on the end times than ever before. Now that the end is getting closer, there is a greater need for us to know these things. We all need to be united now, looking for His coming at any day and any hour.

Second, some of the overlooked details in Scripture are finally coming to light. They were there all the time; we just haven't noticed them before. Anyone can pay attention to the details of Scripture. Scholars are not in a class by themselves. In our church a young mother proved some scholars wrong by spending just fifteen minutes with her concordance. She was willing to take the time and she discovered the truth about a certain word. Even brand new Christians at Berea took time to check up on the apostle Paul (see Acts 17:11). Meditation on the details of Scripture leads to deeper truth.

Historically, the process of discovering the overlooked details about the rapture has taken some time. To begin with, the study of the end times was not taken up in earnest until the 1800s. Since that time it has taken an interplay of minds and ideas on all sides in order to arrive at some of these discoveries.

Today we need this interplay of minds because you may see something in Scripture which I don't see. And I may see something that you haven't seen. Together, working as a body as the Lord intended, we can arrive at the unity of the faith even though the interplay of minds and ideas takes some time.

THE CHURCH AND THE TRIBULATION

When I study a subject in Scripture, I am not content to study only the evidence, the bare facts. I also like to ask, *Why?* As a capstone to this study we ask, *Why did God design the tribulation period?* Here are five reasons for the tribulation period:

First, to glean out the last possible person who will be saved. The "hour of testing" produces a polarization in which men are forced to choose Christ or antichrist. The winnable are won, while the disobedient are hardened even more (Revelation 3:10; Daniel 12:10).

Second, to give birth to Israel. This is the "time of Jacob's trouble" which will produce the spiritual restoration of the na-

Now What?

tion (Jeremiah 30:7; Zechariah 13:9).

Third, to call out righteous people from all nations who will enter the millennium in their natural bodies.

Fourth, to call out guests to attend the wedding feast Christ is preparing for His bride.

Fifth, to provide a dispensational test. Men will no longer have the excuse, "But, God, if You had only given me a taste of hell, I would have repented." God gives them a taste of hell on earth to prove once and for all that men are still stubborn at heart (Revelation 9:20-21).

I find no reason in the Bible for the church to be in the tribulation. I find no exhortation for the present-day believer to prepare himself to endure the last seven years of tribulation. Christians do not lack courage when they rejoice in the assurance that Christ will come to rapture them before the tribulation. Nor do we excuse laziness. As Christians we face and endure tribulation every day. These daily trials shape our character so that we will become more and more like Christ. We are strengthened by today's tribulations, not tomorrow's. Let us make the most of them so God can perform His perfect work in us that we might be perfect and complete, lacking nothing (James 1:4).

But I do find reason for the church to be raptured before the tribulation:

First, to reward those who have received and kept His Word (Revelation 3:10).

Second, to display His mercy and grace. Although it is a reward, God was not obligated to promise this reward. Sheer goodness gives us the pre-tribulation rapture!

LAST WORDS

The last page of the Old Testament leaves ringing in our ears a prophecy of the coming of Elijah. After those last words was a long gap of 400 years. But the *very next thing to occur* was the fulfillment of that prophecy as John the Baptist appeared in the spirit and power of Elijah.

THE PRE-TRIBULATION RAPTURE

The last page of the New Testament leaves ringing in our ears a prophecy of the coming of Christ. After those last words has been a long gap of 2000 years. But the *very next thing to occur* . . . .

Appendix I
Outlines of First and Second Thessalonians

Making an outline was one of the things the Holy Spirit used most in opening up my understanding. It was a lot of hard work, but it helped me to see what the passage was really saying, not just what I thought it said.

Try making an outline of your favorite book. The procedure in brief is this: first, mark off the divisions; second, organize the divisions into an outline. Let the outline reflect the actual thought pattern of the author rather than forcing an artificial outline from the outside. This requires much meditation and hard concentration, but I would like you to experience the thrill and satisfaction of slicing the meat of the Word for yourself.

FIRST THESSALONIANS—GOD HAS CALLED BELIEVERS TO HOLY LIVING IN THE MIDST OF AFFLICTION

I. A SUCCESSFUL BEGINNING (Thanksgiving to God) (1:1—2:16)
   A. Thanksgiving for God's calling (1:1-10)
      1. The people—Thessalonians (1:1-2)
      2. The content—faith, love, hope (1:3)
      3. The reason—God's calling (1:4-10)
         a. As evidenced by powerful preaching (1:5) (Explained further in 2:1-12.)
         b. As evidenced by joyous reception (1:6-10)

(Explained further in 2:13-16.)
1) The exemplary result (1:7)
2) The far-reaching result (1:8-10)
   a) Widely known is Paul's entrance (1:9a)
      (Explained further in 2:1-12.)
   b) Widely known is their conversion (1:9b-10)
      (Explained further in 2:13-16.)
      1] To serve God (1:9b)
         (Explained further in 4:1-12.)
      2] To wait for His Son (1:10)
         a] Who rose from the dead
            (Explained further in 4:13-18.)
         b] Who delivers from wrath
            (Explained further in 5:1-11.)

B. Presentation of God's calling (2:1-12)
  1. The portrayal (2:1-8)
    a. Bold preaching in affliction (2:2)
    b. God-pleasing preaching (2:3-4)
    c. Unselfish preaching (2:5-8)
      1) Not throwing our weight around (2:5-6)
      2) Gentle (2:7)
      3) Sharing our very souls (2:8)
  2. The proof (2:9-12)
    a. You remember our labor (2:9)
    b. You witnessed our holy lives (2:10)
    c. You witnessed our tender exhortations (2:11-12)

C. Reception of God's calling (2:13-16)
  1. By belief (2:13)
  2. By suffering (2:14-16)
    a. The example of the sufferers (2:14-15)
    b. The deserved doom of the persecutors (2:16)

(Not only did you begin well, but you have also evidenced a . . .)

Appendix I

II. A STEADFAST CONTINUATION (Encouragement from them) (2:17—3:13)
   A. Paul's previous attempts to visit (2:17-20)
      1. His strong desire (2:17)
      2. His Satanic hindrances (2:18)
      3. His "selfish" reason—joyous reward (2:19-20)
   B. Timothy's preparatory visit (3:1-10)
      1. The purpose of the visit (3:1-5)
         a. To represent Paul in his absence (3:1)
         b. To strengthen them in affliction (3:2-4)
            1) Unmovable in affliction (3:3a)
            2) Appointed to affliction (3:3b)
            3) Forewarned of affliction (3:4)
         c. To make sure they had not fallen (3:5)
      2. The result of the visit (3:6-8)
         a. The reported faithfulness (3:6)
         b. The resulting encouragement (3:7-8)
         c. The renewed prayer (3:9-10)
            1) Of thanks (3:9)
            2) Of request (3:10)
               a) To visit
               b) To perfect
   C. Paul's plan to visit (3:11-13)
      1. His desire for God's direction (3:11)
      2. His desire for their growth (3:12)
      3. His desire for their establishment (3:13)
         a. In holiness
         b. At the Lord's coming

(May your great beginning and your steadfast continuation extend into . . .)

III. A SANCTIFIED FUTURE (Exhortation to them) (4:1—5:28)
   A. Serving God (4:1-12)
      1. Bodily sanctification (4:1-8)

        a. What God wills (4:1-6)
           1) No fornication (4:3)
           2) No heathen lusts (4:5)
           3) No defrauding (4:6)
        b. Why God wills (4:7-8)
           1) His righteous character
           2) His holy call
              a) Disobeying means rejecting God
              b) Disobeying means rejecting His *Holy* Spirit
    2. Brotherly love (4:9-10)
        a. I do not need to teach you (4:9a)
        b. God teaches you (4:9b)
        c. You are already doing it well (4:10)
    3. Busily working (4:11-12)
        a. The exhortation (4:11)
        b. The purpose (4:12)
           1) For no criticism without
           2) For no needs within
  B. Waiting for His Son (4:13—5:11)
    1. Who rose again—comfort (4:13-18)
        a. The desire of Paul (4:13-14)
           1) Not for hopelessness (4:13)
              a) In ignorance
              b) In sorrow
           2) But for hopefulness (4:14)
              a) Based on the resurrection of Christ
              b) Focused on the resurrection of their dead
        b. The new revelation from Paul (4:15-18)
           1) Its content (4:15-17)
              a) The dead have not lost any advantage (4:15-17a)
                  1] The descent of the Lord (4:16a)
                  2] The ascension of believers (4:16b-17a)

Appendix I

                a] The dead rise first (4:16b)
                b] The living join them (4:17a)
             b) All are destined to the same place (4:17b)
          2) Its comfort (4:18)
    2. Who delivers from wrath—edification (5:1-11)
       a. A reminder concerning the day of the Lord (5:1-3)
          1) It comes as a thief in the night (manner) (5:1-2)
          2) It comes with sudden destruction (result) (5:3)
       b. Our relation to the day of the Lord (5:4-10)
          1) Our identity—we have no part in it (5:4-5)
          2) Our consequent duty—be wide awake and sober (5:6-8)
          3) The reason for our duty—we are delivered (5:9-10)
             a) Appointed not to wrath (5:9a)
             b) Appointed to salvation (5:9b)
             c) Appointed to live with Him (5:10)
       c. The result of our relation to the day of the Lord (5:11)
          1) Comfort
             (Explained further in 4:13-18.)
          2) Edification
             (Explained further in 5:1-10.)
  C. Concluding exhortations to holiness (5:12-22)
    1. Honoring church leadership (5:12-13)
    2. Helping church members (5:14-15)
    3. Personal exhortations (5:16-22)
       a. On rejoicing in prayer (5:16-18)
       b. On good and evil (5:19-22)

Salutation (5:23-28)
   God Himself secures our holiness

THE PRE-TRIBULATION RAPTURE

Greet with an holy kiss

SECOND THESSALONIANS—GOD DELAYS PUNISHMENT OF THE WICKED IN ORDER TO PRODUCE PATIENCE IN THE BELIEVER

I. COMFORT REGARDING THE JUSTICE OF GOD'S JUDGMENT (Patience is worth it) (1:1-12)
   A. The rejoicing of Paul for their patience (1:1-4)
   B. The result of persecution (1:5-12)
      1. Result introduced (1:5)
         a. Justice will come in due time (1:5a)
           (Explained further in 1:6-9.)
         b. In the meantime, patience produces worthiness (1:5b)
           (Explained further in 1:11-12.)
      2. Result explained (1:6-12)
         a. God's righteous judgment (1:6-9)
           1) Judgment introduced (1:6-7)
              a) For unbelievers: tribulation (1:6)
                 (Explained further in 1:8-9.)
              b) For believers: rest (1:7)
                 (Explained further in 1:10.)
           2) Judgment explained (1:8-10)
              a) Fiery vengeance on the disobedient (tribulation) (1:8-9)
              b) Glory given to believers (rest) (1:10)
         b. Paul's prayer for their worthiness (1:11-12)

(Even though God's judgment is fair, that does not mean it will come right away. I want to give you . . .)

II. CORRECTION REGARDING THE TIME OF GOD'S JUDGMENT (Patience is necessary) (2:1-17)
   A. The plea introduced (2:1-2)

Appendix I

      1. Its basis—both aspects of the coming of Christ (2:1) (Explained further in 2:13-14.)
      2. Its object—a patient and worthy attitude (2:2a) (Explained further in 2:15-17.)
      3. Its substance—the day of the Lord is not near (2:2b) (Explained further in 2:3-12.)
  B. The plea explained (2:3-17)
      1. The destiny of unbelievers is delayed but certain (2:3-12)
         a. Their destruction is delayed (proof) (2:3-7)
            1) Two preceding events introduced (2:3)
                a) The departure
                    (Explained further in 2:6-7.)
                b) The revealing
                    (Explained further in 2:4.)
            2) Two preceding events explained (2:4-7)
                a) The revealing of the man of sin (2:4)
                b) (No excuse for not already knowing these two events) (2:5)
                c) The departure of the Holy Spirit who withholds (2:6-7)

(Lest you think, "If destruction is delayed, how can we be certain it will happen at all?" I want to tell you that . . .)

         b. Their destruction is still certain (reassurance) (2:8-9)
            1) Destruction of the man of sin is certain Why? The coming of Christ consumes him (2:8-9)
            2) Destruction of the followers of the man of sin is certain. Why? They follow the deception of the man of sin (2:9-12)
                a) Satan: immediate reason for deception—lying wonders (2:9)

b) Self: personal reason for deception—chose unrighteousness over truth (2:10)
c) God: ultimate reason for deception—God gives Satan power to deceive so that all will see His justice when He punishes them for their personal choice (2:11-12)

(In contrast to unbelievers . . .)

2. The destiny of believers is salvation and glory (2:13-14)

(In light of the destruction of unbelievers and the reward of believers . . .)

3. Live worthy of your destiny (2:15-17)
   a. Live according to Paul's teaching (2:15)
      (Explained further in 3:6-15.)
      1) By personal word
      2) By letter
   b. Live according to God's power (2:16-17)
      (Explained further in 3:1-5.)

III. COMMAND TO LIVE WORTHY OF GOD'S JUDGMENT (Patience is commanded) (3:1-18)
   A. According to God's power (3:1-5)
      1. In their prayers (3:1-3)
      2. In their lives (3:4-5)
   B. According to Paul's teaching (3:6-15)
      1. Teachings introduced (3:6)
         a. By letter: "withdraw from the disorderly" (Explained further in 3:11-15.)
         b. In person: "traditions ye have received" (Explained further in 3:7-10.)

Appendix I

   2. Teachings explained (3:7-15)
      a. In person (3:7-10)
         1) Paul's example: I worked hard (3:7-9)
         2) Paul's words: you work hard (3:10)
      b. By letter (3:11-15)
         Withdraw from those who will not work

Salutation (3:16-18)

Appendix II
Points to Remember When Studying the Bible

(With Examples)

1. Remember to rely on what the Bible says; it won't deceive you (for example, see pages 18 and 176).
2. Remember to take the language in its normal sense; figurative expressions still convey a normal meaning that people understand in ordinary everyday language (page 216).
3. Remember to study the key words in a concordance or other reference book (pages 95, 96 and 235).
4. Remember the context; search out the progression of thought in the context to see how every part fits in (pages 113 and 209).
5. Remember the purpose and theme of the book; search out the author's reason for writing to see how each section fits in. Making an outline will help here, as well as for the context (page 145 and Appendix I).
6. Remember to check parallel passages and related passages (pages 181-184 and 198).
7. Remember the historical situation; put yourself into the

shoes of the original readers (page 142).
8. Remember that God reveals truths one step at a time, planting the seeds in Genesis, displaying the full flower in Revelation (pages 93 and 161).
9. Remember that the simplest most obvious interpretation is usually the correct one (pages 138 and 170).
10. Remember that prophecy often has double reference; when things don't fit otherwise, look for the double-reference (pages 151-155 and 233).
11. Remember to admit your ignorance; some things we just don't understand (pages 200 and 224).
12. Remember to pray for understanding, to know all that God wants you to know (pages 232-233).